A HISTORY OF THE CENSUS TAKERS

A HISTORY OF THE CENSUS TAKERS

Recording the Nations

MISH J. HOLMAN

Pen & Sword
FAMILY HISTORY

First published in Great Britain in 2026 by
PEN AND SWORD FAMILY HISTORY
An imprint of
Pen & Sword Books Ltd
Yorkshire – Philadelphia

Print ISBN 978 1 39906 133 9
ePUB ISBN 978 1 39906 135 3
ePDF ISBN 978 1 39906 137 7

A CIP catalogue record for this book is available from the British Library.

Typeset in Times New Roman 11/14 by
SJmagic DESIGN SERVICES, India.
Printed and bound in the UK by CPI Group (UK) Ltd.

The Publisher's authorised representative in the EU for product safety is Authorised Rep Compliance Ltd., Ground Floor, 71 Lower Baggot Street, Dublin D02 P593, Ireland.
www.arccompliance.com

For a complete list of Pen & Sword titles please contact
PEN & SWORD BOOKS LIMITED
George House, Units 12 & 13, Beevor Street, Off Pontefract Road,
Barnsley, South Yorkshire, S71 1HN, England
E-mail: enquiries@pen-and-sword.co.uk
Website: www.pen-and-sword.co.uk

or

PEN AND SWORD BOOKS
1950 Lawrence Rd, Havertown, PA 19083, USA
E-mail: uspen-and-sword@casematepublishers.com
Website: www.penandswordbooks.com

MIX
Paper | Supporting responsible forestry
FSC® C013604

Contents

Foreword

> If the cream of the tales of the day's encounters that could be told by the 40,000 enumerators throughout Great Britain were to be collected, I feel sure it would make a volume at least as attractive to most people as the Blue Books of Census figures that is promised some two years hence.[1]
>
> *Hampshire Telegraph*

"The enumerators in some quarters had a lively time when getting the papers in yesterday", wrote one newspaper columnist in 1901. "Some of them can tell some funny stories; but whether they are all 'gospel' or not is another thing."[2] Elsewhere, it was similarly observed that "It is only natural that the taking of the census should be held responsible for many stories. Some of them are true, some are doubtful, all are probably exaggerated."[3] The enumerators themselves were not the only culprits blamed for such embellishments – and I do think it is fairer to say there were embellishments rather than complete fictions – the press was also accused of chasing readership by exaggerating situations when reporting.[4] However, it was the rather dubious practice of offering a prize for the best enumerator's story that ruffled the feathers of some observant commentators who noted the hypocrisy, the tawdriness of a cash prize, as well as the lack of professionalism from a government official. And of course offering half a guinea to a tell-tale would surely encourage those individuals to come forward with ludicrous and apocryphal accounts. As Rory O'More writes:

> Even the press, who counsel their readers to place full confidence in the secrecy of the census, turn somersault and offer a money

> prize to census enumerators who send in for publication the most entertaining incidents of their experience. This money not only "mak's the mare tae gen", but it likewise opens a door for census enumerators to enter tell-tale competitions.[5]

In his letter, O'More makes another important observation stating, "It is a simple thing to poke fun at other people's expense ..." Indeed, this was a familiar trope running through many of the stories with the poor and the working class at the centre of the enumerator's or journalist's scope. While the middle class didn't escape the disdain, it certainly was those at the bottom of society's ladder who were the objects of the most derision. Standing from their lofty position and their assertion that the job enabled them to comprehend and empathise with a world that was foreign and distant from their personal predicaments, enumerators wrung every bit of bathos from their "comic" encounters. It was the working man's ignorance, his lack of education, his multi-faceted employment record, his home and his familial relationships, that were scrutinised and ultimately turned into hilarious compulsive copy. Even when there was empathy for the poor man and poor woman's plight, one can't help but sense a certain disgust in the commentary.

As this book is replete with such newspaper accounts because, let's face it, there are few other sources where we can learn about how enumerators organised their work and how our ancestors responded to their intrusion, it is fair to say we should proceed with caution. Knowing there were embellishments, it is wise to have that awareness at the forefront of our minds when reading these accounts and to make allowances for a few fictions.

It does pose the question can we trust any of it? Well, yes we can. Quite a lot actually. There is plenty of corroborative evidence from other sources. For instance during the 1911 Census, the enumerators reported that households were writing the fertility information on the wrong row. A quick check of the census schedules can verify that this was indeed widespread. Both institutional enumerators and ordinary enumerators suspected the elderly overstated their ages. The statistics, according to the census report authors, did support this suspicion for the over sixty-fives. Enumerators and the press also stated some householders completed the schedule by writing across the entire page (ignoring the columns) or squeezing as much as possible into one column. An example of writing mostly in a single column can be seen in the extant 1841 Census schedules held by the Shropshire

Archives. Tales of ladies supplying their schedules to enumerators in sealed envelopes meant only for the eyes of the Registrar General or the local registrar, then becoming irate when the enumerator tore open the envelope, were also prevalent. And you're probably thinking these tales are fiction. Well you're wrong. This was corroborated by Registrar Frank Tupper in his testimony to the Treasury Committee in 1890.

Similarly, enumerators described to the press they were treated with suspicion and were obstructed during their duties. Here, enumerator Charles White confirms this when he told the Treasury Committee in 1890:

> In the evening, say after half-past five, especially in the neighbourhood where there are dock labourers – unless you treat them properly; that is the secret of the whole matter – if you call you make these people very suspicious, sir. Some of the poorer classes are very suspicious. They do not believe in inquisitorial examinations and so forth ...[6]

There are numerous other examples of corroboration from other sources which indicate much of what follows can actually be trusted.

With his words, Charles White indirectly nails my whole reasoning behind this book. It is this reaction to officialdom, to bureaucracy that gives this book its purpose. For in my quest to understand my ancestors through the surviving documentation, I reasoned I could not understand the answers they gave, the information they chose to share or hide, without knowing how they reacted when encountering officialdom. It should be regarded equally with the social pressures and burdens they faced every time life events took them outside of propriety and the classic expectations of behaviour. Both are entangled together and it is through this entanglement that our ancestors reveal themselves delineated closer to their true selves.

Acknowledgements

As ever with endeavours of this magnitude, it is necessary to express grateful thanks to individuals and organisations. My gratitude goes to Emma Jolly, Amy Jordan, Kim Rose, the late Audrey Collins, Jane Roberts and her wonderful website, Nigel Butler, my mum and sister, and all those from the genealogy community who have given their encouragement and who have inspired me to continue on during difficult times. I would also like to thank The London Archives, the National Archives, the National Library of Wales, the West London NHS Trust, the British Library, SOAS and the British Newspaper Archive for their kind permission to use quotes from primary sources. Finally, I am indebted to the NHS for saving my life.

Chapter One

Knowing Thyself

> [Enumerators] reminded you of mosquitoes – they were created for a brief time, and were a trouble to you while they lived.
>
> *Liverpool Evening Express*, 4 April 1911

The 30 March 1861 was a dull day. Rain had fallen persistently upon the streets of Glasgow and a dark thunderous sky let loose a single flash of lightning. There had been a brief fall of sleet and snow, perhaps enough for the market traders and merchants in Candleriggs Street to dash indoors, and the men appointed as enumerators to hasten through the sand-coloured portico of the City Halls.

A thousand men entered the Halls that day, listening to the Lord Provost Peter Clouston, extol the benefits of the census and thus emphasise their duty to undertake their work for both country and empire. For what could be better than to communicate to the whole world, the progress of the country and to assist the government in providing provision for the poorest in society? There was no need for him to offer advice, he trusted that each one of them had been selected on merit and capability, however some may encounter difficulties and should prepare wisely. They may be accused of collecting tax or preparing the way for conscription; householders may view them with suspicion and they may encounter recalcitrant females averse to providing their age or an accurate age. This troublesome issue of age, familiar to both the experienced enumerators and the initiates, caused laughter and applause to break out among those seated. Clouston added they must therefore provide assurance to the reluctant and suspicious householder that confidentiality was guaranteed throughout the process. It was in their interest to use tact and diplomacy to persuade those from the lowest stratum of society they may receive healthier dwellings and lower mortality rates because of the census.

To aid the enumerators as much as possible, it was hoped clergyman would give notice of the census from their pulpits and impress upon the congregation the need for their cooperation; that in every marketplace and every square, placards would be posted informing the public, so no one could claim ignorance of the census.[7]

These Lanarkshire men, their compatriots and their counterparts in England, Wales, and Ireland were about to walk the enumerator's path that so many had travelled before. This path was not a linear one and those who traversed it were not always engaged in census taking. To enumerate is simply to "mention [a number of things] one by one" according to dictionary definitions and so it's necessary to recognise the predecessors of these Lanarkshire men, who were called upon to enumerate individuals for all manner of reasons, not just censuses as we may recognise them.

In the preface to his book *Pre-1841 Censuses and Populations Listings*, genealogy pioneer Colin Chapman describes his journey in bringing together into one chronology a catalogue of censuses and other population records. He is somewhat apologetic about including very basic enumerations in conjunction with lists most readers would not view as censuses or similar to censuses, but does not doubt their value to historians. In the decades that have passed since Chapman's publication, his view has been validated by serious family historians recognising the need to place their ancestors in the context of the local, county and national situation.

In fact, their usefulness goes further than helping family historians identify and understand their ancestor within the context of their environment or in response to national events. A study of the records and their administration helps family historians recognise the importance of the parish as an administrative unit, one which superseded a waning manorial court and acted as a local authority up until the 1830s. Though the parish's functions were far-reaching and required a structure in which to operate, it was always working within the hierarchy of government. Both the monarch and the Established Church made use of the parish organisation for religious and social policy. They would engage the services of church or lay officials, who were already part of the infrastructure of local administration when they needed to gather information about communities. As a consequence, when the kingdom proceeded to initiate its first national census, a framework for it was already in place.

While it's not possible to discuss every type of list the historian may encounter, it is useful to examine a few and understand why they existed and the method of the undertaking. When studying the procedures, responses and outcomes, it is possible to see the parallels and differences with what is known in regard to the nineteenth-century censuses.

A journalist writing for the *Coventry Evening Telegraph* in 1901 certainly thought of making the comparison, albeit to contrast a time gone by with his own era. In an article about the 1901 Census and the history of census taking, the writer postulated that the men who took William the Conqueror's Domesday survey between 1085 and 1086 encountered similar difficulties contemporaneous enumerators faced when examining a household. This was of course a clever writing device allowing him to inform his readers about Coventry in 1086... and my how Coventry had grown since these former times!

William the Conqueror was fortunate in that he inherited an incredibly powerful and efficient state when he took the throne and was able to proceed with alacrity in sizing up the condition of the nation. In comparison with later attempts to survey the land or its people, Domesday's coverage of most of the kingdom south of the Tees was thorough, extensive, and initially completed in 100 days. It went through three further stages of checking and reorganisation, ostensibly turning it into a "database" of landholding which enabled William to maximise his income. Even though only heads of household were included and there were omissions including members of religious houses and the inhabitants of castles, the survey was one of the most remarkable feats of government bureaucracy in Britain and it would take centuries to be emulated.[8]

Land value, tithes, and taxation on both personal and real estate were some of the main drivers behind bureaucratic record taking from the medieval period onward. In 1188, a moveables tax known as the Saladin Tithe was imposed on individuals' personal estates. The value of a person's goods was assessed by jurors or declared and sworn to be correct by the owners of the goods themselves. At other times, there were many smaller enumerations conducted at county, hundred, city and parish level for reasons other than tax. In some instances the justification for these are unknown, for others it may have been requested by a landowner, by the church, or government officials.

The journalist from the *Coventry Evening Telegraph* passes over the city's contribution to census taking in Britain. He only makes fleeting references to its population in the sixteenth century, but it's possible Coventry's census or in this case the "dearth", is the earliest surviving record of an exact census of any urban population in Britain resembling those of the nineteenth century. Following a wet summer in 1520, a very poor harvest coupled with rising grain prices led the city government to order a numbering of the people and an account of the grain stores.

The Coventry 1520 Census covered the city's ten wards and was repeated again in 1523, when the total number of the people in each ward was noted along with the names of each householder.[9]

In churches across the kingdom, rectors were instructed by higher authority or by their own volition to take down the names of individuals when it was deemed necessary. On 9 April 1676, William Sampson, rector of Clayworth in Nottinghamshire read a brief to his congregation requesting they subscribe for the relief of Northampton which had suffered a disastrous fire. He records in his register, "I took occasion to enquire, at the same time, the names of all my parishioners" and thereafter he entered them by household with the surname of the head of household in alphabetical order and so "avoiding envy". Sampson's list may have originally been intended as a record of subscribers and then extended, as Chapman suggests, in response to the Bishop of London, Henry Compton's request for details of parishioners. Compton's aim was to discover the number of Anglicans, Catholic recusants and Nonconformists in England and Wales, but the results of the survey were inconsistent. The instructions given to the deaconries and archdeaconries were often misinterpreted and individuals were either omitted or recorded twice.

The brief William Sampson read from the pulpit was essentially a call to action issued by the monarch. Briefs were commonly known as Letters Patent, King's or Queen's Briefs or Letters, Orders in Council, Patents of Alms, Fire Briefs, Church Briefs, and so on. In addition to collecting money for those who suffered loss due to fire, flood, plague, and shipwrecks, writs were also issued by the monarch on behalf of individuals affected by fraud, robbery or even persecution. They were used in circumstances where money was required for repairing the fabric of the church or for building or rebuilding bridges, houses of correction, and hospitals. After the brief was read and the church service was concluded, a collection on behalf of the cause was made and the money collected was either entrusted to an authorised travelling collector or handed over during the bishop's visitation. If authorised, churchwardens were allowed to collect money from each householder by going door to door, which may have coincided with their usual rate collecting duties.[10]

In 1642, churchwardens, overseers of the poor, and sheriffs were engaged on behalf of the Crown to collect relief for Protestant refugees after civil war had broken out in Ireland. They were asked to

> ...go from House to House to every the Inhabitants of the said Parishes respectively, and as well to collect and gather the free and charitable Benevolence of all the Inhabitants thereof... [they were to write] down in a Schedule thereof indented, as well the Name and Names of the several Givers as of the Lenders, with the several sum and sums of Money which shall be by every of them lent or given: And the said Churchwardens and Overseers for the poor, having subscribed their Names at the foot of one part of the said Schedule indented, shall deliver that part.. unto such Person or Persons as shall be therefore employed and entrusted, by order of the... Committee.

At Harleston in Suffolk, the collecting for distressed Protestants in Ireland was coordinated to correspond with the Ash Wednesday fast and the taking of the Protestation Oath which was passed by the Commons on 3 May 1641. Though the motion was passed in the May, it was not fully implemented until after the Speaker's letter of January 1642 demanding a nationwide subscription. Thereafter, all males (and some women) over 18 were requested to take the oath in support of the Crown and the Protestant religion. While the coordination of taking the oath and giving relief was not widespread it certainly was frequent enough in Buckinghamshire and Surrey to suggest some premeditation. The oath taking usually followed a reading of the oath's text by the minister and then each parishioner made the oath in the "sight and hearing" of the minister and the parish officials. In Roseland, it was recorded by parish officials that "by their dyscretion [they] have seene and heard all the persons abovenamed to make vow and declare the same protestacon."[11]

Many subscribers raised misgivings about the purpose of the oath and in some places local officials interpreted it as a new test for recusancy. In many instances this led to the name of any individual refusing to take the oath being marked as a recusant. Surviving returns for the Protestation exist for all counties in England except Gloucestershire, Herefordshire, Rutland and the East Riding of Yorkshire. Cornwall and Devon have almost complete coverage, whereas Essex and Hampshire have a handful of returns.[12] There are no returns for Wales except for Denbighshire.

Compton's census and the Protestation Oath are examples of how instructions given to local officials were open to misinterpretation or were loosely followed, resulting in inconsistency. This problem would occur again during the nineteenth-century censuses. In Scotland in 1831, enumerators were entering occupations in the wrong classes because of the ambiguous terms of the question. A few decades later in the more densely populated quarters of Edinburgh they were given instructions to enumerate one side of the road within their district because another enumerator's district incorporated the other side of the road, but were also told to include house numbers inclusive. The result of this misinterpretation led to some householders receiving two schedules. Later, there was further confusion over the term "uninhabited" and use of Gaelic in the language column.

The Protestation Oath was followed swiftly by the Vow and Covenant and the Solemn League and Covenant in 1643. The purpose of the Vow and Covenant was to test the support for continuing the Civil War, while the Solemn League and Covenant bound the oath takers to the defence of the Church of Scotland and the reformation of the Church of England. The Vow and Covenant was first ordered to be taken in all the parishes of London and then expanded on 27 June to encompass the rest of the kingdom. The procedure was essentially the same as the Protestation whereby it was initially subscribed at the local market town by the ministers and parish officers before justices of the peace. It was then taken into the parish and individuals were asked to subscribe to the oath.[13] Unlike the Protestation Oath Returns and the Solemn League and Covenant, where lists of subscribers survive for many English counties, there are far fewer extant records for the Vow and Covenant. The returns only survive for parishes in London, Norfolk, Essex, Kent, Sussex and Suffolk.

In Scotland, the Solemn League and Covenant was preceded by the widespread swearing and signing of the National Covenant of 1638. It was drawn up by the nobility together with the lairds, burgesses, lawyers and church ministers who were aggrieved with the religious and political policies of the king, Charles I. Orders were issued that each shire, baillery, stewartry or distinct judicatory should be provided with the Covenant or

"Confession of Faith" as the document was generally known. Initially, the principal persons in the community signed followed by those admitted to communion in every parish. Any illiterate parishioner was required to sign through a notary. Although it was mainly men who signed and women only swore to the covenant, there were exceptions and women's signatures can be found. At the Lasswade Kirk sessions, it was recorded that "the confession[n] of faith was publiclie red with great joy & hands holdine up" and at Menmuir it was stated that "This day the confessioune of faith and covenant with our God [was] openlie read, subscryvet, and swore unto." The practice of subscribing to the Covenant varied across the nation and many interpreted it as being a renewal of an earlier declaration. Some copies of the Covenant have survived even though there is a low survival rate of Kirk sessions and presbytery records from the seventeenth century as a whole; David Stevenson's *The National Covenant: A List of Known Copies* is a useful guide to availability.

In Scotland, the barons and gentry were at the forefront of a functioning local government in the rural parishes. They paid teinds in church as heritors and sat as elders on Kirk sessions. The sessions were responsible for burials, the funding of schools, and the appointments of schoolmasters and ministers. It was also accountable for the administration of poor relief. Away from the rural parishes, the civil equivalent of the Kirk sessions was a town or burgh council. It consisted of local gentry, merchants, and craftsmen and was responsible for any matter concerning trade, health, schools, and the punishment of offenders. It was not uncommon for men who sat at the Kirk sessions to also hold office on the town councils. Among the session records are communion rolls – lists of the members of a church's congregation who attended the annual or twice-yearly communion service – and rolls of adherents (parishioners not taking the communion at a given time).

Besides the incumbents, in England and Wales there were four principal offices required for the parish to fulfil such functions effectively: the churchwarden, the constable, the surveyor of highways, and the overseers of the poor. These roles were unpaid and compulsory service was required for a year with exceptions for peers, justices of the peace, attorneys, and the military etc. The method of who and how a person was selected varied from parish to parish. In many instances it was by nomination and in others, officers were chosen by house-row in rotation throughout the parish. In some rural areas where "ancient order" was maintained, it was dependent on the occupation of certain properties. In 1657, it was recorded in the register for Stoke-on Trent that the three churchwardens for Burslem, Sneyd and, Hulton were "the occupiers of certain ancient messuages and farms in those three townships ... [and] were bound to serve the office in rotation."[14] As the Webbs point out in their study of English local government, this may explain why women were sometimes elected as churchwardens or overseers. Thus the ownership or tenancy of a particular property was something of an equaliser when it came to women and roles in office at a local level.

Up until the end of the sixteenth century, it was the constable rather than the churchwarden who was regarded as the senior official. They were the ones entrusted with the general supervision of the parish. There were regional differences in terminology when it came to the title of the officeholder, coming no less from the division between Wessex, Mercia, and the lands settled by the Jutes. This gave rise to a host of alternative names for the role including headborough, thirdborough, borsholder and tithing man. Furthermore, many were given the dual role of surveyor of highways and were known as waywardens.[15] Originally the role was not affiliated to the parish, but to the manor or perhaps the tithing and in some areas of England continued to be appointed at the Court Leet up until the first quarter of the nineteenth century. When the manor ceased to exist in some areas, responsibility for appointments fell to justices of the peace.

Aside from their normal duties, the constables also maintained the parish butts and supervised the contribution of both men and money to the militia. Keeping track of the local men qualified to serve in the militia produced numerous lists of individuals now preserved in archives. The pretext for muster to arms by county and hundred was derived from the Statute of Winchester of 1285, which itself owed its existence to the ancient Anglo-Saxon Fyrd developed by King Alfred. This enabled the calling of all men aged between 15 and 60 to be assessed and sworn to arms according to his land and personal estate. In the eighteenth century, the militia acts – a response to the Seven Years' War – saw men aged between 18 and 50 chosen to serve by ballot.

Constables were engaged as enumerators in 1787 when justices of the peace in Westmorland and Cumberland requested a census of the inhabitants of the region. The information was organised and entered into columns drawn up by the constables themselves. These men were also engaged for tax collecting purposes across the nation. Following the Restoration of the Stuart monarchy in 1660, a supplemental tax was imposed in England, Wales, and Ireland to make up the shortfall in annual income of the royal household. The Hearth Tax was charged according to the number of hearths or fireplaces in a property. Unless individuals were exempt for reasons of poverty, all householders were taxed at a rate of 2s per hearth. The tax was collected from the occupier of a premises in two instalments, on Lady Day and at Michaelmas by the parish or ward constable who drew up lists of householders, recording their names and the number of hearths. It was an unpopular tax and was abolished in 1689,[16] but continued in Ireland until the nineteenth century.

The tax was levied in Scotland in 1691 by the Scottish Parliament at a rate of 14s per hearth (with exemptions) in an attempt to reduce army pay arrears and to clear debts to the shires and burghs. James Melville of Cassingray was appointed collector for Scotland and a number of sub-collectors were employed to compile lists in their area. They encountered great difficulty collecting the tax in some of the more remote areas and consequently the exercise was delayed several years.

Alongside the Hearth Tax, the parish constable also assisted the commissioners collecting the Window and Land taxes. Countless other taxes including subsidy rolls, the poll tax, horse tax, window tax, farm horse tax, valuation rolls etc., plus land and property surveys such as the Liber Assedationis and the Liber Episcopi on the Isle of Man, all led to the collecting of information about individuals from local officials.

The tithing system also gave rise to numerous enumerations. The Ludlow Easter Book of 1725–1734 records in alphabetical order all of the householders in the four city wards with their wives, servants, and children over 16 as well as the relatives and lodgers who lived with them. The officials collecting the payments went street-to-street visiting every household along the route. It is clear from some of the entries they used ledgers from previous years to follow the same path around the townships. In larger parishes, several trips were made in order to collect all payments and deal with arrears.

These lists together with various parish, diocesan and religious surveys, are detailed in a number of books and articles concerning records of inhabitants. Among the highlights are Chapman's aforementioned *Pre-1841 censuses and population listings;* Emma Jolly's *Tracing Your Ancestors Using the Census* and Jeremy Gibson and Mervyn Medlicott's *Local Census Listings, 1522–1930.* Also of great use is material published by the Cambridge Group; their work is often included, among other excellent articles on the subject of population listings, in the *Local Population Studies* journal.

The move towards a national census did not come until the eighteenth century and had its precursors elsewhere. In the second half of the seventeenth century, temperatures cooled and the rain fell heavily and frequently across the Northern Hemisphere in a period known as the "Little Ice Age". Summer frosts and wet weather led to crop failure, starvation, malnutrition, and disease prompting some nations to take action to mitigate the effects on their population and the economy. In the north Atlantic, Iceland, then part of the Kingdom of Denmark, sent one of its chancellors Lauritz Gottrup to meet with King Frederick IV of Denmark. They spoke of the harsh conditions endured by the Icelandic people and as a consequence a commission was set-up to investigate, resulting in a count of the Icelanders and their livestock. The commission appointed professor Árni Magnússon and vice chancellor Páll Vídalín to undertake the survey from December 1702 to June 1703. The "winter census" was then extended to a livestock count between May and June 1703. A Register of Estates was simultaneously compiled over a period of twelve years, from 1702–1714.

The responsibility for administering the census fell upon magistrates (sýslumenn), the highest authority in each county, who then submitted the results to the commission during Alþingi (parliamentary session at Þingvellir) in 1703. The magistrates appointed local administrators (hreppstjórar) to collect the information for their districts and instructed them to count and record the population into three groups: families, paupers, and vagrants. Inland, where there were a few scattered farms and houses, bogs and lava fields, the administrators discovered the terrain was far more easily crossed when frozen in winter. However, with most of the population living by the coast, they mainly travelled by sea. In each household, everyone was to be recorded by their given name, patronym and age, and their position or employment was to be noted. Individuals who were outside their own county, at sea or visiting relatives, were to be recorded in their place of residency.

During the course of the 1703 Census, 670 local district administrators and 21 magistrates were employed, which was approximately 1.4 per cent of the Icelandic population. As far as it is known, these local administrators conducted the first comprehensive census of a population anywhere and it is thought to be an accurate and reliable record of the Icelandic people. However, there were some problems: the task took six months to complete and there were instances of births and deaths during the period; some children who were born after the census were added to the report before it was submitted, and students listed at home were also recorded overseas simultaneously.

Despite these minor problems, it is considered a remarkable record and can be searched online at the National Archives of Iceland website. Delving into the document reveals some tragic and personal stories including that of Katrín Þorvarðsdóttir, who was recorded on the census in her home, Hvítanes, in Skilmannahreppur in Borgarfjörður on 2 April 1703. She was listed as being 33 years old. When Alþingi was in session from 9 to 20 July, they considered a case against Katrín for murdering her child. In her defence, she said the baby was stillborn and, as she was not in her right mind, she kept the birth a secret. The court decided against her, and she was executed by drowning at Þingvellir on 12 July.[17]

Over the next one hundred years a number of European countries plus the USA would undertake their own population surveys in one form or another. In Britain, where population and vital statistics were defective due to the reliance on information collected for other purposes, controversy slowed the progress of any move towards a census. Webster's *Account of the Number of People in Scotland in the Year 1755* had proved to be a fairly accurate outlier in terms of estimating the population of Scotland at 1.265 million. However, in England and Wales the use of parish records and taxation for population data provided no useful basis for estimating the numbers of inhabitants in those regions.

The administration of parish records had been the responsibility of the Church of England following Thomas Cromwell's injunction of 1538. Apart from two very brief periods, the local clergy of the Established Church recorded the baptisms, marriages, and burials of members of their congregation in parish registers. As a consequence dissenters and members of other faiths were largely omitted from the records resulting in an incomplete picture in terms of population estimates. Other methods including counting the number of houses and guessing household size also fell short of satisfactory. These defects did not go unnoticed by individuals interested in population statistics and those questioning whether the population had increased since the Glorious Revolution of 1688.

During the second half of the eighteenth century, the debate rumbled towards a resolution, but not without a number of objections along the way. In 1753, both *The Gentleman's Magazine* and *The Scot's Magazine* provided publicity for Thomas Potter's census and civil registration bill as well as coverage of some of the debates in Parliament. By all accounts, Potter, a

Member of Parliament and son of the late Archbishop of Canterbury was not the most endearing of characters, though his peers regarded him as a speaker of more than middling ability. When he swaggered into the Commons to present his Bill, he immediately provoked resentment, however it was later conceded the Bill was well worthy of a place in history.

The practicalities of the proposed legislation and how it was received are worth examining in light of later enumerations. Potter proposed that the numbering of individuals would be undertaken by local government officials on 24 June 1754 or within ten days following and would be repeated on the same day every year. Overseers of the poor of every parish, township and extra-parochial jurisdiction would proceed from house to house within their district and demand to know the number of people resident in the house for the 12 hours next preceding. They were to distinguish separately for males the numbers under 20 years of age, those aged 20 and under 60 years, and those aged 60 years and over. They were asked to do the same for married persons and to note the number of poor, both male and female in receipt of alms during the previous year. The overseers were entrusted to prepare a schedule, using an example provided by Potter, on which the numbering would be recorded. After the census was taken they would swear before the church minister that a true account of the people had been made.

Further checks for accuracy would be implemented. After divine service on the second Sunday in the July following the count, the minister, churchwardens and other principal inhabitants were to assemble in the vestry to examine the schedule. Once it was agreed the information was correct and all those present attesting to the fact it was faithfully made, it was to be signed off by them and returned to the Overseers.

In addition to the census, Potter proposed a system of civil registration, which incidentally would have provided genealogists and researchers with a wealth of material. Ministers were to create a notice for every birth, marriage, and death within their parish and then transfer the information into a register book. It is particularly noteworthy that in regards to deaths, they were to be registered within fourteen days of an individual's decease and would record their full name, sex, age, cause of death, names and residences of both parents "as far as the same can be known or conveniently obtained." Marriages would also include the names and residences of the bride and grooms' parents as well as the names of the bride and groom, and the date and place of marriage. The minister would receive 6d. for each notice of a birth or death and the overseers would receive 20s. which would come out of the parish accounts. Abstracts and duplicates of the notices would be made and on 10 August 1754 and every year following, the overseers would then deliver the schedules, abstracts and duplicates to the chief constables of their hundred or division, who in turn would pass them to the Clerk of the Peace at the next general or quarter sessions. From the Clerk of the Peace, they would be forwarded to the Board of Trade in London and a complete abstract would be annually laid before Parliament.

Local government officials were empowered to deal with any individuals who refused to comply with the act. They could call before a county Justice of the Peace any person who refused to provide information or who wilfully obstructed the officers in their duties; guilty offenders would face a penalty not exceeding 40s. on their goods and chattels. Likewise, if the officers themselves neglected their duties, made wilful omissions or false entries, the Clerk of Peace could summon them before justices and they would pay a levy of up to £5.

In Scotland, the numbering would be undertaken by the clerk of the Kirk sessions, who was paid 20s. to complete the schedule, and who would upon the same day in June go house to house and record individuals in the same vein as the English and Welsh overseers. A register book for notices of births, marriages, and deaths would also be created along with duplicates and abstracts. The minister, elders, and heritors of the parish would then meet in the July and sign off the schedules and documents arising from the registration system. Once that task was completed the documents would be sent to the sheriff depute, who would forward the duplicates to the sheriff clerk. These would then be transmitted within twenty days to the secretary of police in Edinburgh before making their final journey to the Board of Trade in London. Sheriff deputies were empowered to levy and impose penalties for failure to comply with the act to the sum of 20s. for individuals and for neglectful officials of up to £5.[18]

The reception to Potter's Bill was exceptionally cool from some quarters. William Thornton's address to Parliament generated the most publicity, citing an infringement upon civil liberties and a general concern the kingdom's weaknesses would be exposed to foreign powers. Others criticising the Bill, were concerned with an outcome of increased taxation or conscription leading to a standing army.

Matthew Ridley, a Member of Parliament for Newcastle was in favour of registering births and deaths and ascertaining the numbers of the poor, but was against the enumeration. In his address to the house, he spoke of letters received from individuals who claimed the Bill filled them with imaginary terrors, and that such superstitions may manifest themselves as violent behaviours and lead to riots should the Bill pass. If the superstitions also arose after an epidemic or divine anger they would endanger the peace, if not the government. His constituents also informed him it would be wise for the overseers taking the census to be accompanied by as many soldiers as possible; without them, they said, people would just laugh in their faces instead of giving a true account of their families. And as a consequence, the justices would become overwhelmed with all the fines they would have to issue.

Ridley's address was met with counter-arguments by supporters of the Bill, doubtful of large outbursts of public anger, believing the public would acclimatise to the process once they saw the Bill in practice. They argued further, the results of any census, as well as knowing the number of births and deaths etc., would surely lead to better informed debates; it would also facilitate deciding whether a general naturalisation was desirable and allow authorities to estimate the size of an army should the need arise. Further, it would help with the attraction of emigration to the colonies and give an accurate assessment of the burden of the poor upon the kingdom – an issue that would reappear come 1800.

Along with all the major issues and general disquiet voiced by the respective Members of Parliament were grievances about how the Bill would work in practice. Thornton was concerned that overseers, many of whom were elected to the office from the poorer illiterate inhabitants of the parish, would be penalised for errors or neglect of duty purely because they were unable to read or write. He also considered the use of force by Constables heavy-handed; should anyone refuse to say they were in receipt of alms or in the case of women, asked to give their age and marital status, they would be exposed to insults and abuse as well as severe penalties.

Ridley too had his doubts. What about the London merchant with a house in town and a house in the country, who would be staying at his house in the country when the overseers called on the Monday morning? All they would find was a servant maid? Or vice versa? The Overseers would visit the country home and find only the gardener. The merchant and his family would never be accounted for. Conversely, he might be counted twice if he visits both homes during the course of the census and is seen by the overseers in both places. And what of the itinerant worker, the stage coachmen, the waggoner, the bargeman, the pedlar, do they stay in any one place for twelve hours?

Ridley agreed with Thornton about the level of literacy expected of the overseers, suggesting they required a learned clerk to accompany them which would be of great cost. If the clerk was less than learned, the overseers may themselves be penalised for inaccuracy and neglect. If there were two overseers for each parish, Ridley declared, perhaps they should go around the parish together, but would they divide it in half? In which case, if one made a mistake would the other be liable?

In Parliament, Potter responded to the issues raised by both Thornton and Ridley, saying that a few people missing from the census would not make much material difference to the total. In any case, anyone not at their residence would be accounted for in the days allowed after the census and itinerant workers would be counted in with their family at their usual residence. And given that illiterate overseers already employed clerks to assist with accounts, even the most ignorant among them should have the skills to fill in a printed schedule.

Unfortunately for Potter, there were yet more queries about the practicalities of the Bill, this time coming from Thomas Pitt. If the census takes place at the end of June, it would coincide with the migration of workers from Ireland to assist with the hay and corn harvest. There would also be a number of parishioners not in their usual residence for the same reason. Pitt argued that such migrations would deflate and inflate the real numbers at a local and national level; conversely, many of these workers were not resident in any house, but slept in barns and dressed their victuals in fields or alehouses. How could an overseer account for these when even the farmer did not know how many haymakers slept in his barn? The same applied to day labourers who rarely lived at their master's house, and if married, both the husband and wife were often out working, so where would they be counted? And what about people who are liars or careful with the truth?

> ... does the law oblige people to answer the question truly, or does it punish them if they answer wrong? Or, when an ignorant country Overseer finds a whole family at their house in the country, can it be imagined, that he will think himself empowered to depart from the express words of the law, and omit putting them down in his account, because they tell him they have been already numbered at their house in town?

All these issues would be pertinent and mitigated in some way by the later Victorian censuses. The residence problem was ironed out by enumerating people wherever they were on the night of the census; enumerators and police would visit barns, caravans, railway cars, railway arches, barges and so on to record the homeless and the nomadic traveller; hotels, lodging houses, guests houses and public houses would all receive schedules to enumerate the itinerant and seasonal worker; enumerators would report visiting homes over and over until they were finally able to speak to the householder and collect the schedule, and when it came to the question of truth, well some householders would both intentionally and unintentionally obfuscate and deceive. These things never went away, but there were mechanisms in place to deal with them. As Potter told the House of Commons, such obstacles would not vitiate or impact the results to a greater degree.

Despite the opposition to the Bill it passed in the House of Commons, but was stalled in the House of Lords after being referred to a Committee. The parliamentary session ended before the Committee could convene and from thereon in the Bill was forgotten. The arguments for and against population statistics continued and individual thinkers outlined their thoughts in published pamphlets. Arthur Young (1741–1820), a writer with an interest in agriculture, economics, and social statistics, wrote in his *Proposals in Legislature for Numbering the People*, published in 1771, that a census should classify every man or family into three occupational classes of agriculture, manufacturing, and commerce. Further to this, it should distinguish between those receiving regular and occasional poor relief. After collecting the data and arranging it into a table which he perceived as an essential component, Young argued the government would be able to ascertain how well tax revenue was generated and "comprehend at once the causes of such prosperity, the means of advancing it, and of preventing a decline."[19]

While some individuals proposed the population numbers were falling, others believed they were climbing in the opposite direction. The increasing burden of poor relief on local rate payers and the rise in food importation led to fears concerning unmanageable growth as encapsulated in Malthus' Essay of 1798. The turning point was the poor harvest of 1800 when wheat prices rose to such a degree, potatoes, potato flour, and rice were used as substitutes for bread.

Four years earlier, civil servant John Rickman had written a memorandum on "the utility and facility of a general enumeration of the people of the

British Empire." Rickman's original was no doubt in manuscript form, but an annotated published version appeared in 1800 in a journal Rickman edited entitled *The Common and Agricultural Magazine*. In the piece, he expressed his belief a full enumeration was unnecessary saying attempts by Prussia, the USA, and France had been fraught with problems and expense and that accuracy in a fluctuating subject was not attainable nor required. Instead, he suggested utilising parish registers for an abstract of the total number of births, marriages, and burials for the previous decade. In addition, the authorities should select three or four isolated parishes, where every inhabitant was likely to be buried, and complete a full enumeration of those parishes.

Rickman's original memorandum was forwarded by MP George Rose to Charles Abbot, MP for Helston in Cornwall. Abbot took some of Rickman's proposals and included them in a Population Bill introduced to the House of Commons in 1800. The Bill entitled an "Act for taking an Account of the Population of Great Britain, and of the Increase or Diminution thereof" passed in the House of Commons on 31 December 1800 with no recorded opposition.

The enumeration would take place the following year and become the first official census of Great Britain. The man in charge was John Rickman, who entrusted the process of ascertaining the information required to church officials and local parish officers, just as Thomas Potter had envisaged in 1753.

Chapter Two

The Evolution of the Census

In 1666 the fire of London tore through the city and reduced to rubble and dust a number of churches including St. Nicholas Acons. The church was never rebuilt and the parish was united with St. Edmund the King in Lombard Street following the devastation. This area of London, close to the Royal Exchange, was a thriving hub of trade and commerce. Here, money lenders provided liquidity for traders, and brokers set out their stalls in the numerous coffee shops that lined the narrow thoroughfares.

At the turn of the nineteenth-century tea dealer Benjamin Heseltine and broker of goods John Kennion were working from their offices in St. Nicholas Lane – one of a handful of streets within the parish of St. Nicholas Acons – when Abbot's census Bill passed through the Commons. The two men were accustomed to dealing with the bureaucracy required for running a business: Kennion produced printed catalogues for his imports of Carolina rice, indigo, Jamaican cotton and ginger, while Heseltine made up his ledger of accounts for tea imports and sales. Both men were churchwardens and were active participants in the parish administration together with the rector, curate, and five overseers.

A decision was made between them to produce "housekeeper schedules" for the forthcoming census and have them printed by J. Abrahams of nearby Clements Lane. Their intention was to have the housekeeper complete the schedule and the Overseer of the Poor would collect it on 10 March 1801. The form they prepared asked John Rickman's census questions, but they were expanded into seven proper sentences, presumably as Paul Dobraszczyk suggests in his article *Give in your account: Using and Abusing Victorian Census Forms,* to help the housekeeper understand the form. Dashed lines were added after each of the sentences to allow the reader to follow the direction of the writing and then write their answer in the corresponding spaces to the right of each question. Instructions were provided underneath the questions explaining there was a £5 penalty for refusing to answer or for giving false information, the default of which would result in a three-month prison sentence. Further to this they requested the housekeeper "sign this Paper with your proper Name, Number of your House, (if any) and Place of Abode, so that it may be then ready to be delivered as your Answer and Return..." The form was dated 6 March 1801 and was signed by Heseltine, Kennion and each of the overseers.[20]

Dobraszczyk argues the commonly used printed legal documents such as marriage licences, marriage certificates, affidavits, and indentures where sentences were printed with blanks to be filled in, were more familiar to individuals than the tabular format. Hence the decision by the churchwardens et al. to proceed with this configuration. The extant returns show the parish officials correctly put their faith in the housekeepers' ability to understand the form and to complete it accurately. Out of the forty-six forms deposited at The London Archives only seven have crossings-out or over-writing. This faith in their comprehension and literacy was in contrast to Rickman who opposed householders filling in the forms themselves. And like Ridley and Thornton who both argued against Potter's 1753 Bill, Rickman was even doubtful the overseers and other officials were capable of the level of literacy required to complete the form.

The officials at St. Nicholas Acons once again employed J. Abrahams to print the 1811 Census schedules for their parish, but dispensed with the fully posed questions and adopted a tabular format in keeping with the examples provided by Rickman. This style of form was used for the duty on hair powder in 1795 and between 1801 and 1811 was widely used after the Invasion Act of 1803. The possibility of a French invasion led to the publication of a number of forms aimed at ascertaining supplies of bread and equipment for the army.[21] Despite this format gaining widespread use, the inhabitants of St. Nicholas Acons made a number of errors when they were asked to complete the form in 1811, indicating this type of data entry confused them. Parish officials kept faith with the tabular format for the 1821 and 1831 censuses, regardless of the errors, and again requested that householders fill in the forms themselves, ready for house-to-house collection by the overseers of the poor. After the collection, the overseers would then transfer the information into the summary format required by the census Bill.

The returns for St. Nicholas Acons survived because they were administered locally and were kept together with other parish chest material. There are a number of similar examples for other parishes which have found their way into the local Poor Law records in archives across the country, though many are nominal lists compiled by the overseers. The majority of the official returns sent to John Rickman have been destroyed. The exceptions to this are the 1831 Clergyman's Returns now held by the National Archives in HO 71. According to correspondence from the Registrar General's office dated 21 October 1891, the 1801 and the 1811 censuses had *long since been destroyed* and the 1831 Census returns had certainly been destroyed by 8 May 1891.[22]

When Abbot and Rickman first joined forces for the 1801 Census, there was no central Census Office, and each census was taken on an ad hoc basis following a separate act of Parliament. The instructions provided with each act and on the prescribed forms set down by the census administrators did not differ greatly between 1801–1831 and utilised the established framework of parish officials to undertake the survey. As well as overseers acting as enumerators in England and Wales (the islands of Guernsey, Jersey, Alderney, Sark, and the Isle of Man were included in the censuses from 1821), it was also requested that churchwardens, sidesmen, parish clerks, vestry clerks, and, if necessary, "constables, tithingmen, headboroughs or other peace officers" should be available as assistants. In Scotland, the responsibility of going house to house to collect the information fell on schoolmasters or "other fit persons" who were appointed by the justices of the peace and the sheriff deputes or stewart deputes.

The enumerators were given a set of questions to gather information about the number of inhabited and uninhabited houses in their parish, township or place and to note how many were occupied by families; they were also asked to provide the number of persons and the ages of individuals within the limits of their parish excluding serving militia and seamen. To almost echo Arthur Young's suggestion that individuals should be classified into three classes: agriculture, manufacturing, and commerce, the enumerators were to provide the number of persons employed in agriculture, trade including manufacturing and handicrafts, and how many were not engaged in those occupational areas.

In order to facilitate answering these questions, the King's Printer was instructed to send copies of the act and a proforma answer form to the Clerks of the Peace and Town Clerks. They would then distribute the same to justices of the peace. Copies of the forms were distributed to the high constables or other proper officers at the Epiphany or Easter Quarter Sessions, who would then ensure they were received by the overseers of the poor or other substantial householders. Separate forms were also issued to the clergy for parish register abstracts.

After the census was completed and the answer form filled up, the overseers were called to meet with their local justices of the peace before a fixed date and attest and affirm the form. Justices could adjourn meetings if the forms were thought to be less than satisfactory and request corrections. Forms that were fully attested were then submitted to the high constables together with a complete list of the names of the enumerators. The returns were then sent by way of the clerks of the peace or town clerks to the principal secretary of state for the Home Department where they were to be "digested and reduced to Order by such Officer as such Secretary of State shall appoint for the purpose." The Census Act instructed that the local accounts made by the overseers while preparing the Answers and Returns should be preserved by the churchwardens, or other persons in Scotland, and their successors. In Scotland, the sheriff deputes or stewart deputes called meetings between the justices of the peace and the schoolmasters or other appointed persons who acted as enumerators, to receive the Answer and Returns forms and to administer the oath contained in the schedule.

In 1801, clergymen were required to provide parish register abstracts for the number of males and females baptised in each decennial year from 1700 to 1780 and provide the same for burials. For the years 1781 to 1800, they were asked to write down the number of separate male and female baptisms and burials inclusive and to state the number of marriages in each year from 1754 to 1800. For the next four censuses, the clergy were asked to provide the number of male and female baptisms and burials for the preceding decade and to give the total number of marriages that occurred within the previous ten years (e.g. 1811–1820). In 1831, the questionnaire was extended to elicit information about deaths between 1813 and 1830, together with the number of illegitimate children born in each parish in the year 1830. Due to the lack of parish returns from Scotland in 1801, the questions were not asked in 1811.

The clergy would provide parish register abstracts in 1841, but it was recognised that this data would quickly be superseded by the Registrar General's Annual Reports and Tables. The new civil registration system would generate more reliable statistics and therefore the 1841 parish register abstracts were the last of their kind.

For their trouble, local and parish officials received compensation for expenses necessarily incurred for undertaking the census. In 1801, at the Michaelmas sessions in England and Wales or the Michaelmas meetings in Scotland, justices of the peace ordered payments to be made by the receiver general of the Land Tax in England and the receiver general in Scotland to the enumerators for their respective counties. In 1811, changes were made to the expenses payment system for officials in England and Wales; overseers, householders, parish clerks or vestry clerks would be paid directly from the parish poor rate. In 1831 some enumerators undertook their duties voluntarily or were paid in kind, e.g. treated to dinner.

Amendments were also made to the schedules for the next three censuses. Questions regarding occupations and housing in 1811 were modified and retained for the 1821 Census schedule, however the occupation question was expanded much further in 1831. A question about ages was added to the 1821 Census. Enumerators were asked to obtain, at their discretion, statements of age in five-year and ten-year groups for members of a household. Even though this information was voluntary and the results of the exercise deemed fairly successful, Rickman did not repeat it for the 1831 Census. Instead, the age columns were extended to include males upwards of 20 years old in total and in occupational groups. To cope with the additional information required for the 1831 Census, enumerators were provided with tally sheets to assist with counting. They were instructed to take with them when "proceeding from House to House ... the printed Formula papers in a Pasteboard or other convenient Cover" and if using ink to use blotting paper.

Any enumerator found guilty of wilful default in terms of their census obligations were subject to fines ranging from 40 shillings to £5. Such penalties were issued at the discretion of the justices after a complaint had been made. Householders could also be fined the same amount for wilfully giving false answers or for refusing to answer at all. Any unpaid fines could result in a prison sentence of three calendar months.

The End of an Era

The rise in influence of the London (and later the Royal) Statistical Society coincided with Rickman's exit from the census stage. Rickman had been involved in the initial planning of the 1841 Census, drafting a census bill along the lines of the earlier censuses. He considered utilising the officers and boundaries of the new poor law and was involved up until June 1840, but fell ill and died in the August.

The London Statistical Society's committee suggested ambitious adjustments to the census in Britain and Ireland in its report of April 1840. The report recommended an overhaul of the procedures, including the adoption of a household schedule designed to enumerate the names of each individual together with a broader set of questions. The committee viewed both the reorganisation of the poor law (Amendment Act 1834) and the formation of the civil registration system in England and Wales by the Act of 1836 as an opportunity to pursue change. The new system of administration would possess the capacity to deliver a census that befitted the country. The committee sent their report to the Home Secretary and the response was positive, resulting in the withdrawal of the original Bill for the 1841 Census and a replacement was formulated. The *Society* continued to meet frequently throughout the nineteenth century to discuss changes to the census in terms of questions about sex, ages, religion, marital status, date of marriage, occupation and employment, ability to read or write, school attendance, birthplace, and housing. They also suggested a quinquennial census, but this was rejected and not included in any legislation until the Census Act 1920.

Following Rickman's death, the Home Office contacted Thomas Henry Lister, the first Registrar General, to open up discussions about his office undertaking the census. It was a pragmatic move to appoint the Registrar General as one of the three census commissioners of the census after the establishment of civil registration. The Registrar General's office had become responsible for producing statistical reports concerning public health and vital events and the new registration district system was apt for the census. The registration district was divided into sub-districts and a registrar was appointed to each of them. He or she would divide them into smaller numbered enumeration districts. In theory, each district was of a size an enumerator could cover within one day.

Initially, the enumerators were expected to gather the information required from a household during house-to-house visits. This, Lister believed, would mitigate any problems caused by illiterate householders. Following a pilot enumeration in London, however, he discovered the process required too many enumerators at far greater cost. Hence, the adoption of the scheme where householders completed the schedule themselves.

The resulting schedule no doubt reflected Lister's doubts concerning householder literacy plus given his late appointment to the role, he was given limited time for its development. The schedule was divided into columns with simple headings requesting basic information: forename and surname only, age (rounded down to the nearest five years if over 14 years), sex, profession, trade, employment or of independent means, whether born in the same county (yes or no), or whether born in Scotland, Ireland or "foreign parts". Upon receiving the schedule, each householder was required to complete it for every individual sleeping in the house on Sunday, 6 June. The schedule was then handed to the enumerator when he arrived to collect it. The penalty for failure to comply with these instructions was a fine of not less than 40 shillings and not more than £5.

Setting aside those examples from St. Nicholas Acons and elsewhere where householders completed forms from 1801–1831, the 1841 was the first official census in Great Britain where heads of household were asked to complete the forms themselves. The extent to which enumerators helped with the process of completing forms across all the censuses will be addressed elsewhere.

In England, Wales, and Scotland the schedule for the 1851 Census settled into a tabular format which would only see minor changes for a number of decades. Questions on sex, age, marital status, relationship to the head of the household, birthplace and nationality, professions, trades, occupations and infirmities would become all too familiar to householders. In addition to the regular census of 1851, authorities planned to include two important enquiries about religion and education. They hoped they would be empowered by the Census Act of 1850 to pursue the questions, but objections were raised in the House of Lords about the penalties imposed for withholding information. A decision was made to proceed with the surveys on a voluntary basis and individuals were informed they would not be compelled by law to answer. There were few refusals, but the religious census proved to be controversial and was not retained. It was not until 2001 that a question on religion made another appearance.

The 1861 Census was the first to be taken under the powers conferred by three separate Acts of Parliament, applicable to England and Wales (in the Channel Islands and the Isle of Man, the Census fell under the same Act, but was taken under the auspices of the respective lieutenant governors acting in conjunction with the English central office), Scotland, and Ireland. In Scotland, with the passing of the 1854 Act of civil registration, a separate Registrar General in Edinburgh was appointed who would be responsible for census administration. Local registrars were to divide their districts into units for the purpose of enumeration and forward their plan of division to the sheriff of the county or the chief magistrate of the burgh. As with England and Wales, each parish was divided into enumeration districts of a manageable size to ensure they could be conveniently covered by the enumerator in one day. The enumerators were usually schoolmasters or other fit persons in each parish.

The separate acts for the censuses of 1861 to 1891 kept to a standard format with regards to the basic questions asked and to the tabular style of the schedule in each country. It also allowed for Scotland to put forward additional questions. In 1861, the enumerators were given instructions to enquire with the householder about whether there were any individuals temporarily absent or present from their household. The schedule would also require the householder to provide information about school attendance and the enumerator to note the number of rooms with one or more windows. In 1871 this was rephrased to exclude rooms with "borrowed light". In 1881, a Gaelic language question was written in a fold on the back of the schedule: "In column 6 (headed 'Where Born') the word 'GAELIC' to be added opposite the name of each person who speaks Gaelic habitually." Matthew Woollard in his essay about the 1881 Census of Scotland describes this as an afterthought.[23] This hastily added question was included on the front of the tabular schedule for the 1891 Census.

After having argued against any further expansion of the schedule and wanting to concentrate on the quality of data collection, the General Register Office of England and Wales was pressurised into making amendments for the 1891 Census. In 1890, the Treasury Committee on the census met to consider implementing additional questions. Social scientist Charles Booth and economist Alfred Marshall appeared at the hearings, seeking further details regarding employment and changes to the classifications of occupations in the census reports. This resulted in three extra columns for check boxes added to the schedule, headed "employer", "employed", "neither employer nor employed". Other changes implemented were an extra column for the insertion of the number of rooms occupied by the household, if under five, and a schedule for language in Wales and Monmouthshire. Here householders were to write "English" if they only spoke English, "Welsh" if they only spoke Welsh, and "Both" if they spoke English and Welsh.

The 1901 Census marked the centenary of census taking in Britain and reunited England, Wales, Scotland, the Channel Islands and the Isle of

Man under a single act. The questions from 1891 were repeated, but the employment check boxes were removed, and the householder was asked to write whether they or members of their household were an "employer", "worker", or working by their "own account" in a separate column. Another column was added to the schedule about home working which the Home Office considered useful with regards to regulating sweated trades.

In 1911, there was a major development in all four countries when questions on fertility were added to the census questionnaire, but were not retained in England, Wales, and Scotland for the 1921 Census. This enquiry was designed to provide data on whether the poorer classes were producing more children than those higher on the social ladder. It was a concern of eugenicists, who were intent on discovering if Britain was in the midst of genetic deterioration at a time when its imperial ambition was in crisis. The reasons given for its removal from the schedule vary. One suggestion is that keeping it while adding the place of work and child dependency enquiries (the latter was thought to be more important) meant the schedule exceeded its practical limit; elsewhere, the 1921 Census report explained the data arising from the fertility question was long range and the analysis hadn't finished. Meanwhile, a newspaper reported the data arising from the query was too imperfect to be of service, possibly indirectly quoting Registrar General Sylvanus P. Vivian. Nonetheless, the enquiry returned in another guise on the 1951 Census schedule for women under 50 when individuals were asked about their date of marriage and children born alive to the present marriage. It was repeated in 1961 for all women.

The 1911 Census schedule also included an enquiry asking about the industry or service where a worker was engaged. This question was designed to gain information about potential recipients of unemployment benefits under the 1911 National Insurance Act should their industry be affected by a downturn. In the Channel Islands, heads were asked to supply the place of birth of their fathers and to repeat the same for all members of their household.

The Census Act of 1920 removed the requirement for separate census acts every decade. It gave the Census Office authority for the taking of a census when necessary, with the date of each census to be authorised by an Order in Council. The original date set for the 1921 Census was 24 April, though there had been discussions during the census conference in 1920 of opting for a day in May.[24] Many enumerators spoke of their difficulties when undertaking their collections and checking the schedule in fading light or in the dark. Even though April became the favoured date, industrial action by mine and transport workers, forced the postponement of the 1921 Census to 19 June.

Having dropped the question on fertility, the importance of the place of work enquiry was circulated and imparted to the press. Registrar General Vivian stated the conflict of 1914–1918 had caused widespread socio-economic changes, adding: "You cannot tell where your houses are to be built unless you know where the people who occupy them will work", he told the *Western Gazette* in 1921. For him it was vital to understand the consequences of increased urbanisation, how the place of work in relation to residence had an important bearing on housing, schools, and transport.[25] No such enquiry was included on the schedule for Scotland, instead column "M" was given to a question about National Health Insurance asking "If the person has a right to medical benefit under the National Insurance (Health Acts)." While this question was viewed as significant for the Ministry of Health in England and Wales, it was the Scottish Board of Health who pressed for its inclusion as a priority. They suggested the registers for the apportioning of benefit funds to insurance companies and medical practitioners were flawed, quickly out of date owing to mobility and death, and too costly. The Board viewed this particular enquiry as a means to overhaul a failing bureaucracy and to replace it with a streamlined apparatus of administration.

Questions about orphanhood and attending school for all those in part-time or whole-time education were added to the 1921 schedule and for the first time on a census, women who worked from home, were recognised as having "home duties". The age column was also tweaked to record the age of individuals within the household of over one month old in months and years. New confidential returns were used for the first time in 1921 and in 1926 in Northern Ireland. Concerns about individuals suffering hardship due to disclosing their particulars to the person completing the schedule led to confidential returns being introduced.

The additional enquiries added to the 1921 Census schedule – apart from the new age format – did not reappear for the 1931 Census. It did, however, contain a new column for usual residence and in Scotland, the length of residence was asked of all persons not born in Scotland. The query about usual residence may have reflected concerns about the June 1921 Census skewing the results of seaside towns or holiday hotspots and was thus repeated.

At some point prior to 1942, the 1921 Census schedules suffered water damage while in storage in government facilities in Leonard Street (they would also be treated for mould and lice infestations). The schedules were eventually dried out and scattered over various parts of Somerset House in London until they were brought together and conserved. The 1931 Census of England and Wales schedules did not fair so well, they were destroyed during a fire at the Hayes Office of Works government facility in mid-December 1942. An investigation tried to establish the cause of the fire and how it had spread so rapidly through the facility despite the installation of special hydrants and six paid fire watchers. The investigators concluded it was impossible to find the cause due to the damage, however the police report of March 1943 suggested it may have been due to a lighted cigarette thrown by one of the fire watchers.[26] This was not sufficient proof and no further action was taken. It should be noted the fire only affected the schedules for England and Wales, Scotland's schedules were kept separate and were therefore undamaged.

The second half of the twentieth and into the twenty-first century saw further changes to the schedule and its administration. In 1951 householders were asked to supply details about exclusive or shared access to piped water supply, cooking stoves and ranges, kitchen sinks, water closets, and fixed baths, indicating the authorities were interested in householder access to home sanitation and utilities. By 1971 the schedule had evolved to include twenty-nine questions and by 2021 there were fifty-one for each individual plus fourteen household questions.

As the ambitions of the census administrators grew, the operations in Britain required the coordination of an administrative apparatus and an efficient workforce of enumerators, registrars, and temporary clerks. They also need a cooperative public, a curious press and, a vast mound of paper.

Chapter Three

Paper Mountain: Forms and More Forms

> Allowing two schedules to one sheet of paper, this will mean that 4,500 reams of paper will be required. If these reams were piled on top of each other they would make a stack about 750 feet high ...
>
> *The Glamorgan Gazette*, 9 September 1910

Imagery such as this served to inform the public of the enormity of the task overseen by the census administration. Elsewhere, in an attempt to convey the same magnitude, column space was devoted to the cost and statistics involved in undertaking a census. Figures, designed to impress the reader, were quoted when a census was imminent: "4,000 plans of division, 3,000 books of instructions for local officers, 60,000 enumerators' application forms, 10,000,000 household schedules, 50,000 enumerators' memorandum books, and 50,000 enumerators' books besides multitudes of circulars and all the forms required for the apparatus of tabulation." Further to the mountain of stationery, the costs of taking the census were also disseminated. In 1891, the fees for registrars, superintendent registrars, and enumerators amounted to £91,900 according to one newspaper,[27] with an estimated total cost for the census of £123,000.

The sources for much of the material printed in the newspapers were either the previous census reports or memorandums and circulars sent to the press directly from the Registrar General's office. In 1901, the *Evening Express* informed its readers that an accurate census was of great significance, as even small mistakes or omissions, which might seem trivial to most people, can collectively undermine calculations crucial for much social work. Errors could cost thousands if not millions of pounds because of the way the census was used by actuaries and insurance societies. It was therefore part of a citizen's duty in which the Registrar General was entitled to ask for wholehearted co-operation.[28] In 1911, the *Sheffield Independent* endorsed the idea of duty and citizenship by telling its readers if a citizen embraces the census he will regard it just as important as giving his vote.[29] The use of this psychology on the literate population was clearly intended; messaging was key to public compliance. The taxpayer might be more inclined to comply rather than have his money wasted if he felt obliged by duty and was aware of the numbers involved.

A circular sent on 16 March 1881 by the then Registrar General, Sir Brydges Henniker, underlines how important the Census Office considered the cooperation of the press. Henniker emphasised the census was an arduous undertaking and he trusted the press would inform the public of the very careful preparations for a successful census, adding, the press contributed to the success of the previous census.[30] Accompanying the circular was a three page memorandum (basically a press release) explaining the purpose and processes of the census. The success of the census it explains, depends not so much on the Registrar General, on his officers, or the enumerators, but on the 6 million heads of families.

The memorandum called upon the influential classes of society to explain and disseminate among the poorer communities, and in persuading them, or even assisting them, to furnish exact returns.[31] Among the influential classes were the clergy who were asked to sermonise the census from their pulpits, members of the Boards of Guardians, teachers, and other administrators. Some circulars were sent to the Board of Agriculture and the Miners' Union.

Even though imagery, statistics, and public messaging played their part in improving the relationship between the householder and the census officials, there was another factor: education. When Registrar Alfred Gibbs gave testimony to the Treasury Committee on 10 March 1890, he informed them the enumerators were having to complete fewer schedules. This was due to the educated older children of householders taking on the task.[32] Later, when asked if householders could cope with an expanded schedule, he reiterated, saying children were becoming better educated and capable of supplying more information.[33]

Almost a year later, the *Burton Chronicle* was endorsing a "contemporary" who suggested teachers drew up a schedule on a blackboard to show children how to complete the form.[34] That contemporary may have been Superintendent Registrar for Preston, John Aspinall who wrote to the Registrar General asking for a supply of 150 household schedules. Each schedule was to be marked "specimen" and disseminated to the seventy schools in his district with a view that the older scholars would receive a lesson on the census. This would assist the illiterate parents and achieve greater accuracy while making sure the schedule was ready for the enumerators.

The day after Aspinall's letter arrived on Brydges Henniker's desk, he received a reply from secretary Noel A. Humphreys informing him he could proceed. Henniker concurred that such a scheme was of great advantage and a delivery of 150 schedules would be forwarded to Aspinall. Within days the Preston Superintendent Registrar had issued a circular to the head teachers of all the schools in his district requesting their assistance.

There is no evidence the scheme was rolled out across the rest of the nation in 1891 despite official approval. Aspinall's suggestion probably arrived too late to be implemented widely, but it was certainly thought to be advantageous a decade later. In February 1901, following an agreement between the Board of Education and the Registrar General, a circular was issued to schools along with two copies of the schedule and a memorandum on teaching totalling 46,000 copies.[35] The circular suggested that a skilled teacher would be able to provide a short lesson adapted to the age and capacity of the children in his or her class. Indeed, there was no prescriptive directions about content, only that such lessons should be aimed at older children and those attending evening schools.

In Leeds, a schoolmaster told his boys: "You must not be frightened when the man calls with the blue paper, for its nothing to do with the Town Hall, or making soldiers of anybody. But you must tell your fathers and mothers to be very careful filling up the paper."

Putting up a blackboard and drawing the columns of a schedule in chalk, he explained the contents of each column to the class. He soon discovered many of the schoolchildren had no sense of when they were born and were reduced to using associations, such as the same year the tram cars started running along some street, or the same year as a well-known local event. Occupations were also a problem: many children had no idea what their father did for a living.[36] This was unfortunate because the authorities aimed to correct the occupational descriptions by educating children on differentiating between various types within the same profession.

By 1911, it was fairly clear to the Census Office, the assistance rendered by schoolteachers delivering lessons to schoolchildren was having the desired effect.[37] That year, prior to the 1911 Census, teachers were issued with explanatory notes detailing the objects of the census and emphasising the confidential nature of the returns.

During a House of Commons question and answer session in April 1921, it was considered the expense of producing the circulars and notes was justified from an educational point of view. Past experience had shown "that very great advantage has accrued from interesting and instructing the children, and through them their parents, as to the meaning and importance of the census."[38] That year, the explanatory notes for teachers were contained in a 24 page booklet complete with a large sample schedule and illustrations of the automated key punch machines and tabulated printers. A similar, but smaller booklet for the 1931 Census in Scotland is held by the National Records of Scotland.

In some schools, teachers took the opportunity to hold census lessons which encouraged further engagement. At a school in Kensington, pupils were asked to dress up as typical members of a household.[39] Educating children about the census was not only conditioning them to assist their parents, but to prepare them for a time, when they as adults, would be required to complete the form themselves. The ultimate aim for the Census Office was a complicit householder, one who understood why the census was taken, who did not fear it, and knew how they needed to play their part.

The use of public information films during the mid-twentieth century, radio broadcasts, documentaries, and TV dramas all served the same purpose. In 1951, radio broadcasts were scheduled to take place in the run up to the census. On 13 March, a programme entitled "Focus on the Census" was transmitted, this was followed by two talks on "Woman's Hour" and a final fifteen-minute broadcast called "Can I Help You?" on 7 April, the day before the census.[40]

Technology and traditional methods were also used for enumerator training. The Further Education Department at the BBC produced two television programmes aimed at enumerators employed for the 1971 Census. The programmes were broadcast along with a fully integrated compulsory training scheme consisting of instructional booklet and classroom activities. In 1980, two twenty-minute training films "The Doorstep Drill" and "Reaching the People" were commissioned from writer Chris Langley showing the many different scenarios an enumerator may encounter during the course of his or her duties.

Labour MP George Foulkes suggested enumerators visit Coronation Street, Eastenders' Albert Square, and other fictional locations including Ambridge (from *The Archers* radio drama). The purpose of this was to show millions of people what to expect and what to do if they were worried. Many of the TV soap writers had already ventured into this territory: a *Coronation Street* character refused to complete his census schedule in an episode aired in 1971. In 2001, the soap returned to the subject showing the character Norris Cole acting as an enumerator.

The adoption of social media and the widespread use of hashtags during the advance of the 2021 Census brought messaging firmly into the modern age. But despite such widespread endeavours informing the public about the census during the course of the twentieth and twenty-first century, there were still failures of engagement.

The deadline for the 2021 Census of Scotland was extended due to the slow completion rate of the survey. Before the extension, only 79 per cent of homes in Scotland had completed the census with the figure increasing by just 10 per cent after the deadline was extended. Despite issuing up to five further reminder letters, postcards, and increased media and marketing activity, in a survey of non-responders, 16 per cent said they were unaware of the census.

Following the 1961 Census, enumerators were asked to complete a survey and give an account of their experiences. From a sample of eighteen surveys taken, nine enumerators expressed their frustration at the lack of publicity. One commented that the publicity accompanying the census placed too much emphasis on the IBM computer used for the first time to process the data, and not enough focus on informing householders someone would call to collect the schedules. Some householders believed the enumerators were local government officials or rate assessors and many regarded the census takers with suspicion to the extent of being obstructive. For enumerators, this meant more time standing on doorsteps explaining the reasons for the census and why they were asking such personal questions.[41] One enumerator only managed to deliver 61 schedules in 6 hours due to such delays. These grievances were not new, enumerators had complained about them for decades. They also complained about the size and weight of materials they had to carry. A bundle of 200 schedules, unwieldy memorandum books plus enumerator's record books (in 1961), were described as heavy and awkward to handle.

The evolution of the stationery produced for each ad hoc census can be seen in the increase in the separate documents printed for the 1861 and 1871 censuses. In 1861, sixty-three documents were printed including enumeration books, circulars, expenses forms, and instructions to registrars and enumerators. By 1871 this had increased to 122 unique documents. While the collective weight and number of schedules printed increased throughout the nineteenth century, the design of the schedule remained consistent. For fifty years the table for the householder's information was printed on a single leaf foolscap. On the reverse in England, Wales, and Scotland, was a smaller table for the householder's name and address together with instructions for completing the form and a warning of a £5 penalty for inaccuracy and non-compliance. In terms of design, it wasn't until 1921 that the form saw a new tick-box system added for recording the ages of children under 16.

The drafting of the schedule usually occurred in between the passing of the census act and the late summer/autumn before the census took place. The passing of the act authorised the questions to be asked and made provision for the funding of what was a temporary census apparatus. This was the decennial cycle until the Census Office became a permanent administration in the early twentieth century. The actual printing of the schedules may have differed from census to census, but in 1851 it began in the January by Ford and Tilt of Long Acre, Covent Garden and was barely finished in time for the enumeration.

During the six months or so prior to taking the census, the General Registrar Office (GRO) administration began preparing their officers for the event. Circulars were sent out to superintendent registrars, registrars, and other organisations informing them of their obligations with regards to the census operation. For the 1911 Census, the preparation had actually begun nine months before, the earliest it had ever been up to that date. Throughout the preparatory period, officials were diligently drafting and revising instructions for the census officials. Arrangements were made for the hiring of temporary clerks who would be entrusted with extracting the data for processing and reporting. In February 1901 the permanent census staff of four at Somerset House were transferred to buildings close to the Tate Gallery to join a maximum of 30 clerks already in situ. In 1911, the number of clerks involved were 200 or so.

These men, women, and boys, aged between 15 and 50 were usually hired via the Treasury and were required to sit an examination by the Civil Service Commissioners. In Scotland, they were only examined after the Registrar General had deemed them competent. This resulted in a satisfactory pool of fairly intelligent and efficient clerks. In England and Wales, many of the individuals applying for positions had found themselves unemployed and were desperate for jobs, but as Dr William Ogle (Superintendent of Statistics) testified to the Treasury Committee in 1890, most were unfit for the level of literacy and diligence required of a census clerk.

For censuses prior to the 1911 Census, the clerks had abstracted data from the enumeration books and transferred it onto large sheets. Occupations were abstracted on to another large sheet with occupational headings vertically and age ranges horizontally. But in order to analyse the fertility data, the Census Office introduced the use of Hollerith machine tabulators. The machine was developed in the US for the 1890 Census, and its use in Britain for the 1911 resulted in a number of different work roles within the Census Office. Many of the roles were undertaken by cheap female labour. For the 1931 Census, following a move to new offices in Acton, brand new machines, designed by British engineers, were installed to undertake the tabulating and counting of punch cards.

Plans of Division

At a local level, the census brought great stresses and disruption to the usual operations of local registrars' offices. In 1890, the Treasury Committee discussed giving superintendent registrars, most of whom were working solicitors, more responsibility for selecting enumerators and checking their work. However, the idea was rejected by Ogle who suggested the Superintendent Registrar was a mere medium by which senior census officials communicated with registrars and vice versa and much of their census work was actually completed by junior clerks. Indeed, the superintendent registrars' responsibilities were minimal: checking the registrar's plans of division, reading and approving the lists of prospective enumerators, and ensuring the registrar had performed their job by briefly checking the enumeration books. In addition, they were to oversee the payment of wages to registrars and enumerators once an order had been sent from the paymaster general. By 1911, the instructions sent to superintendent registrars were revised and separate headings were inserted to emphasise the importance of specific duties. Among those of significance were checking the enumerator's signature for his/her abidance to their statuary obligation to serve as an enumerator and the transfer of the census documents from the registrar to the Census Office.

In a similar fashion to the superintendent registrars, most registrars of births and deaths held other positions; many were doctors, relieving officers, clerks on the Board of Guardians or were school attendance officers. When the census arrived, it was therefore another set of duties on top of all the other roles and responsibilities they undertook. If their area was large, they often had to travel and hold registration days at specific spots. It is therefore likely some registrars may not have had their minds firmly committed to the census. In some quarters, they were even considered incompetent at registration and there were many instances of incomplete or badly copied causes of death on death certificates.[42]

On 23 October 1900, the Registrar General for England and Wales, Reginald MacLeod sent a letter to the registrars of births and deaths in London regarding the formation of enumeration districts. He was concerned that under the provision of the Local Government Act of 1899, the numerous boundary alterations of Poor Law Unions and parishes in the metropolis would require a redrawing of sub-districts and consequently, enumeration districts. His letter was a pre-emptive action; despite the act not coming into force until the follow year, he wanted the registrars to immediately recognise their revised sub-districts and arrange their enumeration districts accordingly. If necessary they would receive help from their Superintendent Registrar and the clerk of guardians.

The redrawing of boundaries was the bane of a registrar's existence. In 1890, Dr Ogle confessed to the Treasury Committee the "doubts and difficulties as to boundaries and their bewildering complexity adds enormously to the work at the Census Office."[43] A great deal of time was spent (and wasted) by the temporary clerks and other officials owing to the confusion surrounding boundaries prepared by registrars. In addition to local government instructions, boundaries could be changed at the behest of the Board of Guardians and it was the registrar's job to ensure any change was properly marked out, but many failed to do so.

In Scotland, there was sympathy for the plight of the English and Welsh officials, with some commentators acknowledging they had been spared the disruption of various Local Government Acts enacted in England and Wales during the previous two decades. Even though boundary changes to civil parishes and counties were in process during the 1891 Census of Scotland, following the Local Government (Scotland) Act of 1889, administrators retained the previous jurisdictions for pragmatic reasons. The delayed pain occurred a decade later after the boundary commission had finished its amendments. Out of 881 parishes, 287 were affected by boundary changes with the demarcation of ecclesiastical boundaries causing the greatest difficulties.

Some changes, however, were to benefit both registrars and enumerators. For the 1871 Census, the then Registrar General sent a letter to the local authorities in England and Wales requesting they co-operate with naming and numbering streets. Hitherto, many streets were privately constructed with rows of cottages numbered without any regard to the numbering further along the street. In Nottingham, a long street repeated Nos. 1–3 up to thirty times; this resulted in one resident giving his address as the fifth number three on the right-hand side of the road. Private construction had also led to unique names such as "Matilda Place" or "Eliza Cottages" being swept away. In rural communities, where mining resulted in rapid growth and the consequent construction of cottages alongside lanes and by-roads, it was feared that without proper naming and numbering, these habitations would be missed by the census takers.[44]

In 1900, the Registrar General reminded authorities and borough councils that by provision of the Public Health Act (38 and 39 Vic., c. 55) they should cause all streets to be named and houses numbered. He went on to state it would be a great advantage to all concerned if the names and numbers were plainly visible on every street and house. If there were any instances where there were houses unnumbered and streets unnamed within a council's jurisdiction, he trusted the matter would be resolved with urgency.[45]

All of these considerations were on the minds of the registrars when they readied themselves for their first census duty: drawing up the plans of division for their district. To facilitate their preparation they received instructions from the Registrar General and a copy of the plan of division they or their predecessors created for the previous census. This was a useful guide and one upon which any amendments to the new plan could be made. No land, inhabited or uninhabited, was to be omitted and if necessary they were required to use a map on which they could mark their enumeration district boundaries before providing a written plan. Enumerators could then be instructed to make an outline or sketch of the map for his or her district. In Ireland, Ordnance Survey maps were utilised by both superintendents and enumerators for each census, but it wasn't until the 1911 Census they were officially used in England and Wales. Prior to this the Census Office could call upon local sanitary authorities to assist with the provision of maps for sub-districts.

Each district was to contain no more than about 200 inhabited houses and the enumerator should not have to travel more than 15 miles. For rural parishes containing less than 200 houses, registrars could unite more than one parish into a single enumeration district if deemed necessary. Conversely, if the parish was very populous it could be divided into two or more districts. In 1911, registrars received instructions that any plan of division used for the 1901 Census could not be reused unless it conformed to certain criteria. The idea was to avoid the smaller enumeration districts used at previous censuses. So in urban areas the enumeration district should contain 1,500 to 2,000 people subject to the condition of its boundaries not conflicting with other boundaries such as wards, civil parishes, ecclesiastical parishes, and parliamentary divisions; it was also necessary for the enumerator to be able to collect the schedules in one day. In rural areas, registrars needed to take into consideration the number of houses and distances traversed, but it was a requirement, subject to the boundaries, to ensure the enumerator was fully occupied collecting schedules on Monday, 3 April 1911.

For many registrars, drawing up their plan and apportioning their districts meant a visit to every street in their sub-district. In Manchester, Mr Hallsworth took six weeks to tour his area making notes and completing his arrangements every day until one or two in the morning. Even after a registrar thought he had finished the task, new developments would suddenly appear: in Levenshulme, in 1901, over 200 houses materialised after the districts were planned.

In Scotland, officials in 1841 were directed that an enumeration district must contain one parish and should not contain any part of two parishes. Parts of a parish that were within a burgh were required to have a separate district, while Quoad Sacra parishes had to be specifically defined.

Registrars and their equivalents were asked to write full and precise descriptions of their districts. The instructions for the 1901 Census required them to describe the dividing line, a well-defined street, in instances where part of a parish is included in an enumeration district. In cases of an enumeration district forming part of a civil parish, the districts were to be described as bounded on the North by the centre of ____ street, on the East by the centre of ____ road. The registrars were required to provide an exhaustive list of streets, roads, groups of houses and detached houses included in each enumeration district. It was impressed upon them the description of the contents and boundaries were to be as clear and intelligible to the enumerator as possible, thereby ensuring accuracy and efficiency during the census process.

After having carefully considered their plan of division with the guidance of the superintendent registrar, or sheriff or chief magistrate in Scotland, they were required to prepare it for submission to the Registrar General. While doing so they provided their best estimate for the number of houses and families in each enumeration district and the number and names of institutions and vessels to be enumerated. Once completed, they submitted their plan, usually well before Christmas to the Registrar General. They could then concentrate on their usual duties until the instructions arrived pertaining to the recruitment of enumerators.

Chapter Four

A Rather Poor Lot

Well, they are on the whole a rather poor lot.

So said Dr Ogle about the quality of enumerators in England and Wales. His scathing opinion may have been a little justified and in marked contrast to the Registrar General for Scotland, Stair Agnew, who viewed his enumerators with satisfaction. In his testimony to the Treasury Committee in 1890, Agnew testified his enumerators – who were appointed by local registrars upon approval by the sheriff – did very well and he could find no fault with their work.

In Ireland the method of enumeration was through the Royal Irish Constabulary and by the Metropolitan police in Dublin with assistance from schoolmasters to great effect. It is highly probable that Ireland's cohort of enumerators fitted the job description published in the English and Welsh press in 1900. Each potential enumerator was required to be a good writer and a capable man, well trained to business habits, and possessing adequate knowledge of the locality and its industry. The instructions supplied to the registrars in December 1900 went further, specifying that the selected enumerators must be intelligent, trustworthy and active with no signs of infirmity or weak health. He must write legibly and have a good knowledge of arithmetic. He must not be younger than 18 years of age nor older than 65 and must possess the character traits of temperateness, orderliness, propriety and civility. It was also suggested his ordinary occupation should add to his fitness for office; individuals who were clergymen, ministers, professional men, schoolmasters etc., were considered perfect candidates. At this date, women were eligible to work as enumerators and had been since 1891, except in areas where local conditions deemed hiring women impractical, according to one source.

Apart from the eligibility of women, the attributions and qualifications did not vary much from census to census, nor were there additional or different requirements in Scotland. By the 1931 Census, however, the age range for candidates had changed to between 20 years of age and 60 years of age. Registrars were given some flexibility if a candidate was older than the upper range and had observed his duty commendably during a previous census.

Unfortunately, registrars did not always stick to the qualification guidelines and were not averse to appointing their friends and acquaintances in need. This habit, described as "petty jobbery" by one individual, was considered detrimental to the recruitment process and resulted in low quality enumerators. In a letter sent to the *Morning Advertiser* in 1841, the anonymous correspondent accused the parochial authorities of favouritism when selecting enumerators for the position.[46]

Registrar Frank Tupper appointed three friends who were fellow clerks and five other enumerators who were either commercial or civil service clerks in 1881. He also appointed a French polisher of reduced circumstances and a house decorator. He recalled that another registrar had appointed a newspaper seller who sold his papers at the starting point of the South Hackney omnibuses and who managed to lose half of his schedules on the day of the census. While Tupper's French polisher managed to complete his work with some efficiency, he made errors with regards to the three ecclesiastical districts that made up his enumeration district. As a consequence, he was made to start again and complete a fresh enumeration book.

Registrar Alfred Gibbs reappointed individuals who had served under his predecessor after receiving their names and studying the districts in his area. Among them were overseers, tax collectors, deputy registrars, and vaccination officers. When asked about their appointments, he said they were all trusted public officers.

In 1871, the Oxfordshire Registrar George Brunner appointed a number of individuals from various backgrounds including the diocesan secretary, banker's and solicitor's clerks, post office clerks, several accountants, two attorney's clerks, a schoolmaster, a rate collector, and an auctioneer's clerk.

It was universally accepted clerks of any kind made superior enumerators, but for commercial and business clerks like Charles Davies, the census occurred at the wrong time. After having signed up as an enumerator, he soon discovered his census duties coincided with the end of the financial year. Most of the censuses during the Victorian era either fell just before the conclusion of the fiscal year, on it, or just after. Writing to his friend in 1881, Charles who lived in Leith in the north of Edinburgh explained that a mixture of stock taking, preparing the annual balance sheet, and his enumerator duties left him with no time for missives. Just prior to the census, when he was required to deliver his schedules to householders, he was working overtime for the business. accounting for stock including 9,000 bags of flour. Then, having collected his schedules he had a whole day "clerking", only to return home to the additional work of copying schedules into the enumeration book until 1 am in the morning. He later admitted to his correspondent the work was greater than he had anticipated.[47]

It was also considered that clergymen were in a superior position to assist the census authorities by dispelling ignorance and acting as enumerators. They knew their parishioners and were trusted with information, they also were keen to act for philanthropic reasons. In 1861, the *Monmouthshire Beacon* reported applications for the role of enumerator in many London districts were over-subscribed. This was due to the large number of clergymen and scripture readers keen to enumerate districts inhabited by the poorer classes.[48]

Schoolmasters were also known and trusted by the householders. Prior to civil registration in Scotland, the sheriff depute or provost of every burgh appointed the schoolmaster or other fit persons to undertake the census work and to divide the parish into enumeration districts. Then, a list of potential enumerators was compiled to assist the schoolmaster. An 1851 list of proposed enumerators for districts in East Lothian shows a mix of schoolmasters and constables, police officers, surgeons, and ministers, a postman, a gardener, and a joiner.[49] In 1861, there were over a thousand registrars made up mainly of schoolmasters in the rural areas and other professional men in the burghs. They picked 8,075 enumerators drawn from various occupations to assist them. In Edinburgh, 300 enumerators were taken from the city's Volunteer Regiment.[50] Thirty years later, one source reported enumerators were drawn from a number of occupations including: students, collar-makers, coopers, dairymen, doorkeepers and storekeepers, bookbinders, compositors, plus the usual clerical staff with an emphasis on postmen. By 1939, individuals working in their day jobs as fancy corsetieres, commercial travellers or teachers of music, signed up to be enumerators for the National Register.

Many individuals clearly enjoyed or suffered the experience for their own reasons, returning to undertake their duties again and again. William Gilchrist aged 67 wrote to his local registrar at Milngavie requesting to be considered for the 1931 Census after having served in 1921.[51] He was duly appointed. Come 1939, he applied for the (later cancelled) 1941 Census at the age of 74! At Llanfihangel Glyn Myfyr, enumerator Mr C. Lloyd acted as an enumerator for the sixth time in 1881 after receiving special permission from the Registrar General on account of his age. Mr H. Woolley, of Moulton was enumerator for the 1831, 1841, 1851, 1861 censuses and registrar for the 1871 Census, following on from his father who took the 1821 Census and his grandfather who took the 1811 and 1801 censuses![52]

In the February of 1951, Mr Young wrote to his MP about the opposition he had received regarding his application to be an enumerator at the age of 66. It was only when he had told the registrar he had served as an enumerator on every occasion except one "since 1899" that he was accepted. Many other applicants wrote to their representatives or to the Registrar General with similar complaints about being excluded due to age. One gentleman wrote "You will be surprised to know that men holding good positions have applied and as in elections we older men have been pushed aside."[53]

As far as the authorities were concerned, while a lower and upper age limit was prescribed, it was not to be rigidly applied and individuals below and above the limit could be appointed at the discretion of the registrar. Registrars had to make judgements about an individual's health and ability to undertake the long hours required during the delivery and collection of schedules. In one case, a husband and wife, both aged over 70 made applications to be enumerators, but were rejected by the registrar because he was not sufficiently satisfied with their physical fitness.

Many war veterans made applications to be enumerators. One wrote to his MP Anthony Wedgwood Benn in 1951 asking for his assistance after the veteran's application had been rejected on account of his disability. In a reply to Benn's enquiry, an official from the Census Office explained that given the arduous duties of the enumerator, the risk of breakdown at the last minute through physical disability couldn't be accepted.[54] Questions about employing enumerators with disabilities had arisen some thirty years earlier when the census administration came under pressure to employ First

World War veterans registered at labour exchanges. The recommendation for utilising the Board of Trade labour exchanges had actually occurred a few years prior to this in 1910. Mr Samuel W. Scott from the Carlton Place Labour Exchange in Glasgow wrote to the Registrar General's office in Scotland suggesting they used the facilities offered by the exchanges for finding reliable and trustworthy men. The census authorities were highly sceptical about using this method to find suitable candidates. In an internal memo, the suggestion was thought to be unfeasible and given the types of the men on the exchanges' books such as labourers and industrial workers, the so-called men of the lower orders, it was considered the nature of clerical work was beyond them. As a compromise, the census authorities in Scotland advised the labour exchanges to encourage unemployed men with clerical experience to apply directly to their local registrar.

For the 1921 Census, the Registrar General's office faced thousands of unemployed ex-servicemen desperate for work as enumerators. Despite a great deal of agitation in the press, from unions, and questions in the House of Commons endorsing their employment, ministers and officials were able to dispose of the proposition. Thinking they could return to their original plan, made in an agreement with the Board of Education in England and Wales, to employ teachers as the sole enumerators for the 1921 Census, they were forced to change. Many teachers had been engaged for the National Registration Act 1915 and in some areas schools were closed for a prolonged period to allow for the work to be completed. In 1921, the agitation to employ unemployed ex-servicemen had induced local education authorities to backtrack and withdraw their cooperation. Teachers were not allowed to serve. Eventually, the census authorities were forced to recruit local government officials and private individuals.[55]

Where possible, the Registrar General tried to find jobs for the unemployed at census headquarters, but enumerator roles were deemed impractical. The census authorities argued applications for the position were made and signed off a few months prior to the census and what amounted to a few days' work in the future, was unsuitable for the unemployed in the present. By signing the declaration to serve and then defaulting because of finding employment, not only led to a £10 fine, but it would also cause major disruption to the census machinery.

Ten years later in the midst of the Great Depression, with unemployment higher than in 1921, the same argument returned. It was agreed by the Census Offices of England, Wales, and Scotland, that applications from the unemployed should be considered if they were deemed suitable for the work of enumeration. This decision, however, did not go far enough for some campaigners who wanted the 40,000 enumerator positions entirely filled by the unemployed. To the chagrin of Registrar General Sylvanus Vivian, many local authorities concurred and restricted their own officials from serving as enumerators. Yet again, the Census Office had to make up the numbers from the retired and employed with no special training or aptitude to fill the roles.

After the census was concluded, Vivian's report on the matter highlighted the predicted difficulties they faced. Out of the 40,000 enumerators appointed by census officers, 12,250 were unemployed. Shortly after their appointment, many withdrew and had to be replaced. Those who undertook the work thinking it was no more than leaflet delivery, saw the paperwork and the nature of the duties, then withdrew; others who had gained regular work quit on those grounds. One enumerator disappeared in the course of the enumeration with his enumeration book and partially collected schedules. Another enumerator prepared fictitious returns to avoid the difficulty of obtaining them from the public. It was also noted, in a small number of cases, there were substantial omissions. All these problems were rectified by other officers, but the inconvenience of finding 2,316 replacement enumerators for various reasons was detrimental to the census operations. The census authorities felt vindicated by their initial reservations in appointing the unemployed, but were quick to give praise where it was due, admitting many coped admirably.

Women were under pressure to avoid making applications for positions while unemployment was high, and many themselves considered it inappropriate. They had officially been involved with the census taking for decades, some in their capacity as registrars, others as enumerators both officially and no doubt unofficially during earlier censuses. Wives assisted their husbands when it came to schedule delivery and collection; some may have burnt a few candles copying schedules into enumeration books before they were authorised to do so. Daughters made great assistants too and can often be found listed as such in the enumeration books.

In 1871, an anonymous account appeared in the *Islington Gazette* by a female describing her experience as an accidental enumerator. The woman was Maria Butterfield, wife of William Butterfield, who had occupied the role of registrar for thirty-seven years. Maria believed "man is said to be the stronger, not the weaker, vessel; and ... that [a] woman's proper sphere is home." It is of no surprise then, her account is somewhat apologetic – that finding herself in the enumerator's role at the age of 40, was not a position she had imagined for herself.

In that year, her husband was overseeing his fourth census, and, like many other registrars, he was grappling with the challenges brought about by changes to the ecclesiastical districts after a decade of church building. Each of his eighty-one enumerators was assigned a district or block of houses recorded in their memorandum book. They were also given the names of two or three fellow enumerators working on either side of them to ensure no household was overlooked. From 7.30 am on Monday, 3 April, all of the enumerators assembled in their respective districts and William left to attend their supervision. He hadn't been gone long when Maria was informed an entire terrace had been overlooked and no schedules had been distributed to any of the homes. She was unsure what she should do. Her first thought was to contact the superintendent, but he lived some distance away. Eventually she picked up some schedules and pencils and ventured to the terrace and began to enumerate the houses. Having completed this task she headed home, but heard the following day, two other streets had also been omitted. Again she took it upon herself to see the job done, writing in the newspaper that "had the enumerators paid proper attention to their instructions, this would not have happened." After completing all of her duties, Maria returned home tired and weary, satisfied she had done her duty and having "the gratification of knowing that a woman had, for the first time, assisted in taking the census."[56]

In July 1890, the *Pall Mall Gazette* advocated for women enumerators, arguing they would be happy to receive the equivalent of a labourer's wage. The correspondent also suggested the requisites of tact and pertinacity were surely characteristics that gave women an advantage over men.[57] He then quotes a passage from the Treasury Committee report of 1890 citing it as evidence women enumerators were used in Ireland in 1881. However, the passage he refers to references twenty-five women clerks who were hired via a women's Work Society in Dublin to assist with the post-census tabulation.[58] The Committee *had* commented that women were eligible to serve as enumerators to some advantage. Many newspapers agreed. The *Yorkshire Post and Leeds Intelligencer* pointed out they may excel in the information they were able to obtain about a family and families in a given time. In addition, the newspaper suggested, they could bring their knitting and have a confidential chat with the householder; there was no limit to the acquisition of information about children, vaccinations, and measles etc., to say nothing of what she would learn about the eccentricities of the neighbours.[59]

In October 1890, a secretary in the Census Office wrote on behalf of the Registrar General to the Superintendent Registrar of Ruthin, informing him women were not eligible for the role of enumerators. By December 1890 this had changed and women were invited to become enumerators at the next census.[60] While there were a number of applications for the role of enumerator among the female population in 1891, it was exceeded in 1901 according to one newspaper. The *Newcastle Daily Chronicle* wrote that it was the first time female enumerators were to be employed on a large scale. In terms of their work the *Manchester Evening News* reported the 1901 female army of enumerators had made it through their ordeal exceedingly well; in fact, their returns were, almost without exception, models of neatness, completeness, and accuracy.

By 1911, with a number of local government roles filled by women including health visitors, sanitary and district inspectors, and infant protection officers, the reception to female enumerators on thresholds across the country, was one of familiarity and respect. Though, like their male counterparts, they still continued to face doorstep refusals and obfuscation during their duties.

Many enumerators hadn't anticipated this when they signed the application form or offered their name. From 1841, registrars in England and Wales were required to make a list in duplicate of the selected enumerators including their ages, occupations, residence and the number of the enumeration district where they resided. These lists were due by a specified date and sent to the Superintendent Registrar. He would then appoint persons he saw as the most fit to serve. This system required the registrar to select more candidates than were actually needed. He was advised to make sure the men were resident in their own district to avoid commuting, however this was not a rigid requirement. Once selected, enumerators were required to sign a form of agreement which bound them to their duty; failure to act after signing the form resulted in a penalty. Substitute enumerators would need approval from the Superintendent Registrar or equivalent and the Registrar General, but if the enumerator reneged just prior to the census, the registrar could find a replacement without approval. The Census Amendment Act of 1841 assisted registrars who faced difficulty finding enough candidates or substitutes to act as enumerators by binding constables, tythingmen, headboroughs, peace officers (including police officers) and relieving officers in any Poor Law Union, to act as enumerators or face a penalty.

In 1890, the Registrar General Brydges Henniker wrote a forthright letter to the Registrars of Births and Deaths in England and Wales informing them their enumeration districts for the 1881 Census were too numerous and unequal in size. He also complained the boundaries were imperfectly defined and they had not taken sufficient care when selecting enumerators. Many of the latter had performed their duties in a slovenly manner and were guilty of writing illegibly. Henniker emphasised that for the 1891 Census, registrars should seek to select schoolmasters, overseers, or those from the higher stations in life.[61]

The 1890 Treasury Committee suggested numerous ways to improve the quality of the enumerators, from selecting schoolmasters and sanitary officials to postmen, school board officers and even the military. For the 1901 Census, it was agreed to commence with application forms because it was believed they would indicate a level of intelligence plus they would evidence the legibility of the enumerators' handwriting. As to any form of training, registrars were asked to interview the enumerators, either individually or as a group after they had distributed the memorandum books and schedules. This was to ascertain whether the enumerator understood the boundaries of their respective enumeration districts and the extent of their census duties. Alfred Gibbs, a registrar from Witley near Godalming chose to interview his enumerators individually. Frank Tupper brought his enumerators together and worked through the instructions with them. Enumerator Charles White recalled his registrar gave some instructions to him alone and did not address the enumerators as a group.[62]

Some registrars went above and beyond the guidelines given to them. In 1841, Thomas Yates the registrar for East Leicester sent a letter to the *Leicester Chronicle* asking for the public to have their schedules ready when the enumerator called. Mr Hallsworth, the registrar for Ardwick in Manchester made sure he had personal knowledge of all his enumerators drawn from various callings including carters, iron moulders, and photographers. While simultaneously coaching each enumerator, Hallsworth prepared seventeen supplemental instructions to those issued by the Registrar General. Of note are:

> 11. Let the writing be as plain as possible, write a simple round hand without flourishing or embellishment.

15. Let me have your books, accounts, and the schedules open and flat (not folded) as soon possible.

17. Finally if in doubt on any point, see me, don't be afraid of giving me trouble, realising, as I trust you do also, the great importance of this work ...[63]

Frank Tupper also offered his enumerators tips and assistance. He supplied sketch plans with the enumerator's notebook and also suggested to his enumerators they number the schedules in pencil before they left home to start their deliveries. They should then re-number them in ink upon completion of the collection to obviate difficulties caused by issuing new schedules to newcomers on census day. Tupper also advised his enumerators to check the schedules before they left the household because many errors would not be detected by the enumerator or registrar at a later date. Mr Watkins, registrar for Cardiff had specially prepared at his own cost, a small map showing the boundaries and every name of every street in Cardiff and Penarth. Mr Strange, in 1901, thoughtfully and carefully marked out his enumerator's route and best direction to travel. In 1871, George Brunner the aforementioned registrar for Oxford made a personal tour of the poorer parts of the town, suggesting to families who understood the returns to aid their neighbours who could not.[64]

During the course of the nineteenth century, the instructions issued to registrars in regards to their duties had grown significantly in scope and detail. The enumeration and memorandum books containing descriptions of boundaries and contents of an enumeration district, had to be legibly copied by the registrar or enumerator from the plan of division before census day. The registrar had to make sure the enumerator had enough schedules and a number in reserve, had his or her claim for allowances form and that schedules/enumeration books for institutions were supplied to the institutional officers. He also had to ensure his enumerators were aware of the institutions in their district and that each enumeration book had the number of the enumeration district written in the appropriate place. In the week following the census, registrars had to procure from each enumerator in his sub-district all the schedules, numbered and arranged in order from No. 1 to the last number entered in his enumeration book, the enumeration and memorandum books, and the enumerators claim for allowances.

His next duty was to check the handwriting in the enumeration book to make sure it was clear and legible. He could insist the enumerator make another copy, if the book was poorly written. Registrars were also required to compare meticulously a sample of schedules with the entries in the enumeration book to ascertain if they were accurate and without omission. In the book, he checked each page for the correct parish township, ecclesiastical district, city or borough, etc., and that the house's name or location was accurately noted in the appropriate column. He ensured the boundaries of parishes and townships were clearly defined in the book and that no house in the district was missing, and if any were, he would ask the enumerator to complete the return. The registrar also checked that the lines separating the houses and individual occupiers were accurate and the column entries were consistent. He was also supposed to ensure ages were recorded in the appropriate columns. Additionally, he verified the "Rank, Profession, or Occupation" column was completed according to the rules, that the totals of houses and individuals at the bottom of each page were accurately recorded by the enumerators, and the summary of totals and other essential details were properly addressed.

In 1890, Frank Tupper admitted to the Treasury Committee he was unable to minutely examine the schedules for errors before they had to be surrendered to the superintendent registrar and another registrar said he was unable to check if the occupations were in the correct format. In Scotland, the enumeration books were checked by the clergy prior to civil registration, then the sheriff clerks or the sheriff, but it was only a cursory examination.

After having supposedly completed all checks of the enumeration books, the registrar had to sign the certificate at the front of the book and then make up further statistical summaries regarding Total Population and Housing etc. on forms provided to him or her. Claims of allowances by enumerators had to be verified and signed off before all the documents, excluding the household schedules, had to be sent to the superintendent registrar by a specified date. The schedules were to be forwarded directly to the Census Office by railway or carrier. Additional duties were added in 1921 when registrars were required to bind batches of approximately 500 schedules between covers provided to them by the Census Office.

The anxieties of taking the census and the number of duties involved took its toll on many of the officers. In 1871, Superintendent Registrar of Alderley Jonathan Downes committed suicide by drowning due to the onerous duties of the census on top of his usual commitments. The death of a Glasgow registrar in 1901 was attributed to the stress of the census.

Registrars were also vulnerable to assaults by their employees and members of the public. Frank Joseph Lockyer, the registrar for Hoxton was punched by householder Joseph Bailby when Lockyer called to collect the schedules for the 1911 Census. Bailby's defence was that he believed Lockyer was a trespasser. In 1851, Thomas Plenderleath the Superintendent Registrar for Longtown was murdered by enumerator William Kirkpatrick. The dispute concerned Kirkpatrick's wages for his census duties.

Such stresses must have led to incompetence. It was clear from Brydges Henniker's letter concerning the problems with the 1881 Census some registrars were inadequate and the problem needed addressing. The 1890 Treasury Committee made a suggestion that bonuses could be used as an incentive to produce higher quality work. From 1901, registrars were given bonuses for care in the selection and supervision of enumerators and accuracy in the revision of their work. This, however, did not remedy all the problems with the registrar's work. In 1931, Mr Beeching the registrar for Dover was docked £2 in respect of his unsatisfactory performance during census duties. In that same year, major errors and omissions were made by the registrars in North and South Kensington. The registrar for North Kensington did not check the 26,000 schedules or make corrections before dispatching them to the Census Office and the registrar for North Kensington made the same mistakes he had made in 1921! To say the Census Office was livid is an understatement. Their only recourse was to request the enumeration of those districts again in the July and August of 1931, though the suggestion was met with some resistance by the enumerators.

Following this debacle, the Census Office conducted a review of the work done by the registrars for the 1931 Census. They found few faults and just thirteen registrars were penalised for poor work.[65]

It can be argued that while many enumerators were simply not up to the job, the competence of the registrar was a significant factor in their capacity to be efficient. If their enumeration district was too large, the content description not detailed enough, or as one 1961 enumerator found, their boundary map was next to useless, the enumerator was more likely to fail. Their duties were onerous enough without these added burdens.

Chapter Five

Tomorrow is "C" Day

> When it is completed I shall be able to say with pride, not un-mixed with disgust, 'Alone I did it!' It will remain in the archives of my country a monument to my industry and perseverance under most trying circumstances.

Just prior to the 1891 Census, a Cardiff man visited his local registrar's office to receive the first instructions regarding his enumeration duties. A friend suggested he might like the work, for it was an opportunity to use his spare time *profitably*. This was a sentiment echoed elsewhere: for some it was the chance to put aside a little cash for a holiday or to add additional income to the household coffers. While many heard about the census work via an acquaintance, newspapers, or posters at the town hall, some did it as a good turn for a registrar who happened to be a friend. After all the work was done, a few enumerators expressed the opinion they had been "induced" and perhaps blind-sided into undertaking the duties by the acquaintance or registrar; they felt the work was just too hard and the pay too little.

For every grumbler, there were individuals who were motivated to undertake the work just for a glance of life behind the curtains, to learn about the lives and circumstances of others better or worse off than themselves. Census-taking afforded these individuals the opportunity to wander through tenements, courts, and warrens they dared not enter at any other time. Whatever their personal incentives were, it is likely their motivations were accompanied by their own biases. "It seemed as though ... I had come upon a people of another race", wrote one enumerator when entering a working-class district. These unspoken prejudices emerged when they ventured into the poverty ridden tenements or stood in the gas-lit vestibules of the middle classes hoping to be shielded from the worst elements of the weather. For even the middling sort did not escape their disapprobation.

The Cardiff man was a grumbler. After all his duties were done, he considered himself deluded for having taken on the enumerator's role. That day in the registrar's office when he was confronted with all the apparatus of his duties, the realisation of what the work involved fell upon him hard as if he had been hit by an enumeration book. Elsewhere, up and down the country, his fellow enumerators were having the same thoughts when they first encountered the census paraphernalia and the dreaded instructions.

There was amazement and disquiet at the volume and size of material the enumerators had to digest and carry with them. The deluded Cardiff enumerator estimated the books were about 2 feet long and queried with the registrar whether he was expected to carry them everywhere.

"Haven't you a bag?" asked the registrar.

"A bag!" answered the deluded one. "You mean a trunk!"

Eventually the deluded enumerator reached home with all the materials, but made successive trips in order to do so. It was only then that he was able to turn his attention to the "closely printed" instructions.

At this point, he discovered he was urged to use a bag to carry the materials whilst undertaking his duties and to take an elastic band or string to tie the schedules into number order. Such helpful hints were not included in the instructions for the 1841 Census, possibly because of the rather hurried decision to print schedules between the original 1841 Census Act and the Amendment Act that followed. When it came to delivering the schedules in 1841, registrars were told they must cause "a Householder's schedule paper to be left at every house in his district ... [and] to be left by person or persons as he pleases." Therefore the registrars could take it upon themselves to deliver the schedules, use the enumerator assigned to collect them, or appoint someone entirely different. Certainly the table of allowances for enumerator's pay (see Dangers, Troubles and Death) does not include payments for the delivery of the schedules.

Other instructions for enumerators in England, Scotland, Wales, and the Islands covered basic points with regards to recording jurisdictions, housing, names, absentees, age and sex, profession, trade, employment, and where born. Clearly, in response to feedback from registrars and enumerators, from unanticipated problems arising during and after enumeration, and from the additional questions asked as the census evolved, changes were made to the instructions.

Clarification as to what constituted a household and in which circumstances a house would be classed as uninhabited were further elaborated upon over a number of censuses. While the content remained more or less the same before 1901, with a few additions and some rewriting, changes were made to the third person voice in 1861, switching it to a clearer and more forceful second person voice. In 1871, the paragraphs were numbered and remained so up to 1901 with a few additions increasing the paragraph count. From 1901, an individual clearly enthusiastic about dividing paragraphs into sub-divisions for easy reading proceeded to break-up those "closely-printed" instructions, thus providing greater clarification and consequently making the content more readable.

In addition to the separate circulars and the book of instructions, a precis of the directions were printed at the beginning of the enumeration books in Great Britain up to and including 1901. While Scotland continued to use enumeration books, England and Wales dispensed with them for the 1911 Census and the enumerators were given memorandum and summary books as well as the householder schedules. The memorandum books also included instructions particularly pertinent to the delivery of the schedules.

Enumerators were asked to make themselves fully conversant with all these materials and the extent of their districts. Initially, they were advised to consult the enumerators in districts either side of their own, making sure they understood where their boundary started and where it ended. In 1891, this was changed to suggesting they should take measures to remove all doubts they had about the confines of their district. Once sure of their area, they needed to settle their route and the order in which they intended to visit all the houses in their district.

Mr Deluded Enumerator was rather exasperated with all these instructions, however he had made his oath to fulfil his duties and that was that. Before delivery day, he wrote on the outside of each schedule the name of the civil parish, the borough, and the urban sanitary district in which his own district was situated, and numbered each schedule starting from number one consecutively. He also added the number of the enumeration district, to which was later added the numbers of the registration district and the sub-district.

He could start his delivery in the week commencing 29 March 1891; unfortunately for him the weather in Wales had turned bitterly cold and wet.

Apart from a summery 1841 Census and a dry and chilly 1881, it was often the case that enumerators had to battle the elements: Edinburgh escaped the worse of it in 1891 and delivery took place during a fine spell, but 160 miles or so further south, the collection of the schedules was impeded by a blanket of cold and wet weather. In 1901, the county of Yorkshire was hit by a weather bomb comprising of hail, snow and bitterly cold blizzards which curtailed any attempts at delivery the week beginning 25 March. Many enumerators sat out the day, hoping to sally forth on the 26th, however the weather turned even worse and some did not start their deliveries until 28 March.[66] Further south, a Norfolk enumerator pushed through the wind, snow, and rain which quickly turned the ground treacherous with mud. Just a week later, the weather in the south turned more clement and the collection was undertaken in more favourable conditions.

When the weather was very grim it could seriously impact an enumerator's duties. They were required to complete the memorandum book in either pencil or pen and ink as they proceeded from house to house and to enter the name of the street, the name or number of the house, and the name of the occupier of the house where they delivered each schedule; and in the event of two or more families occupying one house, they were to leave a corresponding number of schedules and note them in the book. If it was cold and dark, many householders would not come to the door to enable the enumerator to fulfil these duties, and during collection time, writing and checking the schedules in adverse weather, when they were not offered a space inside, was onerous. Some enumerators reported that in the wind and rain they could only offer a cursory glance at a schedule to check to see if the information was entered correctly. This was emphasised in the 1951 Census Preliminary Report, where it was stated that due to the bad weather: "... the enumerators were naturally reluctant to examine forms at the door, and some deficiencies in the quality and completeness of some answers may result; it is much more difficult to get deficiencies put right a few days after the schedules have been collected."

Bad weather also brought bad light and dark spring evenings. Enumerators were unable to see the schedules in dark areas and check them as instructed. Even though many reported revisiting households for this task, no doubt a few went unchecked.

Enumerators travelled mainly by foot and horse, but took up the bicycle, the pony and trap and later the automobile to complete their rounds. While the pony and trap was a popular mode of transport, it could sometimes become a cumbersome burden. One enumerator was driven by his friend to a distant part of the district, but both were impeded by mud and bad weather and the two men were subsequently observed carrying the vehicle while the pony walked on serenely in front. For those on foot, their days on duty could be long and tough. Calling at 200–300 houses, asking for the paper, examining it to check for incorrect entries and making the necessary alterations involved a good eight or ten hours of walking. Streets with backyards, courts, alleys, ginnels or squares were preferred and meant the enumerator was at advantage if they or the registrar had marked out an exact path to follow. If the enumerator was careful they rarely went wrong. Parallel streets, on the other hand, with little front gardens and iron gates which were permanently latched meant four times more walking than passing unhindered from door to door. Tenements with three flights of stairs inevitably made enumerators grumpy due to the extra effort and also cautious when navigating darkly lit landings filled with detritus. Yet the more packed in the householders were, the happier the enumerator was in general.

Those in rural areas could take in the spectacular vistas of their district, some so thinly populated they had only a dozen or so households to visit. These were so dispersed and scattered about the hills, enumerators were forced to walk miles traipsing through fields soaked with rain and through bogs. In Scotland, John Cameron the enumerator for Morven in Argyle wrote that the majority of the inhabitants in his district were around Lochaline, but there were four families he visited that were so far apart, he had difficulty traversing the rugged landscape in the time allocated.

For the 1911 Census in Boston and Skirbeck, each enumerator averaged nearly 400 houses, and some walked a distance of 20 miles. These were outdone by the enumerators of Bramley in Surrey who calculated they had walked 30 miles for the 1901 Census. However the winner of the "most miles walked" surely has to be poor Mr Wilkinson the enumerator for Foulness Island who allegedly walked nearly 60 miles over roads which were no better than cart tracks.

It was widely reported that as well as suffering from blisters, enumerators were frequently met with suspicion and received a great deal of resistance by householders in some areas. As a consequence, enumerators learnt that tact, diplomacy, knowledge, and sometimes a few tricks resulted in them getting the required information quickly and efficiently. Enumerators who were not only local, but who also held employment positions within the community such as school board officers, teachers, or those working for the Board of Guardians were at an advantage when it came to knowledge of individual households. They may already be aware the householder was a landlord or landlady with a lodger upstairs who required a schedule even though the householder was loathe to admit it; they knew that the man who said he was a cooper was in fact a cooper's labourer, because he had already confessed to this when he appeared before the Guardians.

The enumerator's official instructions requested they explain to each householder the objects of the census if necessary. By doing this, they hoped to allay any fears the occupant may have about the questions, inform them of the penalties if they did not complete the form, and to assist them in understanding the schedule. Some enumerators decided that pre-emptive action may serve them in this matter. In 1891, a Sussex enumerator wrote to his local newspaper with instructions and an example census schedule showing exactly how the form should be completed. He added he would have very little time to spare, and it would greatly assist him if every householder had his or her census paper clearly written out and ready for prompt delivery on collection day. Hopefully, the people of his district were paying attention because elsewhere householders were convinced the papers were summonses and that the enumerator was a bailiff.[67] This was particularly so when the schedules were printed on blue paper akin to that used for court documents. Many enumerators expressed their discontent at the decision to print on blue paper, pointing out it was a hurdle in the completion of their deliveries. One enumerator even hoped the next census form would be printed on bright pink paper.

Having endured one or two hostile encounters, it was often necessary to hide evidence of the blue papers when going house to house, but householders often caught wind that someone was visiting their street on official business and would not open their doors. This necessitated leaving the schedules with next-door neighbours who were less suspicious.

On occasion, some householders would answer the door saying they had already received the papers, at which point the enumerator would explain these were in fact census papers and not summonses. If the enumerators weren't mistaken for bailiffs, then they were considered to be someone else the householder needed to avoid. It was commonly thought nothing good ever come from a paper bearing the Queen's arms – the equivalent of the twenty-first-century brown envelope. Enumerators were thought to be school board officers, agents from Dr Barnardos, rent and rate collectors, chasers of dog licence defaulters, postmen, army recruiters intent on conscripting the men of the household (particular in 1901 during the Boer War), a German spy during the 1915 National Registration, insurance canvassers, gas men, and a vaccinator – at a time when the country debated the merits of vaccination. In addition, they were mistaken for either the milkman, the greengrocer, the circular deliverer, or an itinerant vendor and were often met with a "Not today, thank you" through the letter box. However, sometimes they were welcomed. Householders thought they were salesmen returning to their tenement with cheap wares for sale or during the 1911 Census, bringing news about pensions. And if the newspaper reports are to be believed, they were sometimes met at the door by certain females in a state of undress, believing them to be the doctor or someone else; or kept waiting for twenty minutes by a lady titivating herself because she believes the enumerator to be her current crush, the minister.[68]

Children, while out playing, acted as lookouts in the courts and yards of some districts. Upon spying the enumerator, they informed a parent and word quickly spread to the neighbours an official was nearby. People retreated into their homes and doors were slammed shut and locked. When children were receiving school lessons about the census, enumerators reported a contrasting scene of being accompanied by groups of kids while they were collecting schedules in the tenements and courts. The parents could be seen waiting patiently on the balconies and in stairwells with completed schedule in hand. Despite educated children and a better-informed public, suspicions remained in some working-class areas.

If a door was locked and the householder was absent or refusing to answer, second and third visits were necessary in the week leading up to the census day, and in one case as many as seven calls were made before the enumerator was able to deliver the schedule. Enumerators quickly discovered the postman's double knock was a way to bring the reticent and suspicious householder to their door. If performed with sufficient gusto, it would bring the entire terrace out of their houses to find out what was going on. Thus, all the neighbours knew the enumerator was on his or her way.

In some instances, the household was never at home and absent for work purposes, in which case the neighbours could be useful. After knocking on the doors of three empty houses, an enumerator in Halifax found an obliging young woman who gave him all the necessary information about the absentees and even undertook to deliver their papers for him. In case the Registrar General happened to be reading his account, he reassuringly wrote he knew she had fulfilled the task. Some enumerators made use of the neighbour's willingness to offer information about next door and routinely asked for it, that way he or she could jot down the names on the succeeding schedule and record the information in the memorandum book in advance before moving on to the next house.

When there was no householder or neighbour around to accept delivery of the papers, other measures had to be taken. In Acton during the 1931 Census, families were so noticeable by their absence, it was deemed necessary for the enumerators to make postal appointments to ensure the safe delivery of the forms.[69] Many householders though took the responsibility upon themselves to acquire schedules direct from the registrar's office if they knew they were going to be absent when the forms were distributed.

Visiting the registrar was not unusual and individuals grew accustomed to contacting him or her if their schedules were not delivered. Notices placed by registrars appeared more frequently in the newspapers from 1891 onward instructing the householder to visit the office when such scenarios arose. In 1901, Burton Street in Bath and some houses in Reigate were completely overlooked by enumerators and both registrar's offices were besieged with people all anxious to get a census paper.

A good proportion of these delivery errors were also remedied by census officials albeit at the last minute in some cases. In Leeds in 1881, the delivery of the schedules was delayed in some areas and householders did not receive them until the Sunday evening with a few arriving as late as the afternoon of 4 April. During the 1911 Census, it wasn't until 3 April that authorities discovered over 200 people had been left out of the count in Stoke-on-Trent. Also, Bayswater was entirely forgotten until one individual raised the issue and the census authorities became aware of the omission. Almost a year after the 1891 Census, officials in the sub-district of Hadleigh were called upon to investigate the omission of three households. They were supplied with blank schedules and were asked to gather approximate information about the families omitted from the census some eleven months earlier.[70]

Many enumerators were on the receiving end of abuse when schedules were not delivered or their competency was questioned. However, it was not necessarily solely due to individual error and other factors may have influenced omissions. Enumerators who were delayed explaining to every single householder how to fill in the schedule and why the census occurred were often out delivering until 10 pm. In 1901, an enumerator from Manchester bemoaned that out of 250 houses, there were fewer than five where he never had to explain over and over again what the census was for and what was required for the schedule.[71] At the end of this, enumerators were often tired, hungry, and having to finish their rounds in the dark; this led to them occasionally overlooking individual houses and streets. In some instances, enumerators ran out of schedules for their district and had to return to the registrar's office the next day to obtain more and then recommence their deliveries. There were also instances of "pop-up" houses suddenly appearing out of nowhere in the enumerator's district, as well as the changes to boundaries not taken into consideration by the registrars in their plans of division.

After delivering the schedules many enumerators had endured enough already and were unaware the worst was yet to come. It took our Deluded Enumerator four days or twenty-five hours in total to deliver to his Cardiff district; in addition, he spent eight hours preparing the schedules. Elsewhere, enumerators were struggling to timetable their duties on top of their regular employment and many reported having to skip meals while delivering and collecting schedules. One enumerator carefully planned his schedule so he did not have to miss sustenance. He decided to deliver before office hours, get a hurried lunch, and deliver during the time allotted for his dinner. On leaving the office he snacked and worked until 10 pm, then had supper on arriving home. Despite hiring an assistant, he did not finishing delivering his last paper until 9.50 pm on the evening of Saturday, 4 April 1891.

The Registrar General's office was averse to enumerators taking on assistants during the delivery phase of their duties, emphasising in the instructions it was important they did this themselves. By doing so they would become accustomed to every part of their district and have knowledge of the number of occupiers in every house. This would facilitate the collection process on the day of the enumeration. If they were unable to hire an assistant, some enumerators found other ways of dealing with the demands of the job. One fellow intentionally made extra visits to his district in between delivery day and collection day as part of his preparation. By spending two or three evenings in the week prior to the census talking to householders and ascertaining if they were confident enough to complete the forms, he discovered people who were illiterate. He then arranged to visit the householder on the Sunday and fill up the forms for them, thus avoiding delays on collection day. Author Susan Lumas discovered an enumerator who visited every house in his district a second time following the delivery of the schedules to ensure accuracy. He then instructed an assistant to go through the district telling each household to fill up their forms and supply anyone with schedules who may have been omitted.[72] Another enumerator decided to undertake field work with the memorandum book a week prior to delivery, spending Monday and Tuesday fulfilling the task. He then spent Wednesday preparing his schedules and delivered them on the following Tuesday before the census.

Working enumerators were encouraged to take the collection day (Monday) off work enabling them to concentrate solely on their duties. On the day, some of them started as early as 7 am, though the average start time appeared to be 8 am. The workday for many households, particularly in mill towns and other working-class areas, started at 6 am and therefore all residents of a house were likely to be absent when the enumerator called. In 1891 the *Blackburn Standard* suggested householders might like to leave their houses open and have some member of the family old enough to wait for the enumerator and supply him with the information he needed.[73]

When families knew they would be absent, all the schedules in a street or tenement were often left at one house so the enumerator would not be inconvenienced; in some cases the schedules were sent to the residence of the enumerator to save him the trouble of calling. In some households the lady of the house took the precaution to pin, gum, or even nail the schedule to the front door for the enumerator to retrieve it.[74] However, not all families were so considerate: many enumerators were frustrated by the tantalising sight of the schedule within reach, but locked away in the green house or in a glass cupboard where they could not access it without the keys. As a result they would have to call again.

In Manchester, the wives and mothers of the household would frequently return to bed after seeing members of the family off to work and school and did not take kindly to being disturbed by the enumerator. Reports of households still in bed when the enumerator called were widespread and the official had no recourse but to call back later or wait until a member of the family unlocked the door. There was one account of a young lady dropping her census schedule to the official from her bedroom window to save him the trouble of a return visit.

The census authorities encouraged householders via newspaper notices to have their forms fully completed early on the Monday morning and this message was amplified by the enumerator when he delivered the schedules. Still, many schedules were either not available when the enumerator called or were not completed. If an enumerator was unable to make any contact with the householder even after the registrar had intervened, he or she was instructed that under no circumstances should a household be omitted from the census. They must be recorded as "Not Known" in the name column for each member of the household, ages (which were often ascertained from neighbours) must be stated even if approximate and individuals "under 20" were to be noted.

> He would do his writing anywhere – at the foot of the stairs, on the edge of a wash-stand, on the bed, on a chair with its back broken, on a cane-bottomed chair minus the cane, and he would laughingly observe that he could write on his knee ...
>
> *Pall Mall Gazette*, 2 April 1901.

When the enumerator knocked and entered any household he or she were privy to the most extraordinary insights into the human condition. In the poor quarters of Cardiff, it was observed in house after house there was not a vestige of furniture and the enumerator was forced to spread the schedules against the wall in order to complete them. Of course this led to the frequent occurrence of the pen or pencil piercing the schedule due to the uneven plaster. It was not uncommon for the writing to be done in a room with scarcely a glimmer of light. Some rooms had windows with missing glass and a makeshift piece of carpet or cloth hung across the open window space.[75] Where the rooms were dingy, they were also full of disease and filth. Enumerators walked into rooms where the elderly, the chronically and terminal ill were in bed, particularly in those places in the north of Britain where beds were in kitchens. Elsewhere they observed human shapes lying on bundles of rags. The enumerators in Scotland weaved their way past rank wet mattresses left out to dry on gloomy landings and closes in the city tenements. Their greatest difficulties were contending with the shadowy stairs and the darkness of the landings, in many cases having to scribble on the schedules without ever seeing the paper they were writing on.[76]

In a number of areas gas lighting and paving were still missing by 1901. In the rookeries of Norwich, such amenities were late to arrive and enumerators found themselves in a maze of murky passageways where some houses were numbered and some were not, and even when they were numbered, it was with no more than an ephemeral chalk mark. Such was the dimness and complexity of the warren, it was impossible to tell whether a door was a front door or the back door of a house belonging to another yard and in the district of another enumerator.

Yet the tenements and courts were not always intractable places with hurdles to avoid and unbearable effluvia filling the air. Cheery residents would assemble on landings to meet the enumerator even when they were in the midst of their tea. And occasionally the enumerator would stumble upon the incongruous sight of a clean, sanded doorstep and a well-kept looking apartment, the door of which would be answered by "a clean, white-capped dame, whose personal charms had not succumbed to the impurities of the air and the street."[77]

In these homes where families were lucky to receive a letter once a year, paper was a novelty. Budgets barely covered clothing provision let alone a penny for a newspaper or the luxury of stationery. Ink was not a regular household purchase and stationers sometimes found they had a run on penny bottles of ink on the Saturday before the census. For those who had gone to the expense of purchasing ink or a pen, they found that once their neighbours had borrowed them, they would never see them again! It therefore made sense to individuals living in large courts or tenements, to gather at one house, where the ink was made to last by adding drops of water or stewed tea from the teapot, for a schedule filling session. To boot, the form filler might be a scholar who had mastered writing when they themselves were unable to write.

The lack of paper in their lives meant the census form could be of practical use to some, or a recreational outlet for others. The schedule was an ideal format on which young minds could draw their favourite animals or play games. In 1921, one Bedfordshire enumerator discovered many children playing noughts and crosses in column O, the space provided for indicating children under 16 years of age.

In the hands of the young, the schedule was also prone to destruction. A child in Norwich in 1901 gleefully tore the paper to shreds after his father had taken two hours to complete the form, forcing the mother to paste all the pieces back together. A decade later in Sheffield a baby had thrown the schedule into the fire necessitating a visit to the registrar to obtain a new schedule by the anxious mother. It wasn't just the young who were intent on destruction either. In a twist to dogs eating homework, one enumerator in Lancashire in 1951 encountered the family pet had eaten the schedule at four successive households.[78]

Many of the blue or buff papers handed to the enumerator were no longer their original colour by the time the householder had done with them. One old fellow produced his 1891 Census schedule from his pocket covered in grease and grime, spots of blood, and a small burnt hole. Elsewhere an enumerator described the papers as dirty and dilapidated, while another noted the schedule may have been used to draw up a recalcitrant fire or was stuck in a jam pot. In Leeds, a man allegedly lit his pipe with it and in Belfast, one schedule may have carried home butter from the huckster's shop. As a consequence, rats had rather taken a fancy to it. Of course, when schedules were lost, torn to shreds or damaged it was necessary for enumerators to draw on their supply of spare schedules and have the papers filled up again.

Most of the time the schedules were kept clean and free from harm behind clocks or on kitchen tables, but occasionally they were mislaid which put everyone in the house into a mild state of panic. After a search, they sometimes were found, stuffed in dad's coat pocket or in the baby's cradle.

Attempts to interfere with the census process were infrequent, but in most cases the perpetrators often eluded the authorities and ran off with the schedules. In the districts of Kirkdale, Everton, West Derby, and Old Swan, enumerators on their rounds for the 1921 Census discovered schedules had already been collected. About fifty targeted schedules were taken in certain streets within these areas and rumours soon spread that this was the action of Irish activists Sinn Fein.[79] In Bath in 1901 and Wanstead in 1891 an individual or several individuals posed as enumerators and collected schedules which were later replaced by the authorities.

There is no penalty for making a mistake in good faith.

In 1890 Dr William Ogle reminded the Treasury Committee "that in England schedules are not filled up by the enumerators, but by the ignorant rustic or artizan." This type of individual he added, does not understand "column" in the context of a printed table, rather he only thinks of the word in terms of architecture, as in part of a building. How the schedules are to be filled up, Ogle continued, are absolutely unintelligible to the rustic or artisan.

We are reminded of Paul Dobraszczyk's work regarding the error counts in the schedules of St Nicholas Acons for the censuses of 1811–1831, of how changes to the schedules from a question and answer format to tabular style resulted in an increase in errors. During later censuses, enumerators reported some householders wrote all their information in one column, while others wrote across the entire schedule paying no attention to the format and using every inch of space. Sometimes the writing was as large as a thumbnail and at other times it was written in a tiny hand requiring a magnifying glass.

Those who used the format correctly may have been the ones who requested detailed verbal instructions from the enumerators, telling the official they preferred to be told how to complete the form rather than read the instructions.[80] Some individuals would not take the schedule until all of the minutest details were explained to them.[81]

Even when they were able to navigate the columns, many placed the requested information in the wrong column, often mixing up names, male and female ages, occupations and inserting the marriage and children information in the incorrect row on the 1911 Census schedule. Many of these errors were reported in the newspapers and the latter is evidenced by the surviving schedules and disclosed by enumerators in accounts of their duties.[82]

> The most perplexing complications arise from the queer way in which the people do their best to comply with the law, many of them giving quite as much difficultly by their works of supererogation as by their omissions.
>
> A man in filling up the column "age last birthday" takes the trouble to give the precise date of birth all down a long list, for instance, leaving the enumerator to calculate exactly how old he must be. Another creates hopeless confusion by putting the right entries in wrong lines, thus making all the male names stand for females, and putting all the elders at school, while juveniles are the employers of labour or heads of families. That employment column has been a sore perplexity for all concerned, and the information got together at infinite pains must be wholly untrustworthy if I may judge by what I saw of the filling up of the schedules.[83]
>
> *The Daily News*, 7 April 1891

A number of houscholders complained their schedules were not large enough and rather than ask the enumerator for a second schedule, sent away their youngest members of the family to stay with a relative where they would be counted. While it may have been genuinely the case these complaints were about the inadequacy of rows in the schedule, it is also possible the householder misinterpreted the instructions and/or zealously over-compensated by providing more information or *works of supererogation* as *The Daily News* put it. Such actions may have stemmed from fearing a penalty for not providing complete details. According to the *Todmorden Advertiser* in 1891, there was an almost painful conscientiousness with some people determined to tell everything they could.

A study of the surviving 1851 Census schedules for Llandyrnog registration sub-district, Denbighshire by R.M. and G.A. Benwell revealed a similar approach by householders: a number of them gave the exact dates of birth for all members of the household, the names of the houses where they were born, and gave far greater detail about the occupations of farm servants and domestics. As the authors pointed out, so many interesting pieces of information were lost by enumerators editing and filtering information for conformity. The following was added to the bottom of a schedule by 43-year-old labourer John Williams: "the wages are very small in Denbighshire, they are from 3 shillings to 5 shillings and food in the week."[84]

The role of the enumerator as editor was suggested by Donald Davis in his article, *The Householders' Schedules in the 1841 Censu*s which concerned the 493 surviving householders' schedules collected by thirteen enumerators in the Cainham (now Caynham) Ludlow registration district. Davis uses the schedule of Thomas Gilson as one example of enumerators translating, filtering, and arranging information into the required format. Gilson used the first three columns from the 1841 Census schedule to include information about his family, placing their names and occupations in the first column and correctly adding ages to the second and third columns. Starting with himself, a "labering limer" aged 35, he then follows with:

> elesebetch Gilson the wif of Thomas Gilson aged 35; Jon Gilson the son of Thomas an elesebetch Gilson laberin caler aged 10; Hana Gilson ther dater aged 8; sale Gilson ther dater aged 6; Wileam Gilson ther son aged 5; Jan Gilson ther dater aged 3; Thomas Gilson ther son aged 5 Months. Al thes Persons Born in Shropshire.

The enumerator Richard Preece when transferring this information to his enumeration book entered conventional spellings for the names Elizabeth,

John, Hannah, Sarah (Sale), Jane, and William as well as the occupations "lime burner" and "miner in coal".

The nineteenth-century newspapers provide a number of similar examples of schedules (using fake names) written in closely running text, which the enumerator deciphered, edited, conventionalised, and converted into the tabular format of the schedule. One such story appeared in *The Burton Chronicle* in 1891 from an enumerator whose district was a mining area:

> Thomas M – boren In ireland county of Armagh Silver Brige eage 303 (33) To the best of my nolege i Am that eage and I am married the secent time the furst wife Mary C – be longed to ireland County armagh the Sekont Wife be longed to County Dereay hur name was elen M'G – Now her name is elen M – but she run away from me five years and 10 months since and i dont know Wheare she is or if she is Dead or not i havent hard from hur since but if she is Dead i think she wood have sent me woard before now my father was a Farmer and had a gratt power of Land in Ireland and when I came to England i was A navey working In the Cole Pitt but sure enough i am not Working no place now for i got my legs broken 9 weeks and 3 days since gen to morrow.
>
> Rosey M – my sister be longing to ireland is married, and her name now is Misses C____ and hur Eage is 205 (25) years, and she has Fore of a Family the oulest Is tomos C – 7 years of eage And Boren in Ireland newery County Armagh Mary C – aged 6 year gen the sevent day of augest Boren in ireland County of Armagh Elsie C – Fore years gen the 10s May Boren in newcastle england Clety C – 1 yere and 9 month gen Saturdeay Boren in newery ireland and the father of them all is Abel C – Born in england eaged 40 years and was a Soger and served his Quane and his country 201 (21) year now is in the Pit Working and all that sins paper is catholecks.[85]

The punch line to this particular story of Thomas the navvy was that he lived alone.

The anxiety of correctly filling in the schedule led to some individuals waiting by their doors for the enumerator to call. In Hulme in 1901, one woman stood waiting, paper in hand and upon seeing the enumerator approach said, "I hope it's right, sir: me and my master have done our best, and if it's wrong it's not my fault."[86] Others circumvented the anxiety in other ways: they took their forms to a neighbour's house and one literate individual completed forms for the whole street or court; they hired a clerk or a professional person; they left the form for the enumerator to fill in, or they hired some enterprising individual to fulfil the task for them.

Chapter Six

One Penny Per Family

> We do not really know who does fill up the schedule; at the present moment somebody else is probably asked in to assist the householder. You do not really know that it is the return of the householder; somebody may dictate anything, and he may sign it.
>
> Dr G.B. Longstaff, testimony to the Treasury Committee, 1890

"If I'd a-known as 'ow you was a-fillin' up them there papers for nothin', young man", said another "lady", "I'd a syved the sixpence I gev Mrs. So-and-So for writin' mine last night."[87] These words were said to an enumerator during the 1901 Census by a householder who had hired an acquaintance to complete the schedule for her. It seems Mrs So-and-So had managed to get herself a decent little side hustle. She wasn't the only one.

In 1861 the *Star of Gwent* reported that a sharp-witted fellow used his education to good account and spent a number of days visiting the poor to fill up their census papers at the charge of 1d. per family.[88] Forty years later, a local accountant volunteered to assist the landlady of a Swansea hotel and completed the schedule for her and her guests. While in Leeds another entrepreneur charged 2d. to show illiterate householders how to fill up their census papers.[89] Similarly, in the Walcot district of Bath, one enterprising gentleman filled up the papers for 2d. per household.[90]

In 1871, an enumerator discovered it was common practice in his district for one individual to charge a fee for completing the schedule, in fact it was a brisk trade, with each scribe finding his own ink and pens.[91]

Not everyone charged for their services and numerous individuals gave up their time freely to assist their neighbours. Some received gifts for their efforts.[92] An enumerator writing for the *Kirkintilloch Herald* discovered a great number of the schedules had been filled up by a factor's clerk to the dictation of the occupiers. He found them to have been completed correctly.

Elsewhere, in the courtyards and tenements, parents offered up their children to act as clerks. Enumerators would sometimes stumble upon a schoolchild filling up a return for six members of a household, none of whom could write.

Of course some took advantage of the situation finding it amusing to add some colour to the schedule. In Cheshire in 1901, a neighbour who filled in the form for another stated the head of the family was a lunatic and his wife an imbecile.[93] In Dundee, a labouring man was entered as a beggar. When it was queried by the enumerator, the householder said it was a dirty trick played on him by a colleague who volunteered to help with his schedule.[94]

Sometimes the japes could lead to serious trouble. In 1891, Lord James Douglas was called before London magistrates for contravention of the Census Act. On his schedule, it was recorded his wife was a cross-sweep and a lunatic, while his son was a shoeblack who was born in Africa. The Lord was not to blame however, for it seems his two mischievous stepsons thought it was a good joke to hoax the enumerator while the Lord was ill.[95]

Japes aside, there were those who were intent on committing fraud. In 1891, an "enumerator" visited Moser's Detective Agency in the Strand and demanded the firm pay him 2s. 6d. for completing the householder schedule on their behalf. This led to the Registrar General's office ordering the local registrar to investigate the claim.[96]

Assistance

Local postmen were called upon to assist enumerators in areas where streets were unnamed and houses were unnumbered. The police accompanied enumerators if they were entering an area known as a potential tinderbox. But in 1871, it was decided the police in Liverpool, accompanied by members of the sanitary bodies, would co-operate to ensure the enumerators were properly discharging their duties.

About fifty persons from the city's health department, assisted by fifty constables, set out at 9.00 pm on the Sunday evening to see if the enumerators had left with the householders the requisite number of schedules. A printed code of instructions was issued to these men, specifying their duties, with the distinct understanding that in no case were they to interfere with the filling up of the schedule. Their duty was solely to ensure each family was provided with the means of making a proper return. Wherever they found an inadequate supply of schedules, they supplied the householder from the spares they were carrying.[97]

Enumerators were able to hire their own personal assistants if their registrar agreed, as long as they covered the cost from their own wallet. Many turned to family, using sons and daughters who were more likely to work gratis. The French polisher hired by Registrar Frank C. Tupper in 1881 had a son who worked in an engineer's office and who assisted his father by completing the enumeration book. The enumerator for Aldeburgh, stationer and bookseller Robert Turner, was assisted by his 29-year-old daughter Louisa Mary Turner for the 1871 Census.

When enumerators hired outside of the family, it was sometimes difficult finding an assistant willing to wait six weeks for their wage. Enumerators' wages came through slowly because they were not paid until all the enumeration books were returned, checked, and corrected, and from this wage most paid their assistants. In 1841, an enumerator writing to the *Morning Advertiser* wrote he engaged an intelligent lad named Master Burbidge whom he promised half a crown. Unfortunately, the lad couldn't wait for his money and went to sea without it.[98]

If they did find individuals willing to assist, they found them beyond helpful. One enumerator working on the 1891 Census sent his assistant in advance to get the schedules ready before he arrived at the next house. He declared he couldn't have completed the collection without him. They both worked until ten at night for two days, after which the enumerator paid his assistant for his time and for his meals during the long shifts. Of course this hurt the enumerator's pocket, so he completed the collection himself finishing on the Thursday after the census.[99]

Our Deluded Enumerator from Cardiff also hired an assistant to help with the collection duties. "We were for two whole days collecting those blessed schedules", he wrote, "dozens of which we had to fill in, owing to the number of 'illiterates' in the district."

Filling in the Forms

When Registrar Alfred Gibbs appeared before the Treasury Committee in 1890, he was asked if he had encountered any difficulties with the householders' schedules brought before him. "Several that they brought were very imperfectly filled up", he said, "and I was obliged to cause the enumerators themselves to refill them up in my presence. Some, of course, they had already filled up at the houses of the persons with whom they had left them, in consequence of the illiterate people with whom they were left." Then when Gibbs was asked if it was common for his enumerators to complete the forms for householders at their homes, he replied that it wasn't. Later in his testimony he was asked again whether there was a large proportion of schedules not filled in by the householder, but by the enumerator. No, was his response, the majority were in the handwriting of the householder himself, or one of his family. "The enumerators had not many to fill up", he insisted, "and now they will have still less, as people are better educated ..."

The aforementioned study of the surviving 1851 Census schedules for the Llandyrnog registration sub-district, Denbighshire by R.M. and G.A. Benwell resulted in some interesting statistics. In the parish of Llangynhafal, out of a total of 115 schedules, 47 (41 per cent) were completed by the enumerator, though some were signed by the householder or another member of the family. For the majority that were completed by the enumerator, he signed it with the householder's name. Out of the remaining schedules, 30 (26 per cent) were written entirely by the householder and 4 (3 per cent) by another member of the family, which in two cases was the teenage son. A further 22 schedules (19 per cent) were completed by neighbours or relatives not living with the household; 12 of which were completed by agricultural labourer Robert Davies. Ten were completed by a farmer, a shoemaker, and a retired seaman. The Benwells stressed in their study, that it was not possible to be certain about every schedule and twelve schedules could not be categorised.[100]

In Donald Davis' study of the 493 householders' schedules collected by the 13 enumerators in the Cainham district for the 1841 Census, 210 household heads (42.6 per cent) completed their own forms. There were 132 households (26.8 per cent) whose heads made their mark but did not complete their own schedules. These were either completed by the enumerator or by a neighbour. The remaining 151 schedules (30.6 per cent) were either unsigned or signed by the enumerator without any input from the head of household. Davis highlights the diversity of completions rates across enumeration districts (EDs): in ED 4, 32 out of 40 households completed their own schedules whereas in EDs 9 and 10 respectively 42 of

57 and 38 of 44 were seemingly unable to do so. Davis argued this was due to occupational status: ED 4 comprised of literate middle-class clergy, a schoolmaster, and tradesmen. In contrast, those in EDs 9 and 10 were coal miners and their widows who, as Davis observed, were less likely to be literate. Only eight of the coalminers who were heads of household were able to complete their own schedules.

Just occasionally enumerators provided details concerning the number of forms they completed but were somewhat vague in the majority of their accounts. An enumerator working in Portsmouth during the 1891 Census admitted he filled up three-fourths of the 140 or so schedules he collected.[101] In Scotland in 1891, a Dundee enumerator completed the majority of the schedules "and, what was far more difficult, extract intelligent answers from people."[102] In Leeds in 1881, another wrote that in a large proportion of cases he filled up the schedule and few of the householders could sign their returns. In such cases he signed it for them and accepted their mark.[103] Ten years later it was reported in the poorer parts of town enumerators frequently wrote out the schedules and made repeated calls to the same houses before they could get the return correctly completed.[104] In 1891, another Yorkshire enumerator wrote "I need not mention the scores [of schedules] I had to fill in myself" when describing his work. An enumerator collecting schedules in the Quarry Hill Insanitary Area of Leeds in 1901 indicated there had been improvements, telling the *Yorkshire Post and Leeds Intelligencer* that at five houses out of six, the schedules had been filled up by children attending school, and in the sixth case the enumerator did it. However, *at nearly every house*, there were always some blanks to fill in, usually for the occupations.[105] Elsewhere in Leeds, it was reported a great deal of time was lost in certain districts writing out or revising imperfect returns.[106] And in Manchester in a very large proportion of cases the enumerator filled in every particular himself. Not far away in Bolton, while there had been improvements in literacy, the enumerator had written out a number of schedules. This was not because householders were unable to do it, but rather those responsible were either too indifferent or too lazy to do it themselves.[107] That same year, a householder told an enumerator in Woking that he wasn't going to fill up the paper for anyone, adding "You had better fill 'un up yerself; ye're paid for it."[108]

Literacy, therefore, does not appear to be the only driver behind enumerators having to complete the schedules. There were reports of laziness, of ignorance and indifference (as well as anti-census sentiment) – all attributed as reasons for not completing the schedules. There were individuals who could read and write very well, but who could not understand the form and so left all or parts of it blank. In rare instances, when disease infected a household, enumerators were instructed to refrain from leaving a schedule and to complete it themselves when they called on the Monday.[109] It's therefore difficult to make judgements about situations where the schedules were completed by the officer without knowing the context. For example, an enumerator reported he was required to fill in 47 out of 60 schedules during the 1951 Census. It's hard to believe the reason for this was illiteracy in 47 households.[110]

For every report indicating enumerators were having to complete many schedules, there were also accounts suggesting the majority of the public were able and willing to undertake the task. In part of the Aylesford district, the enumerator divulged that out of about 110 houses, only 10 or 11 persons could not fill in their schedules. The *Sheffield Daily Telegraph* reported in 1911 the enumerator had to fill in no more than four papers.[111] But how many enumerators were including partially filled in forms or forms they had to rewrite? Many faced schedules that were so poorly completed they had to be redone, as Alfred Gibbs explained to the Treasury Committee in 1890. He informed the committee the schedules were written out so inadequately he rejected them. Names and surnames were scrawled across other columns, zeros were improperly added to ages, turning 31 into 301, and in one instance, a farm labourer's occupation was written so illegibly it appeared to say perambulator.

These problems were seen elsewhere. The *Halifax Evening Courier* reported in 1911 that information was frequently given in the wrong column and not written in sufficient detail. It went onto say some schedules had been written out without any reference to the instructions, and were so incorrect they had to be destroyed as useless.[112] The enumerator writing for the *Kirkintilloch Herald* in 1901 went as far as saying, even though most of the papers had been completed by the householder, the majority of these had to be rewritten on spare schedules he carried with him for the purpose.[113] Even as late as the 1921 Census, the enumerators in Bedfordshire were remodelling or refilling many forms during their collection rounds[114].

There were no official statistics kept regarding how many forms enumerators filled in, partially filled in or rewrote, however in 1871 an attempt was made to gather some data on the subject. On page iv of the enumeration books, the following was printed at the bottom of the page:

"Of the above Schedules the *number filled up by the enumerator himself* was___." No instructions were given to the enumerator for completing this section and many left it blank. Edward Higgs surveyed a number of enumeration districts and found that in parts of Manchester the proportion completed by the enumerator was 25 per cent. He then turned his attention to Christ Church, Spitalfields and discovered the proportion was 15 per cent. In Colyton in Devon, he found it was 7 per cent and in some Welsh-speaking parishes in Anglesey the majority were filled in by the enumerators.[115] This correlates somewhat with my own findings for Welsh enumeration districts (see below). Higgs also discovered extreme differences of completion rates within a single sub-district. In the six enumeration districts of Greater Missenden, the proportion of schedules written up by the enumerators ranged from 5.3 to 64.7 per cent.

In examining 200 EDs from the 1871 Census, I found the number of schedules completed by the enumerators to be quite low. Nevertheless, the variations identified by Higgs and Davis in their research were also observed in my study, though they were obscured by the average percentage. Of the 200 EDs, 32 of the relevant pages containing the number of schedules completed were either blank, missing from the website (thegenealogist.co.uk) or the writing was unclear. Some enumerators wrote comments which suggests they were not keeping track of the number they filled in as they undertook the collection, writing "about half a dozen", "about 20", "about 62", "more than half", or "the great part". So potentially they may have overestimated or underestimated the numbers. Occasionally they added further comments. The enumerator for enumeration district (ED) 7 in the sub-district of Leeds South East (RG 10/4542) wrote that out of 205 schedules he filled in 8, but wrote he had *partly filled in 116*. The enumerator for ED 22 put down he had filled in 27 out of 198 schedules and a "good many altered say about 30 or 40." In the St. Asaph sub-district, another enumerator completed 23 "beside partly filling up" others from a total of 63 schedules (RG10/5668 ED 9).

The total number of schedules from the study of the 200 enumeration districts was 37,993. The number of schedules filled in by enumerators – again it is unclear whether fully filled, partially filled, or rewritten schedules were included in the enumerator's calculations – was 4,087 (9.7 per cent).

There were some areas where the figure was higher and perhaps align to Davis' diversity of completion rates. In 18 enumeration districts in Shropshire the percentage of forms completed by the enumerator was

19.7 per cent. In 24 enumeration districts in Wales the total figure was 17.7 per cent, but in some of those Welsh EDs the amount completed by the enumerator was close to 50 per cent. These findings warrant a more far-reaching study of the 1871 Census CEBs to see if they reveal other diversity of completions rates.

> ... 30 per cent, of the schedules were incorrectly filled in, in some respect or another.

As part of their duties, enumerators corrected defective schedules, or as we have seen, if a schedule was poorly completed, they would start a new one. But what exactly were they correcting? The 1861 Census instruction book outlined their tasks in respect of corrections:

> You should pay particular attention to the column headed "Rank, Profession, or Occupation", taking care that what is inserted under the head is in conformity with the instructions [on the schedule]. You should also see that the Christian names of the persons described as wife, son, daughter, &c., are consistent with their description as Male (M) or Female (F), and with their occupation, &c.

Upon finding an error the enumerators were told to ask any necessary questions to secure a complete answer, however as the *East London Observe*r put it, "It is not for him [the enumerator] to question the accuracy of the items set forth", though many probably did. If they found a formatting error on the schedules, the enumerators were to "draw a line through the erroneous words, without erasing them, and enter the correct words over them in the proper columns."

By 1911, the enumerator's instructions further elaborated on the troublesome areas of the schedule where the enumerators needed to be vigilant. This, in addition to the new columns, resulted in a resetting to eight paragraphs in the English and Welsh instructions, and ten paragraphs in the Scottish ones. Enumerators needed to make sure ages were in the correct columns for males and females; that marriage and the duration of marriage for each woman was correctly stated, and no children born alive was written as "none"; occupations had to be clearly described and not vague, and for those not born in England and Wales clarification regarding whether they were resident or visitors needed to be added, together with nationality and the year of naturalisation. In Scotland, officials were to state the nationality of foreign-born individuals. Finally, the number of rooms in the dwelling was to be completed at the foot of the schedule. No erasures were allowed when making corrections.[116]

In Scotland, enumerators were also asked to make sure column 5 for "Gaelic" was completed for all individuals aged 3 and upwards, and the "Working from Home" column corresponded with people actually working in their own homes. It was not unheard of for individuals to put working from home when they actually worked as a labourer in a quarry next to their house.[117]

For the 1921 Census, the instructions for corrections had grown substantially with guidance on entering names in their natural order of first name then surname and for checking the age column etc.

Evidence shows enumerators did as instructed with regards to checking columns for the correct information, and as already indicated, they conventialised the spelling of names and occupations when it came to writing in the enumeration books. Any major corrections concerning names and occupations etc., should have been undertaken in the presence of the householder, though it is likely that did not always occur. Further evidence regarding occupations comes from a Leeds enumerator:

> One man describes himself as an – "option" – instead of optician, and a widow writes the word "mangel" under the occupation heading, which is intended to convey that she makes a living by taking in washed clothing to mangle. Among the relationships recorded are "neace", "border", &c.; but in such cases the meaning is obvious and the imperfect spelling easily corrected.
>
> *Leeds Mercury*, 5 April 1881

So most of the information corrected was for uniformity and comprehension, which in turn facilitated the tabulation of the data by the Census Office clerks.

It is worthwhile taking a moment to summarise the schedule filling process based on what has been written so far. Schedules, according to the instructions, were to be filled in by the householders. However, it is clear many were written by neighbours and it was not uncommon in courtyards and tenements for the schedules to be taken to one house. Here they were filled out by the local "scholar", or they were taken to the house because it had the best supply of ink and pens. If a literate local person was not available, householders hired clerks or other individuals willing to sell the service of completing the schedule. Sometimes, they were also assisted by clergy and other individuals such as schoolmasters who volunteered their time.

In other cases, the schedules were filled in by enumerators, however to what extent remains unclear. If partial filling in is included, then it may have been to a considerable degree, but if counting the whole form, it may have been less than 10 per cent. It is necessary to also acknowledge a diversity of completion rates from district to district. Equally, it's important to recognise literacy was not the only reason householders didn't complete the form. Not understanding the instructions, fear of committing an error, as well as laziness and sheer indifference played their parts. And even though a schedule may have been filled in, it may have been so defective the enumerator completed a new form. Though in many instances, he instructed the householder how it should be done.

Enumerators who didn't notice flaws on the schedule while on their rounds were made to rewrite those particular schedules while in the registrar's office. Those who did notice the flaws, corrected the information if it was placed in the wrong column, they supplied a county where it was missing, and they conventionalised spellings.

On the subject of correcting schedules, it was not something enumerators enjoyed because not only did it delay them from completing their collections, they frequently met with opposition. One enumerator suffered a number of unpleasant encounters in one of the more salubrious districts of Edgbaston, writing it was not unusual for him to be told the schedule was right and he was wrong! He later declared he preferred to enumerate the poorer areas any day of the week.[118]

It was frequently noted by these officials there was a distinct difference in attitude between the poorer districts and those of the tradesmen, the middle class, and the so-called "upper tens" – the upper class. The better off classes tended to leave the enumerator waiting. One clergyman from Norwich told the official to call in half hour when he would be at leisure to complete the form; in Woking many from the upper tens had completely forgotten about the schedule and delayed the enumerator while they filled it in.[119] They also made more errors than the poorer classes. In Guildford, it was said there were more blunders amongst the well off than among the poor, chiefly because the former didn't make the effort to read the instructions. Elsewhere the number of errors were ascribed to anxiety and over-confidence regarding the whole rigmarole of the census.

In other parts of the country, the most difficult people were the tradesmen, while the people who gave the least trouble were the middle-class residential population. Their papers were always ready and they were always correct according to one source. The poorer men and women were also ready for the enumerator when he called and had filled up their schedules more intelligently than those in better social positions, proving they had taken the trouble to ascertain what was required of them. Indeed, it may have been a mixture of fearing the penalty for not completing the form, in addition to hiring a clerk or asking a neighbour to complete the schedule, which ensured their readiness and compliance. They could also be helpful and obligingly go halfway down the street to find their charring neighbour on behalf of the enumerator.

Given their long days (one claiming he only slept 4.5 hours each night while on duty) enumerators were grateful for any assistance given. They were also relieved when the collecting stage was over, though many were still unprepared for what was about to come. For the 1911 Census, enumerators in England, Wales, and Scotland were explicitly told that their collections had to be finished by Tuesday, 4 April at the latest. If there were outstanding schedules to collect, they needed to inform their registrar immediately. That same year, Form E.5 in England and Wales, and Form E.4 in Scotland was issued to each enumerator to enable them to inform the registrar they had completed the enumeration of the population in their district. For the 1921 Census, it was renamed Form E.3 in England and Wales and postcard E.3 in Scotland. The enumerators in England and Wales were also required to complete Form A.3 with their registrar. This was to ascertain which of the addresses recorded in the Place of Work column were outside the registration sub-district. The process required both registrar and enumerator to consult each schedule one by one.

> ... by the time I have finished this book I shall have written nearly 40,000 (forty thousand) words.

Census Enumeration Books

After the collection of the schedules, cnumerators were required to undertake the mammoth task of transferring the information from their schedules into the enumeration books supplied to them by their registrar. Enumeration books came in difference sizes and can be identified by their sheet letter. For example, in 1871, Sheet E consisted of 48 pages and Sheet

C consisted of 32 pages. Not all pages were used and any that were not used were removed at a later date.

Enumerators were given one week to complete their enumeration book. Then on the Monday they would take the book, the schedules, their claims form, and the memorandum book to their registrar.

One enumerator did not think about starting to write out his enumeration book until the Friday after the census. And only then he just looked at it probably hoping it would go away. On the Saturday, gradually easing himself into the task he arranged all of his schedules in proper order, but still did not start entering them into the book until the following day. Underestimating the time it would take him, he started the job on Sunday afternoon and wrote, "I am still at it" in a letter published on 21 April 1891. He estimated that after finishing the job, he would have written nearly 40,000 words.[120]

Naturally the Deluded Enumerator of Cardiff had much to say on the task of writing out the enumeration books. He started his work two days after collecting the schedules on 8 April 1891. The books, he said, were two foot long and divided into

> fourteen columns [it's seventeen actually] in which were to be entered the various particulars as to number of schedule, number of house, name of street, dwelling-houses, number of rooms occupied, name, age; condition of marriage--whether head, wife, son, daughter, lodger, servant, or visitor; occupation, – whether employer, employed, or working on own account, place of birth, language spoken, &c. Each page of the book would contain particulars as to 31 persons, and in addition each page had to be headed with the name of the administrative county, civil parish, municipal borough, municipal ward, urban sanitary district, Parliamentary borough, and ecclesiastical district. At the foot of each page totals were to be given of number of schedules, occupied houses, unoccupied houses, houses building, tenements of less than five rooms, number of males, number of females, &c. Each page would occupy half an hour in filling. My schedules WOULD FILL ABOUT 120 PAGES!

And when all the pages of the book were filled and the totals added to the foot of the table, he had to transfer the totals to a "formidable" table on the first page of the enumeration book. After that he made up his final totals. To help him with the entire task he used his assistant. Thanks to this help, he was finished by noon on Tuesday, 14 April 1891 [he stated the 7th in error], thereby missing the Monday deadline. Despite the aid he received from the assistant, he still worked all the previous Saturday night, until 6.30 am on the Sunday morning, and all Sunday afternoon and evening.[121]

For the formidable tables enumerators were asked to summarise the contents of their enumeration books. Primarily this included the number of persons, houses and households recorded on each page plus population increases and decreases. The number of schedules collected, the number of temporary absences and those temporarily present, and tenements of less than 5 rooms (in England and Wales) were later added to the tabular data requirements. In addition, enumerators in Scotland were required to provide the total number of windowed rooms and would continue to provide summaries in their 1911 and 1921 enumeration books.

In 1911, enumerators in England and Wales were provided with summary books to complete after the enumeration. On the nominal pages, they had to supply the usual headings e.g. civil parish, ecclesiastical parish etc. This was followed by the schedule number, kind of building, name of occupier, whether the residence was inhabited, uninhabited and so on. Finally, they had to transfer the totals in terms of population from the foot of the schedules to their summary books, paying particular attention to the correct number of males and females.

In addition to filling in the summary tables in their enumeration books, they were also encouraged to add any explanatory notes or observations to make the description clearer or more complete. Some enumerators took this as an opportunity to either voice their opinion or to genuinely provide more information as encouraged by the census authorities. William Roberts Henderson an enumerator acting in both the 1851 and 1861 Censuses decided he would do the latter. In 1851 he was given district No. 1 for Pontefract and following the registrar's description of his district he wrote:

> The Township of Stapelton contains about 450 Acres of Land Covered with wood and about 1350 Acres of Arable and Pasture Land... The Principal Mineral Production in the Parish is Limestone and Lime, great Quantities of which are used Annually for agricultural purposes and also for Building; and repairing the Turnpike Roads. The Church is a very neat

> Structure Situate about the Middle of the Village of Darrington and built in the Gothic Style, it is Dedicated to Saint Luke...
> (HO107/2330 ED. 1 F.1. p. i)

When he was enumerator in 1861 for the same district, he greatly expanded his notes describing Darrington as containing: "about 230 Acres of Land covered with Wood, also principally Fir, and about 2780 Acres of Arable and pasture Land, the Tenant Right occupation, of the arable Land being under the Customary regulations of the four Crop Course."

Local landowners the Sotheron-Estcourts were mentioned for their ownership of Darrington Hall and to conclude, Roberts Henderson proceeded to describe the church as he had done in 1851 (RG9/3437 F1. p. i).

Enumerator John Hoghton had a great deal to say about his district in the Preston Union for the 1861 Census. It was a notoriously impoverished area, inhabited by a great many Irish families packed together in cottages. Accompanying his description, he commented:

> ... there being Lodgers at most of the Cottages, in many cases there are two families besides other Lodgers living in one Cottage, and in a few cases there are three distinct families living in one Cottage. In No 39. Canal St there were three families besides two Lodgers, being altogether sixteen persons in one Cottage... The Cottages are very dirty and miserable. Indeed there is such an entire absence of social comfort, that few respectable persons would imagine that there was such an amount of misery and destitution in Preston. In Foster's Square about one third of the Cottages had a Bed in the Kitchen, and in some of the Cottages in Canal St, Back Canal St [&c?] there is a Bed in the Kitchen.[122]
> (RG9/3131 ED. 27. F.54. p. iii).

Susan Lumas discovered other examples from various censuses. In 1861, Thomas Berry Christian, the enumerator for ED No. 58 in the sub-district of East Leicester had this to say: "This District being chiefly composed of the lower order of Parish, such as Lodging house keepers, Pedlars, Rag collectors, Chip sellers, Bone collectors, Hawkers of small wares, Beggars &c &c I found it difficult to get at the proper description of some of the parties." (RG9/2291 F. 44. p. ii).

After completing their enumeration books and delivering all their census materials to the registrar, all the enumerators had to do was sit back and wait for their payment. Most of them anyway, some were required to repeat their tasks a second time. In the meantime, the registrars started to check the schedules and enumeration books for accuracy and insert any corrections in black or red ink. It was recommended they check the first six nominal pages of the enumeration book – for it was impossible to check the whole book – and compare those pages to the schedules for accuracy.

It was during this process that many queries arose and registrars were quick to write to the Registrar General's office for advice. From these letters, it is possible to garner an idea of the queries arising from the process which were of concern to the officials. On 29 April 1891, the Superintendent Registrar for Pontypool queried the use of unauthorised abbreviations in the enumerations books and was told that unless the abbreviations rendered the information ambiguous, they should be left alone. On 17 April 1891, the Registrar General's secretary replied to a letter from the Registrar for Stonehouse in Gloucester who voiced his concerns about the quality of the schedules collected by his enumerators. Even though the work of one enumerator was deficient, the Registrar General considered it useless to attempt to collect better information. The schedules, the secretary wrote, "must be accepted and copied as they are into the Enumeration Book."[123] They received a similar query from the Registrar of Pontefract, who complained the household schedules collected by his enumerator gave the place of birth as England only. Again it was decided it wasn't viable to chase the information and the schedules were to be copied into the enumeration books precisely as they appear.[124] On 22 April 1891, the Registrar for Leamington was told the schedules needn't be copied verbatim if his enumerator had amended missing information, i.e. the county in the "Where Born" column. This was acceptable in order to make the return conform with the instructions on the schedules.[125]

However, there were instances when the Registrar General's office shared the concerns of the registrars. The enumerator responsible for enumeration district No. 6 in South Shields had so inaccurately and so carelessly filled up the enumeration book, the census authorities insisted he recopy it and sent a new enumeration book for the purpose. While there were a number of unnamed defects, one of the major omissions was the condition of marriage which was missing from the whole book.[126] The registrar endeavoured to have the enumerator correct his work, but was unable to do so and resorted to employing another enumerator. In Kimberworth near Rotherham, the enumerator for district 37 was instructed to recopy his entire enumeration book due to his misunderstanding or disregard for the example provided on page 3 of the book. His mistake led to an unintelligible mess of Columns 9 and 10 which would have obstructed the tabulation process.

Registrars also reported in their correspondence items missing in transit including all the schedules and enumeration books, though items lost in their entirety seem to be rare. Schedules accidentally lost between collection and the filling up of the enumeration books were forwarded to the Census Office and written in at the end of the relevant enumeration district by clerks in the Census Office.

To end this chapter it is worth reflecting on an account from an enumerator who worked on the 1981 and 1991 censuses. Much of what is found here mirrors the experiences of people who strolled through Sheffield's streets a century ago: the draw of a side hustle, the advantage of closely packed terraces over driveways and front gardens, householders away from home, and as we approach the next chapter, the oddities and vagaries of humans when faced with officialdom.

1981 Census: Sheffield

March 1981, final year of studies on a three-year degree course, six weeks to go before final exams. Time to revise. Then the poster appeared on the noticeboard, 6th floor Heriot House, Pond Street, home of the Sociologists and trainee Social Workers. £500 for working the Census. The poster said the census would be all done and dusted on 5 April. Should we revise, or did we need £500. No brainer, £500 won the day.

Interview & assessment, – a short session at the Victoria Hall in Sheffield. Were we "fit and proper persons" to be employed in such a role? By then we had convinced ourselves that yes, we genuinely did need £500. What a relief therefore when we were "approved".

More meetings followed, mainly to allocate an area that we would enumerate. Sheffield is built on seven hills, like Rome. My friend Christine lived in Walkley, so was allocated the neighbouring area of Crookes, probably the steepest hills in the city, home to students and *Guardian* readers.

I lived at Hillsborough, and was allocated Fox Hill as my enumeration area, a mile further out of the city to the north, not quite as hilly as Crookes but not far off. (To refresh my memory, I've just Googled "Fox Hill, Sheffield", and the first comment I saw was "Not the most attractive area of Sheffield"). It had its fair share of housing issues, some private, some council, but it bordered open moorland as most of north Sheffield does, so it couldn't be all that bad surely.

Stages 1 and 2 were easy for both of us. Check each address against the published lists by delivering a leaflet to each household. We helped each other out on that. Easy. Stage 1 complete. The £ signs are rolling. Stage 2 – deliver the actual census form. No real problems here, other than the hills.

April 6th, time to collect the forms, and it's here that realisation dawns that they can't be collected in one swoop. People not in, out at work, "forgot to fill it in" … "Can you come back later"? or worst of all "what form"? Crooks for Christine wasn't bad as the streets are mainly terraces, so door to door is a matter of seconds. For me in Fox Hill it's semis with driveways, and council type "boxes". Fox Hill is also not the place you want to be after dusk, so I had a self-imposed 8 pm curfew.

Collection turned in to seven or eight trawls round the district, slowly winding the returns back in, with eventually a handful of non-returnees, handed over to my superior, the boss-man enumerator. Job done, £500 to come, and still two weeks left to revise.

The overriding memory of that time, and one which causes flashbacks now and then is of one door opening and the lady was dressed in a sack. A proper sack, the type you would put potatoes in. No socks, shoes etc…. and she says those magic words. "I've not quite finished it, there's a few bits I don't understand, come in" Mistake…. I'm sure even now, forty years later, I could find the exact house where the words "come in" were spoken.

Census finished, exams completed, graduation done and dusted. Participation in the 1981 census saw essential life skills learned – project planning, time management, working to a deadline, perseverance, attention to detail, how to meet and greet people politely to achieve the desired response, and many more.

These skills enabled one of us to go on to a career in teaching and education, and one of us to have a lifelong career in the IT industry as a communications engineer. The skills learned doing the census – particularly 1981 when we were "wet behind the ears" – stood us in good stead.

We spoke about it afterwards though and agreed that although it was £500 hard earned, the money was very welcome. Would we do it again? No way. Absolutely, definitely.

1991 Census: Rotherham

1991. Married, two children aged 4 and 2. Money tight. £500 beckons….. Poster goes up at work again – Volunteers wanted, Census, money to be made. The memories of ten years ago have faded and blurred. I don't remember it being that bad, surely. Oh, of course I'll give it a go.

Training was only a mile from home, and I'm allocated Thurcroft, a mining village, whose pit was to close in the December of the same year, and the village whose Brass band I would join as a player and become Chairman of ten years later. In 1991 the village and its people were angry, but I grew up in a mining village, my family were miners, so an angry Thurcroft with an imminent pit closure did not phase me, and apart from the trawl of collection, this wasn't too bad. In my early 30s by this stage, I was better equipped to deal with most of what Thurcroft could throw at me. The percentage of forms I struggled to get back was probably greater than ten years earlier, as there were some who were really anti anything the Government wanted and didn't wish to cooperate at all.

Would I do it again in 2001?

Nigel Butler

Chapter Seven

Private Life of the Family

"Column 5, with the heading, 'age last birthday', was mistaken by some of the fair sex evidently as 'age last census'."[127]

It could be argued it was the meme of the century; certainly, in respect of the census. Every decade, with the census on the horizon, newspaper columnists dusted down their old stories on the subject of age and asked: would elderly spinsters or women over a certain age candidly reveal the true number? Would seniors in the workhouse institutions up and down the country add a few years on to make them octogenarians or nonagenarians? And when the census was done, those same journalists avidly waited for new tales of recalcitrant females and males (in some cases) who would give nothing away regarding how old they were.

Many householders conveniently forgot their age while others regarded the question as impertinent. There were reports by some enumerators that schedule after schedule were given to them with the age column left blank. It often took a return call and a lot of coercion to make individuals come up with an actual number. If they were not forthcoming, enumerators would ask neighbours, which probably resulted in some laughable guestimates. It was also reported householders intentionally wrote the age illegibly so it could not be understood!

In the middle of the century, the census authorities were aware the ages provided by the population were prone to error. As David Thomson explains in his study of age accuracy, they were sanguine on the matter and considered the figures would eventually balance out.[128] But towards the latter half of the nineteenth century the census authorities started to become more circumspect and concerned about the age gathering exercise.

In 1871, Dr William Farr who initially worked on the registration system and then as a census commissioner knew all too well some sections of society were prone to age mis-statements. In an official paper issued from the Census Office, he remarked that should the stated age of servants, or of others for that matter, "be found by any fatality standing still, or even retrograding, it will be corrected by the heads of families who fill in the return."

Thirty years later, the writers of the 1901 Census report stated there was a "tendency among some portions of the population to incorrect statement of age [*sic*]." It goes further by saying there were those who were guilty of "wilful mis-statement." For example, the domestic servant may mis-state her age in order to obtain higher wages, or an inmate of the workhouse may do so in order to secure a better diet or other advantages such as outdoor relief then available to the elderly.[129]

Younger women in general were also a problem. The numbers returned as aged 20–25 at every census, according to the 1901 Census report, exceeded the number of girls returned as 10–15 at the previous census. The report compilers undertook a detailed investigation, but found explanations of immigration and mortality for the disparity to be unsatisfactory. In conclusion, they reported there was "little room for doubt that a considerable number of females under 20 years of age have returned themselves over 20, and that very large numbers of females between 25 and 40 have understated their ages. The amount of false statement has been greater among women aged 30–35 than among women aged 25–30."[130]

These problems had not disappeared by the 1911 Census when it was found a considerable number of individuals had stated approximate ages. But at the passing of each census, those in charge of the statistical data acknowledged it had grown less of a problem. This was mainly due to better education and steps taken by the authorities to tackle the problem.

For the 1921 Census, the schedule was modified and the householder was asked to provide their age and that of each member of their household in years and months. The census authorities had no intention of tabulating the age by months, it was purely a device to improve the accuracy of age reporting. In the 1921 Census Report they admitted the initiative had been partially successful and by 1931, they had seen a significant reduction in errors. Problems were still abounding with a propensity to state age next birthday instead of age last birthday particularly for children. In addition, there was evident age heaping. This occurs when people intentionally or unintentionally (because they don't know their age) misrepresent their age by rounding it up or down to the nearest number ending in a 5 or a 0.

Following the 1951 Census, there was a genuine attempt by the census officials to measure the extent of the mis-statements of age by attempting to match census records with those of births, marriages, and deaths. When trying to match with the birth registrations, a sample of 1 in 1,000 enumeration districts (no institutions were included) was drawn by selecting the 500th, 1,500th etc., district in a serial list. Certain criteria were then added to the sample until it reached the sum of just over 8,000 individuals to be checked in the birth registers. Cards were used and were grouped together on a family basis, starting with the children. Then as the search progressed, other information was added to the card. Bias was introduced by forbidding common surnames such as Smith, Jones, and Brown plus others thought to be confusing. The names forbidden were estimated to account for 8.6 per cent of the population. In such cases, the next permissible schedule was substituted.

To check the census schedules, names, sex, place, month, and year of birth were noted. When a match was established in the birth register, the date of birth was extracted. For women stating a date of marriage, a marriage card was prepared with dates, husband's name, the ages of both parties, place of enumeration, and the birthplace of the eldest child. This facilitated finding the mother's birth entry.

It was the first time any such operation had been undertaken in England and Wales and the officials were highly satisfied with the result. The study authors did not find widespread errors in individuals transferring from one age group to another, for example those aged 30–35 transferring into group 25–30. In fact they insisted it was quite rare. They did discover a number of individuals born between 9 and 30 April anticipating their birthdays and thereby recording their age next birthday, but errors overall were very small. They concurred that the recording of ages on the census "is subject to a relatively high order of accuracy, the main features being a minor degree of digital preference and a tendency to anticipate the next birthday."

The survey discovered 94 per cent of males and 87 per cent of females ages 65 or more reported their age correctly. For those aged 35–64, the figures were 93 per cent and 91 per cent respectively; all other age groups were in the mid to high 90s.[131]

Other studies have attempted to determine census age accuracy. PM Tillott's comparison between the 1851 and 1861 censuses for Hathersage

(Derbyshire) and Braithwell (Yorkshire) revealed that in 60.6 per cent of cases in Hathersage and 67.5 per cent of cases in Braithwell, the expected ten-year interval between the ages reported in the two censuses prevailed. A nine or eleven-year interval was found in 28 per cent of cases in Hathersage and 22.4 per cent of cases in Braithwell, while a larger interval was observed in 11.4 per cent of cases in Hathersage and 10.1 per cent of cases in Braithwell. Interestingly, errors were more common among individuals over the age of 20, with slightly higher rates among women than men.[132] In a separate study conducted by Anderson, which compared 475 individuals living in Preston using the censuses from 1851 and 1861, it was found that 47 per cent had an age discrepancy greater than ten years.[133] Higg's looked at individuals in Colyton in Devon on the 1851 and 1861 censuses and found in 51.5 per cent of cases for males and 52.4 per cent for females there was an interval of ten years. He did the same for Llangefni in Angelsey and concluded that the standard and accuracy of age reporting varied from place to place.

Some studies have examined the correlation between data from censuses and baptism registers, with one notable example conducted by Razzell in 1972. Razzell's study focused on forty-five parishes and specifically looked at natives over the age of 17, excluding married women. The findings indicated that 46.5 per cent of individuals matched with a baptism record were correct in terms of their age, while 31.8 per cent had an age discrepancy of one year. Furthermore, 10.5 per cent had an age discrepancy of two years, with fewer individuals experiencing greater discrepancies. Razzell also discovered the discrepancies were notably higher among individuals in the 81–90 age group.[134]

Audrey Perkyns' study delved into the total census populations of six adjacent Kentish parishes, namely Hartlip, Newington, Rainham, Stockbury, Upchurch, and Lower Halstow, over five censuses spanning from 1841 to 1881. The study aimed to analyse this data in relation to the information gathered from multiple sources for these six parishes. To achieve this, two different methods of calculation were employed. The first method copied Tillott and involved a straightforward comparison of the given ages of individuals over consecutive censuses. The second method aimed to estimate the probable age of each person whose age could be verified.

Perkyns employed a range of criteria to ensure the data for the second method was checkable, this included dates of birth, baptism, age at marriage,

age at burial, and workhouse records. Recognising the limitations of relying on baptism data, Perkyns implemented adjustments to account for possible inaccuracies. Similar doubts were raised regarding the use of age at burial and age at marriage for comparisons with census data. By employing this multiple-checking method Perkyns found for males in the six parishes, a ten year interval in 79.8 per cent of cases with ages out by one year in 14.3 per cent of individuals examined; for females she found 80.6 per cent accuracy and 13.7 per cent were out by one year. There was a greater tendency to errors as individuals grew older.[135]

David Thomson's study of the census and the elderly focused on two contrasting areas: rural Puddletown, Dorset and the residential suburb of Ealing in Middlesex. His work suggests greater accuracy in rural areas than in towns, but he admitted he couldn't draw definite conclusions. Rather than the elderly not knowing or forgetting their ages consciously, he writes, social pressures may have played a part for reasons such as Poor Law and charity; for other age groups, employment prospects, traditions of family support and conventions as to marriage ages, may all have contributed to individuals not always correctly stating their ages.[136]

The question of age accuracy or not being forthcoming about one's age was not reserved to just England and Wales, nor to just census records. In 1901, the insurance and annuity industry found nearly 2 per cent of soldiers' widows could not, or would not say when they were born.[137] And in order to qualify for a pension following the 1908 Pensions Act, the older generation were reported to have exaggerated their ages. The 1911 report excuses many on the account of them not knowing their age prior to the introduction of the pension and they were then prompted to find out, but the report also suggests this did not account for all the inflated numbers. In Scotland, the 1911 Census revealed a similar situation and rather than place the blame on the Pensions Act, the report authors wrote the decidedly uncommitted comment that the Act "is not unconnected with it."[138]

> A young maiden lady, aged fifty-two, who felt very considerable alarm lest her age should become known in her village, was driven to the necessity, on Sunday week, of walking four miles to the village of Beeston, in the dirt and rain, to sleep at the house of a friend, in order to avoid the dreadful exposure.
>
> *Monmouthshire Merlin*, 18 April 1851

The newspapers of course, enjoyed relaying stories such as the one above to a readership eager for such tales. Many seem so outlandish they are probably true. In 1901, the *Burnley Express* wrote that some women spent the whole of the census night riding around on their bicycles while another sat on a cold and draughty railway station.[139] During other censuses there were those who went on holiday so they wouldn't have to suffer providing their age (or so they thought), while in the well-to-do areas of Belgravia – Portman, Bryanstone, and other squares – as well as in Tyburnia, ladies delivered the census paper to the enumerator tied with red tape, sealed with the family crest, and addressed to the Registrar General, George Graham.[140]

When confronted with the enumerator, some would try to be evasive. One woman informed the official her age was between 16 and 100, while a labourer in a Scottish parish told the enumerator to consult the Kirk sessions books to find his age and place of birth.[141] Another lady wrote on the census schedule "of full age" hoping this was sufficient for the census authorities.[142] And the *Huddersfield Daily Examiner* told of how one old maid when informed she would be penalised £5 if she refused to state her age, said she would rather pay £20 than give it up. The threat of the fine was often enough to make a stubborn individual see sense. However, the assurance of confidentiality seems to have been the main driver in encouraging reluctant individuals to surrender the information. In 1901, the *Bedfordshire Times* stated there was considerable delicacy with ladies disclosing their age, and the secret was only parted with on the understanding the enumerator was sworn to silence, and the Registrar General would never divulge the information.[143]

In January 1921, the Registrar General Sylvanus Vivian recognised that giving up sensitive information may lead to cases of hardship. "A few days ago I received a letter, unsigned, and without any address", he explained.

> ... It is from a servant, who said that she had been compelled to under-state her age in applying for work in order get employment. She was born in a Workhouse; and if she had to state the true facts concerning herself to her employer, she feared she would lose her place. It will be possible... for a person so situated to go the local registrar and get a form, which she will fill up and present to the enumerator when he delivers the household schedules. The enumerator is then bound to admit her claim, and give her a separate schedule, which she would sign and hand direct to him.[144]

Labourers the wrong side of 40 also faced similar difficulties obtaining work and fearing their true age would be exposed, they were reluctant to provide accurate information. Assurances regarding disclosure and the introduction of the confidential schedule for the 1921 Census helped allay any fears.

The enumerator's role, in terms of how they were editors and shapers of the information supplied to them, has already been discussed. But they were also translators of vague and nebulous information. The *Trevecca College Magazine* told of how one enumerator was given a schedule with the age marked as 805 by an old farmer from the parish of Llanveigan. "There must be some mistake here", said the official, "you can't be so old as this." "No mistake at all", was the impatient reply, "I have put it down quite correct – 80 and 5. No mistake about that." In another household in south Wales the aggregate age of the family was 2,320 when the ages were entered onto the schedule in this manner. This form of age reporting was not confined to Wales either and was widely reported across all four nations. Many commentators placed the blame for this on Edward Cocker, whose book *Cocker's Arithmetic: Being a Plain and Familiar Method, Suitable to the Meanest Capacity, for the Full Understanding of that Incomparable Art, As It Is Now Taught by the Ablest School-Masters in City and Country*, was probably on every Sunday school's shelf.

Enumerators also encountered vague and associative age recollections or they had to wait until the householder had consulted the family Bible for the ages of everyone present. For want of a Bible, one mother tried to calculate the age of one child by tracing various removals from street to street. When that didn't work she asked her other children, but they couldn't help.[145] In Scotland, one enumerator recalled being told "I was born the year after the windy Christmas" and another individual stated she was born the day the foundation stone of the Kirk of Wick was laid.[146] And in a Westminster workhouse in 1901 the elderly population reckoned their ages by comparing them with some well-known event in the reign of the life of Queen Victoria.[147]

If after all of these efforts they failed to ascertain the age of an individual or their family, registrars made enumerators guess and write down how old they thought the householder was and enter it onto the schedule.

"Anney, Adia, Rashel and Hahriarte..."

When it came to entering the names of each family member onto the schedule, the family Bible was used once again. Without it some families were stumped. It was reported in Wellingborough there were several cases of men who did not know the Christian names of their wives and women of their husbands. Further, when asked for their surnames, a look of blank ignorance came over the faces of many householders.[148] In Wales, an Irish settler did not know his surname and a letter was sent to his old parish priest in County Cork to enquire about the name.[149]

Nicknames and shortened names were used without care until a conscientious enumerator pointed out that Bessie Brown should in fact be recorded as Elizabeth Brown if that was her name. The correct name was then entered onto thc schedule, but only after the husband had consulted with his wife to check that she was indeed called Elizabeth. In another case in 1901, not only did a Surrey publican forget to add his daughters to the schedule, but he had to locate them to find out what names he and his wife had given them![150]

Newborns were a problem for couples and enumerators. Some children just made it onto the schedule in time. It was reported in the *Berkshire Chronicle* in 1901 that one child was born five minutes to midnight while another was born on the stroke of midnight. However, a number of households forgot or purposely omitted very young babies from the schedule. One child born on the Saturday night before the 1891 Census was not included when the enumerator called. Before he or she left the house the baby was named and duly entered onto the schedule, but only after the parents had argued as to whether it should be called Jack, Bill, Tom, or Harry etc.[151] One couple avoided such problems. In 1901, Robert and Ethel Evans of 10 Pritchard Row, Ystradyfodwg entered their 4-day-old son as "XYZ Evans." In other instances of fresh arrivals without a name, householders and enumerators were told to write "Baby" instead. In 1911 it was also reported that "Tootsie" could be used for very young infants – indeed there are a handful of Tootsies under 1 month old on the census.

Some individuals wrote their names on the schedule backwards, which is why there are a number of examples of people using middle names instead of their first name. Middle names were not required for the 1841 Census – they may have been supplied by the more precise householder, but were filtered out by the enumerator for the sake of uniformity.

On the 1911 Census, the question regarding the number of deceased children posed difficulties for some parents. At Northwich a woman found it necessary to pay a visit to the churchyard to ascertain how many of her children had died. While one man in Dundee wrote "Can't tell. Lost count." Indeed, the Angel of Death was an unwelcome caller to all households and the census did not prevent its shocking visitations. On Sunday, 31 March 1901 George Binfield the storekeeper at Windsor Castle was filling in the census schedule while his wife was dressing for church upstairs. He called out the questions to her and she answered, but when he jokingly asked, "Married or single?" there was no reply. He went upstairs and found her unresponsive. She had died from heart failure.[152]

For some individuals, the census recorded their last moments. Emma Baxter, a 60-year-old widow was seen going about her usual business at Pinkneys Green, near Maidenhead, on the Sunday evening of the 1911 Census. After returning home she filled up her census paper and then proceeded to her bedroom. She was partially undressed when she fell and was found dead on the floor at 8 am the following morning. The coroner decided Emma had a weak heart.[153] James Harding, one of the unfortunate men burned at the Adare Level explosion died at his home in 10 Evans Terrace, Ystradyfodwg when the enumerator called on 1 April 1901. And there were countless others: Ann Blackhurst of Liverpool died on the morning of 31 March 1851; Ann Wharam of Toxteth died 1.30 am on the same day; Ann Wigglesworth died at 7 pm on the census night in 1861 – all were recorded in the enumeration books. There was 14-year-old Elizabeth Souter's mother who died on 2 April 1871 leaving her alone in Devonport; George Squires of Beetham died on 3 April 1871; James Bushell of Leeds died at 11 pm on 7 April 1861, and 9-month-old Louisa Woolf died early Monday in 1871 according to the enumerator for St. James's, Westminster. These and so many others were captured for posterity in a single moment in time.

There were some horrific moments when enumerators encountered the dead while on their rounds or had to notify the police when they received no response to their calls. In the Welsh hills an enumerator asked a woman for the whereabouts of her husband and was told bluntly he was dead in the next room.[154] In 1951 there were two incidents where enumerators raised the alarm concerning possible dead occupants, one was for 63-year-old Wilfred Pearson who was found dead in his living room in Bradford, and the other was Ida M. Bolton, who was well-known to locals in Bramley, Leeds and who was found dead in her bathroom after the enumerator attempted to call.

"So good-bye forever, my love."

On 2 April 1911, there were just a few prisoners languishing in the cells of the Hull Central Police Station. Their names, ages, professions, and places of birth were noted, but the census didn't illuminate their tribulations or misdemeanours, it didn't give a sense of who they were or if they deserved to be punished, or, if in fact, life was dealing them lemons. That's not the job of the census. But in the case of one merchant seaman, his story was revealed to the world thanks to the census. Frederick William Gray was a 22-year-old from Whitstable in Kent who migrated to Hull for work and who settled in Nornabell Street.

Upon receiving his census paper from the enumerator and being in a very depressed state, he set about writing the following note on the census schedule:

> I have not done right you [*sic*], love; but if you wish to go to my fun[eral], say that you knew me, so my father will know where I am, for it is more than I can stand I have "N moon" on right hand. and "S.W.S." on the left hand. So good-bye forever, my love. Paison [*sic*] had taken place. I am at Stoneferry Bridge. You will find me. Death has parted us – W.G.[155]

He then took a bottle of poison and headed down to Queen's Dock. The police discovered him semi-conscious on the dockside and he was promptly taken to the police station where he admitted he had attempted to take his own life. At his house they found the census paper with his note resulting in a charge of attempted suicide. Frederick appeared before the police court a few days later.

In court he gazed listlessly around while others described him as "strange in his mind" and troubled. His decline was triggered by a quarrel with his girlfriend, a local girl from Arundel Street who had been seeing him for roughly eleven weeks. After three weeks together, he proposed and on 25 March 1911 they were due to be married, but the girl asked him to postpone it until he had a better situation. They quarrelled and the girl returned his engagement ring.

The justices ruled Gray should be held for a week while his health was evaluated. Years later, in the summer of 1914, Frederick William Gray attempted to enlist in the East Yorkshire Regiment at Hull; describing himself as a ship's cook, married to Louise, and father to an illegitimate child, he failed the fitness test and was dismissed from service. It seems he suffered from chronic gonorrhoea.

There must have been hundreds if not thousands of examples of individuals writing extra information on their schedules. The census afforded an opportunity for people to express their feelings and opinions in a very direct manner. Householders used the census as a platform where they could share their sense of humour, make sarcastic comments, and exhibit their irritation.

Somewhere near Burnley, a power weaver, who according to his schedule was of "grey texture of late" sat down to write out his 1901 Census paper and wrote after his place of birth:

> Migration through a series of intrigues before and since enactment of Parish Council Bill. Moreover, impeachable induction of instated members in Parish of _____ by heterogeneous combination of consanguinity, etc., obligation virus, obligatory obsequeous [*sic*] and satellites votes ostracised indictment.

Thankfully the local newspaper was able to translate this for their readership writing,

> He was compelled to leave his native place by a series of intrigues after the passing of the Parish Council Act. These intrigues which led to his being ostracised were conducted by successful candidates for the Parish Council --------, who themselves secured election through a heterogeneous combination of relatives and others bound them by obligation and by the votes of satellites and obsequious dependents.[156]

In 1911, medical practitioner Philip Laver wrote on his schedule that in addition to his usual occupation he was an "ill paid" official of the Poor Law Guardians. George Alfred Boreham of Sunderland who was previously an architect and surveyor added, "But have been incapacitated thru ill health for nearly four years, during which time I have lived on private means. Hope to recover health and business." Similarly, Kate Christina Johnson was unemployed due to ill health and was receiving "help from the parish and a few friends." Governess Sarah Chivers who was also sick, kindly informed the enumerator her previous employment was as a companion to a lady and she received an annuity of £15.

In 1881, the *Jarrow Express* reported that a schoolmaster, returned his paper with the remarks, "Permanent endowment, none; voluntary contributions, none; grants from Government, none: school fees, unknown; other sources, energy..."[157] He was not alone in using the census to explore his bitterness. A wife who was left in the lurch by her soldier husband referred to him on the schedule as Royal Artillery Reserve *deserter* according to the *Brighton Gazette*.[158]

Then there were those who refused to take the whole process seriously. Thomas Randell of Leicester decided to either take an impish approach or was at best reluctant to give honest information about himself. He wrote "Head and Tail" in the relationship column, did not provide his age, wrote "anything (nothing special)" in the occupation column, and under place of birth offered "Co. Leicester I believe."

Thomas only had himself to think of when it came to deciding who was head (and tail) of the household. Elsewhere there were couples with simmering tensions arguing over who was head of the family. A lady from Kingston said she was "head" of her family since her husband hadn't worked for years and she was the one responsible for caring for him. Unfortunately, her logic was rejected.[159] *The Leeds Journal* reported in 1881 that a handful of disputes concerning who would take the position of head had to be discussed and worked out.[160] In 1921, an enumerator writing for *The Bedfordshire Times* remembered going to every house with polite enquiries: "Good morning, madam. Who is the head of this residence, and how many rooms are there? Invariably", he wrote, "the first question generated quite a bit of tension." The official left the household feeling quite sorry for the husband. Another enumerator, trying to write out the form for the 1911 Census entered the husband's name and asked Mrs X of Sheffield, "I suppose he is the head of the family?" to which she responded without hesitation, Aye, fathead."[161] For the amusement of its readers, the *Monmouthshire Merlin* gave space to an anecdote concerning a Glasgow housewife who when confronted with the schedule said, "Head of the family; that's me, nae doot. I wad like to ken wha's the head o' the family if it's no me." Then after considering her husband and his role in the family, noted "Doots aboot and does nothing: leaves a' to me."[162]

In 1891 Henry Dyson or his wife Augusta wrote in the occupation column she was "Boss of Household". Naturally, there was some resistance from a census official, and a line was drawn through the text next to Augusta's entry. In 1911 Henry Dawes wrote the same about his wife Mary Ann Dawes, this time however there was no challenge from an official (only the insertion of "wife") and Mary Ann Dawes assumed her rightful place as boss of the household! Elsewhere in 1911 John James Lloyd described himself as "The Boss" in the relationship column with no obvious objection from his wife!

The census posed a further difficult question for many households around the country: who actually should be counted? The 1911 and 1921 censuses have numerous examples of householders including their absent children or dead relatives on the schedule. This confusion was noted by enumerators and reported in newspapers and there were also instances of soldiers away fighting in the Boer War added to the census schedule by their wives. These inclusions occurred during earlier censuses, but were filtered out by the enumerators.

It seems some individuals believed it was necessary to give an account of their whole family, including their pets, rather than just who was in the house on the night of the census. Not reading or misunderstanding the schedule may have lead to these inclusions as well as a touch of sarcasm at the prying nature of the process. Individuals may have also feared the fine or just wanted to be noticed by the authorities:

> It was novelty to some of them to find anyone cared whether they were married or single, or where they were born, or what they did. Assured that the Government – including "beaks", "peelers", parish officers, and other natural enemies – meant them no harm, they jumped with fatal facility to the opposite conclusion, and assumed that the authorities were about to interfere actively for their good.
>
> *Preston Herald*, 1871[163]

In some people's minds there was also the vague idea the monarch took notice and wished to know of their personal circumstances, including who was in their family and how many pets were at home.[164] Genealogist Jane Roberts has tracked down a number of furry additions to the schedules of the 1911 Census plus a few from earlier censuses. Frances Catherine Stone of Heanor listed Timothy the Cat aged 7 and Jack the Dog aged 8 on her 1911 schedule; Jane also found an Airedale terrier called Roger belonging to journalist James Ange Little on the same census.[165]

Naturally, contemporaneous newspapers lapped up such stories too. The *Bedfordshire Times* reported, "several facetious citizens have made inquiries to the necessity of entering the dog or the cat on the list, and a boy wanted to put his pet mice." A Hull journal stated that a man named Matthew residing in the borough of Scarborough, made a return of his livestock to the enumerator as thus: "Matthew Reed, Sanak Reed, son Matthew Reed, thomas Reed, catren Reed, elsebeth Reed, tu poll parets, tu cats, on canare (one canary), and how many Meas (how many mice) I don't know."[166] On one census paper, a London enumerator found two cats, a dog, and a tortoise had been entered as lodgers.[167] In High Wycombe in 1901, lodger Jim the cat was described as aged 1 last birthday and a "mouse-catcher, worker on own account." According to the *Bucks Herald* when the head of the family was asked whether this was a joke, he responded that it was part of his duty to number the animal as one of the household.[168] An official in 1911, most likely the registrar, scrawled in large red handwriting on the schedule belonging to John Charles Belton of Chester, "This is a cat" against the entry for 5-month-old "servant" Peter Tabby, a "mouser" who was of "Persian" nationality![169] That same census Mary Owen of Llanboidy (or someone in her household) listed her cat Sof as a rat and mouse catcher who according to the language column spoke "catawall" (Mary herself was recorded as speaking Welsh and English "when angered"). Mary also obligingly provided Sof's place of birth as Llanboidy.

> Some householders have a desire to improve the dry details of the schedules. For instance, one householder under the heading "Where born", described one of his children as "born in the parlour", and the other "upstairs".[170]

Yet again enumerators were required to perform the role of editor and filterer of unordered and unwanted information when confronted with the place of birth question. One newspaper in Rugby reported that 75 per cent of householders had entered the town of their birth before the county.[171] Enumerators may have corrected this error on the schedules as they went along, but some didn't. Registrars were advised by the Census Office in 1891 that such widespread corrections of schedules was unnecessary; the enumeration books, however, needed to comply with the instructions to facilitate the checking undertaken by clerks in the Census Office.

Enumerators discovered there were householders who were unable to identify their parish or county correctly or even at all. According to the *Pall Mall Gazette* in 1901, the proprietor of one public house professed he didn't know his place of birth. If he failed to deliver the information when the enumerator called, wrote the journalist, he would be fined. However, if he genuinely didn't know, a prosecution was unlikely. If the householder had no knowledge of where they or their family members were born, then they had no recourse but to write England, Scotland, Wales, Ireland etc.[172] Conversely there were examples where individuals entered the actual house number and street or the field or farm of their nativity onto the schedule. Among the amusing anecdotes offered by the press were reports of persons writing they were born in a henhouse, on a seashore, and on a piece of waste land.

In Yorkshire there was a habit of listing places adjacent to where the householder was born like Halifax instead of Todmorden. In Audrey Perkyns' study of birthplace accuracy in Kent, she also found that some individuals had a tendency to give the largest nearby town adjacent to where they were born. She also noted they gave the name of a farm or township on one census and then the parish on another (equally this may have been down to the enumerator), but of course both were correct in their own way.[173]

In her comparison of census birthplaces with residence at the time of baptism, Perkyns discovered that out of 2,351 single entries with baptism records, only 79 (3.4 per cent) had a different birthplace in comparison to the census. Following analysis of these exceptions, Perkyns found that 33 could be explained by a move around the time of birth or baptism, twenty-one were from families who were frequent movers, and six were either orphans or illegitimate children who may have been born in the workhouse. This left only eight remaining cases, five of which may have had incorrect birthplaces due to dittos or being a servant at the time. The last three cases involved siblings aged 6 and 4 whose birthplaces were listed as being in Bobbing while all their siblings' birthplaces were recorded as Newington. However, the baptism records mentioned their residence as "Newington but belonging to Bobbing", Perkyns concluded that overall, census birthplaces aligned with residences at the time of baptism.[174]

When she compared census to census, Perkyns discovered very few birthplace mistakes and believed they could be ascribed to the quality of the enumerators. For instance the high number of errors in Stockbury during the censuses of 1861 and 1871 may well have been due to the dubious literacy skills of enumerators John Jennings, a publican, and Daniel Goodhew, a victualler and farmer who took over in 1871. Although both had decent penmanship, they also displayed a tendency towards spelling mistakes and carelessness. In Halstow in 1881, the enumerator was a young schoolmaster known for being particular and precise, yet even he made errors later corrected by his superiors, proving that not all schoolmasters were reliable.[175] Out of the 369 errors recorded, 116 were dittos which suggests the enumerators may have accidentally, perhaps in a state of tiredness or boredom, lost their concentration in a rhythm of repetition. And while it is reasonable to expect the enumerator to know that Manchester and Newmarket are not located in Kent, it may have been difficult for them to recognise small place names brought by migrants from other counties. Perkyns correctly states it would be unfair to blame enumerators for all of the errors; some mistakes can be attributed to illegible handwriting or miscommunication during interviews.

Parents were particularly adept guardians of the fine detail when it came to distinguishing the birthplaces of their children. It was often found that individuals had an accurate birthplace as long as their parent completed the census forms, but when they become heads of their own household, they would supply the place where they lived as a child, mistakenly believing it to be their birthplace. Perkyns also found some heads of households had a tendency to transpose their wives' birthplaces with their own. Among those who were uncertain of their age, she also discovered a correlation with birthplace inaccuracy.

Perkyns believed farmers or landowners who were listed with different birthplaces on different censuses were most likely holding land in multiple parishes. She found baptism records confirmed this trend among yeoman farmers who held land under the Kentish custom of gavelkind, where land is divided between heirs. Other families, such as military families and bargemen, moved so frequently they often did not know their exact birthplaces.[176] Remarkably, 536 errors and anomalies, which account for over 74 per cent of the total, were located within 5 miles of the alternative birthplace. Additionally, 399 of these, equating to over 55 per cent, were found within 2 miles or in a neighbouring parish.[177]

Another study conducted by Razzell further supports Perkyns findings by cross-matching baptism register and census data from 1851 and 1861. Razzell also found there were more discrepancies in urban areas compared to rural areas, and that migration played a significant role in causing errors in birthplace information. The birthplaces of natives were found to be more reliable than those not born in the census parish.

> Similarly there will be many errors in the "married or single" column on account of wilful misrepresentation. Couples who are merely cohabiting together will, for the sake of appearances,

> return themselves as married persons; while persons of the latter classes, and especially husbands, living in a state of separation, as single persons, will have returned themselves as single.
>
> *Whitehaven News*, 6 April 1871

There was very little written in the press and in accounts about the Condition as to Marriage column in terms of responses and comprehension of the question being asked. In rare cases some householders may not have understood the terminology in a similar vein to not understanding the meaning of the word surname. In 1901, a Welsh newspaper reported that the husband of the household had written down "married-bachelor", and his wife as "married-spinster".[178] And in Bath that same year, it was reported the question of whether "married" or "single" gave rise to *doubt and uncertainty*.[179] The most common situation and one familiar to many family historians, saw couples seeming to appear married when in fact they were cohabiting, either after being separated from former spouses or just choosing not to marry. Those who were estranged from a spouse and who were not living with another partner were sometimes returned as being separated: Ann Binge of Sheffield was described as "separated from husband"; Martha du Frocq was separated from a husband who was living in St. Martin's, Guernsey; and Annie Elinor Ash wrote she was "separated judicially".

Perhaps the most surprising admission or perhaps an insertion by the enumerator, were the women and men shown to be paramours. This was a phenomenon researched by the late Audrey Collins and the aforementioned Jane Roberts. Across all published censuses there are over ninety confirmed listings of individuals who were returned as paramours (and forty plus concubines in England and Wales), which given the millions censused, is statistically insignificant. Yet it is interesting to note the ones seemingly admitted by the householders themselves in 1911 and 1921 including Annie Lawton the paramour of Chas Wilcock; Ann Wardle the paramour of Charles Nolan, and Mrs Gardiner the paramour and housekeeper of boatman Mr Roberts of Chalford. There may be many more hidden under the guise of "housekeeper", a word used to disguise improper relationships akin to some seamstresses and milliners hiding their true occupation of 'prostitute'. And what of prostitutes, where are they to be found on the census?

Chapter Eight

Work, School, and Home

In 1911, a newspaper columnist wrote there were a large number of women in his area who returned themselves on the census as "of independent means", which was no doubt a hint to his readers something was amiss. He was not alone either. Two decades earlier a Portsmouth enumerator expressed the same, writing: "The means of livelihood practised by certain young women living in the district I traversed found euphemistic expression in such descriptions as 'sempstress' and 'laundress'. Three of them, lodging in one house, were returned as 'living on their means'."[180]

Given the small number of prostitutes returned on the census versus the number from official police reports, it can be assumed that females working in the profession were not openly declaring themselves as such, but were putting forward other occupations.

When the householder's schedule was introduced in 1841, the inhabitants of a household were asked to supply details of their rank, profession, or occupation regardless of whether they were actually economically active. The exceptions to this were wives living with their husbands, and children living with their parents who were assisting them, but not receiving wages. The goal was to obtain an accurate record of individual occupations. It must have become apparent to the census authorities the matter was more complicated than expected. In 1851, a sentence was added to the instructions telling the householder to list occupations in order of importance, with the first occupation taking precedence. This still confused some and there were many with furrowed brows trying to decide which of their many occupations was more important.

After having decided to infer the existence of masters in 1841 simply by everyone else adding they were either an apprentice or journeyman, ten years later householders were requested to make the distinction between masters, journeymen, and apprentices. Masters in trade and manufacture were required to indicate their status on the schedule by adding "master" after their occupational description, and to report the number of employees they had on census day. However, not all provided accurate information, leading to incomplete statistics. There were also problems with journeymen as Dr Ogle (yes, that man again), told the Treasury Committee in 1890: "The registrars say people often will not state whether they are journeymen or masters; they are angry if asked to do it. A man does not like to call himself a journeyman."[181]

In response to the criticism that masters were not being distinguished from other workers on previous censuses, the commissioners in 1891 adopted a plan suggested by the Local Government Board. As a consequence, three new columns were introduced with the headings "employer", "employed", and "neither employer nor employed." On the Scottish schedule, an additional column was included for those working on their own account. Householders were asked to mark a cross in the appropriate column for each person engaged in an occupation. The 1890 Treasury Committee debated employment and agreed householders often faced confusion about whether they were employees or employers, because in some cases they were both. Indeed, many individuals failed to mark a column or marked crosses in multiple columns.

In addition to asking farmers if they were masters (employers), they were also asked to disclose the amount of land they owned and how many labourers they employed. In 1851 the enumerators were given additional instructions on the subject:

> The numbers of labourers returned should include waggoners, shepherds, and all kinds of workmen employed on the farm, whether they sleep in the house or not; and when boys or women are employed, their number should be separately given. The male and female farm servants who sleep in the house will be returned in the Household Schedule, and their particular employments as waggoner, dairy maid etc. inserted in the column headed "Occupation".

In the report that followed the 1851 Census, the authorities admitted "Some uncertainty prevails as to whether the farms returned all their indoor farm servants; and women and boys were included in some cases and not in others." In 1861, women were apparently excluded from the numbers employed on farms.

Following his study of farmers and farm servants in Tickhill in 1851, Peter Tillott pondered the difficulties of interpretation. Much depended on how the enumerator interpreted his instructions and how many and what type of farm servants were listed on the census. The size of the family, their available labour, as well as the inconsistent practice of labelling farmer's children as "farmer's son" etc., needed to be taken into consideration. The inclusion of female servants on farms was also problematic, as they were not necessarily confined to domestic duties. In some cases, enumerators distinguished between female domestic and farm servants, but not always.

During the 1871 and 1881 censuses, only men living in the farmer's residence and working on the farm were considered as "farm servants." The exclusion of women continued a decade later, when householders were instructed to only mention sons or other male relatives working for the farmer. There was no requirement to mention a farmer's daughter. Additionally, the census no longer collected data on the size of farms or the number of labourers employed.

> A lady who is member of half-a-dozen committees, honorary secretary to two associations, and an energetic slum worker, was in doubt as to her occupation. So was the enumerator, but they had no alternative save to make it "home duties", although these occupy but a part of her time.
>
> *Dundee Courier*, 22 June 1921[182]

According to the instructions on the reverse of the 1851 Census schedule, women who were householders were required to have their titles or occupations recorded in the same way as men. Women who undertook jobs outside of their domestic duties were also supposed to be noted separately. But those mistresses and ladies of the house whose main occupation was domestic duties didn't need their occupation listed, because that was well understood (the enumerators were told). These instructions were diligently followed by many women or householders according to Tillott in his study. The records show numerous wives working as dressmakers and milliners, widows running their late husbands' businesses and mangle women.

These women may have technically only been working part-time, yet still fulfilled their traditional domestic roles at home.

Tillott also discovered that in most cases, the wives who were not working would leave the occupation column blank and enumerators would simply refer to them by their husband's occupation – such as "groom's wife" or "cutler's wife". However, some of the enumerators in Tillott's study chose to ignore this convention and referred to each wife as a "housekeeper" or even included the phrase "domestic duties" (although this was rare). Yet it is important to note the term "housekeeper" was also used in a different context. In households where there were widowers, bachelors, or married men with absent wives, an appropriate person (such as an unmarried daughter, sister, or mother) would often be designated as housekeeper by the enumerator. For some enumerators it appears the term housewife was synonymous with housekeeper. However, they were not consistently noted as such by enumerators and sometimes their designation was crossed out by checkers.

Despite attempts by census takers in the middle of the nineteenth century to account for women's work there was one area where it was under-recorded. Women in casual or part-time occupations appear to have been overlooked including those working from home creating products for sale and offering services outside their domestic duties. If the service was as a domestic servant then there was also some confusion similar to that of housekeeper. As Edward Higgs points out, "service" in the nineteenth century was a legal term rather than having any occupational meaning; it specified a relationship between employer and employee. As such there is an expectation to see servants described as servants in both the relationship column and the occupation column. But in surveying the enumeration books of Rochdale, Higgs discovered over 40 per cent were not enumerated as servants; instead, they were returned as next of kin.

Higgs proposes several interpretations of this situation. Firstly, it's possible these servants, who resided with their families, were typically hired as live-in workers but were temporarily out of work, which would imply a notable degree of unemployment. Secondly, many were day-servants who worked in their employers' homes during the day and returned to their own families' homes at night. Thirdly, these "domestics" not only lived with their relatives but also carried out household chores for them.

The conclusion to be drawn from this is that the interpretation of servants and their relationship within the household should be regarded with caution. As Higgs noted, if we assume that all the "servants" living with relatives in Rochdale were employed at home, then of the 2,065 people listed as working in servant roles in 1851, only 1,113, or 53.9 per cent, were accurately recorded. If this discrepancy occurred nationwide, around 500,000 women might have been incorrectly listed in the mid-nineteenth-century census reports."[183]

> Some working-class householders may have used "scholar" to conceal the work of their children.

Householders and enumerators were instructed to regard the work of children using the same conventions as for women. Thus, children, who were not receiving tuition, but who were engaged in casual or part-time work such as running errands and harvest work may have been under-recorded. The 1851 Census instructions specified that scholars were defined as above five years of age and were "daily attending school, or receiving regular tuition under a master or governess at home." In 1861, an extra column was added to the Scottish schedule for the householder to indicate the number of children from five to thirteen who went to school the previous week. No such column was added to the England and Wales schedule, in fact the instructions concerning master and governess were removed and scholars only needed to be "attending a school, or receiving regular instructions at home." The new column was moved for the 1871 Census in Scotland to column 8 and guidance was added that only children aged between five and thirteen in regular school attendance or at home under the tuition of a master or governess should be taken into account. The column was gone by the 1881 Census, probably because the information could be obtained from local school boards, however "scholars" were still added to the "Rank, profession, occupation" column. Householder instructions were missing for the 1891 Census in England and Wales, but retained in Scotland. Instructions returned in 1901 for England and Wales where it was stated children attending school "and also engaged in a trade or industry should be described as following the particular trade or industry."

The schooling of their children put pressure on working-class parents because they could no longer rely on the labour of their offspring for a secondary income. School boards and their officers pursued parents whose children were conspicuous by their absence. Hence, there was a tendency for parents to use "scholar" when their child was in fact working.

The 1921 Census for England and Wales included a special section to collect details about children in school and those enrolled in either full-time or part-time further education. This data aimed to identify the number and ages of people engaged in any form of school or institutional learning, distinguishing between those attending full-time (during regular school hours) and those attending part-time (for limited or occasional periods). The collected information helped to determine how many individuals were solely focused on education versus those juggling work alongside their studies. The decision to postpone the 1921 Census meant it occurred during the summer term, a time when evening classes and special courses were not in session. Consequently, the census data did not fully represent the expected attendance levels for part-time education during the winter and spring terms.

Classification of Occupations

The authorities needed a system for tabulating occupations after the census was concluded. In 1851, Dr Farr initiated a classification system and occupations were organised into "Classes" and "Sub-Classes", later renamed as "Orders" and "Sub-orders". An alphabetical list was created to show which Orders and Sub-orders each occupation fell under. This classification underwent a complete revision in 1861 and was accompanied by a guide for the clerks responsible for this task. In 1871, the list was updated using similar sources but remained mostly unchanged. However, in 1881 it was decided that a new dictionary of occupations must be compiled due to many obsolete terms. Up until then, this "special dictionary" contained about 7,000 entries, but thereafter it swelled to 12,000 and had 15,000 entries by 1901. The main reason for this change was the emergence of new industries requiring more detailed categorisations. Additionally, many occupational names in use were merely informal nicknames and were included in the list because householders used them on the schedules.

For workers in regions where there were alternative names for occupations, it meant some adaptation. In 1911, a newspaper used miner-hewer as an example stating that the word "getter" was commonly used in Derbyshire, but householders had become acquainted to entering "hewer" on the census paper.[184] As Higgs points out in *Making Sense of the Census Revisited*, occupational terms had different meanings in different parts of the country citing clothier meaning cloth maker in one area and cloth dealer elsewhere, or bricksetter for bricklayer when in most areas it meant a man involved in brick making.

During the preparations for the 1901 Census, the Home Office and Board of Trade requested additional changes to the classification system in order to align their statistics with other departments. The number of occupational headings, which had varied in previous censuses and stood at 347 in 1891, was increased to 382. The same departments also requested information regarding individuals working from home in certain industries.

Challenges in collecting precise occupational data during the 1881 and 1891 censuses were anticipated to reappear in 1901. To address this, instructions for completing the occupation section on the census forms were updated and stressed to households. Additionally, enumerators received a memorandum containing common vague descriptions and examples of preferred terms to use as a reference.

For the 1911 Census the focus shifted to an interest in the difference between industrial and occupational classifications. The occupation column pertained to personal employment, while individuals who worked for an employer were required to specify the industry or service they were associated with in the corresponding column. In 1921, householders were required to give the address of each person's place of work.

In 1931, those who were temporarily unemployed were considered a priority and were tabulated for the first time. The instructions on the back of the schedules provided additional information to householders on how to report unemployment status: "If a man who follows the calling of a carpenter is in work at Census time he will enter 'Carpenter'. If he happens to be out of a job at Census time he should enter 'Carpenter, out of work', and the particulars given in column L should be those of last employer."

Even though unemployment was tabulated for the first time in 1931, householders were asked on previous censuses to state whether they were "out of employ". In 1881, the *East London Observer* wrote it "was the cause of misunderstanding and much disappointment" in poorer districts because there was a belief it would enable the head of household to claim some kind of poor relief.[185]

It didn't go unnoticed by the newspapers that with each census there was an ever greater requirement for accurate descriptions of occupations from householders. Though, it is probably more accurate to say the newspapers had received the memo. As we have seen, the census authorities relied on the press to spread the word to the population whenever it needed to increase exposure for a forthcoming census.

> An attempt is made to ascertain the precise nature of the occupation followed ... It will not do to describe oneself simply as a "merchant", "broker", "agent", "manufacturer", "contractor", "manager", and so forth. You will have to add that you are "fruit merchant" or "tea merchant", or "stockbroker", or a "furniture broker", and so on ... So strong are the wishes of the census authorities upon this point of classification of occupation or employment that they have solicited and obtained the co-operation of the Board of Education.[186]
>
> *Mid Sussex Times*, 1901

In addition to that department, the Board of Agriculture was also engaged to get the message out to the farming community, appealing to farmers to be careful to obtain an accurate record of the occupations of persons engaged in the various departments of agriculture.

Despite attempts by the census authorities to disseminate the requirements for completing the occupation column, newspapers reported that as anticipated, it was a great stumbling-block and was well-nigh impossible to get the householder to understand. "Time after time", the *Manchester Evening News* reported, "were papers handed in giving the occupation simply as ironworker, labourer, worker in cotton factory, mason, striker, and forth, instead of stating the identical branch of these industries to which the person referred to belonged."[187]

Some householders tried their best while others offered irrelevant information or silliness. One man described himself as a bricklayer working in "bricks, mortar, and beer". Another said he was a fishmonger working "in the fish trade", while a locomotive engine driver indicated he worked at home.[188] He was not the only one perplexed by the working at home column. In south Wales, a man wrote "Coalminer, own account, at home."[189] One enumerator encountered a man who professed to be a clerk, but who could not read or write. After questioning, the man explained he believed he was a clerk because he kept the gate of a yard where vans entered and made chalk marks on a wall as they went in and out.[190]

In 1901, some people found it problematic they couldn't list "gentleman" as an occupation. In Surrey, a number of individuals wished to return themselves as "esquire", "gentleman" and of "no occupation". The census instructions forbade this, instead they made do with "living on our means" as the *West Surrey Times* reported.[191] In Chester, one man actually lost his temper with the enumerator over it. In 1841, the term used for individuals who derived their chief income outside of employment was "Independent" which was abbreviated to "Ind". Then in 1851 householders were instructed to record their former occupation e.g. retired grocer and if they received money from land and annuities to specify they were landed proprietors, fund-holders, and annuitants and so on. In 1891, any retired individual still had to record themselves as such, but "Living on their own means" could be used for all those who were in receipt of pensions, rents, and dividends etc. In 1911 this became the more succinct "private means" and in 1921 individuals could also write "None" or "Not occupied for a living" in the occupation column.

At the other end of the social ladder, The *West Surrey Times* received word from one enumerator that two men residing in a Goosepool lodging house near Chertsey returned themselves as "beggar" and "moucher". The evidence for this survives due to the enumerator copying the information into the enumeration books (RG13/590 F. 88v. p.14).

> In some of the districts inhabited by the very poorest classes, persons renting only one room for themselves and family actually took in lodgers to fill up the few vacant inches in their room.
>
> *Star of Gwent*, 13 April 1861[192]

In their accounts, enumerators barely mentioned housing, though they were required to have a meticulous approach in recording the desired information both in their enumeration and memorandum books. On occasions, they were accompanied by journalists who would write a vignette of the poverty-stricken inhabitants of a slum or rail against the levels of overcrowding they encountered on their rounds:

> Here is an old lady occupying one room about 10ft. by 15ft. She herself was sixty-five, and she had a son and daughter of twenty-three and eighteen respectively – pretty well for one small room; but in addition to these she had two "visitors," a youth of sixteen and a young woman of twenty-three. Down the filthy little hole, with a piece of string by way of a hand rail, and up another.[193]

> It appears that in some five or six-roomed houses, in Sandford-place, as many families, numbering, perhaps, 20 or more, are huddled together... Immediately on entering some of these dwellings, the enumerators were overpowered by a gush of foul air, redolent with noxious particles of animal and vegetable life... The officials found drains neglected, stagnant water in the back premises... decomposed meat, and some other spectacles which are too shocking to describe. On calling at houses of this class, they were at once ushered into the only audience room of the family, where a child, or, perhaps, two, were sick on a pallet; where the wife was awaiting her confinement, or even the corpse its sepulchre.[194]

It was generally accepted truthful admissions regarding the number of persons inhabiting a house or a room were often not forthcoming. The Sanitary Act (1866) gave powers via the Secretary of State to the local Nuisance Authority to make and enforce regulations for "fixing the number of persons who may occupy a house or part of a house which is let in lodgings or occupied by members of more than one family."[195]

In 1891, a letter appeared in the *Morning Post* regarding overcrowding and incorrect schedules:

> Sir. – I have to day interviewed one of the clergy of the East-end, who has a parish of over 12,000 people, one of the poorest and worst in East London. He informed me that the people there have in very many instances given an absolutely incorrect return, in order to avoid subsequent disagreeable proceedings against them for "overcrowding". He instanced one house of six rooms returned in the census paper as having 18 residents, whereas there were, in fact, 28. Another with 22 inhabitants was returned as 10. Another with 20 also returned as 10. In many cases they have returned 10 to 12 persons less than the actual numbers. I would like to ask. How is the Registrar-General proposing to deal with such cases?[196]

Many families were forced into overcrowded conditions because of escalating rents. These hikes in rent took advantage of those displaced through slum clearances and this together with the strict regulations on block dwellings limited the housing stock available.[197] Fear of eviction due to the powers of the Nuisance Authority or anxiety from possible rent increases should they be found subletting, led to householders withholding the number of people living with them. Landlords themselves may have been complicit, fearing an increase in rates relating to the number of persons in their properties or worrying about nuisance convictions.[198] Hence, overcrowding caused a great deal of census anxiety to those fearful of being found out.

With each of the decennial censuses of Great Britain there had been an enquiry into housing. Initially, enumerators were simply required to ascertain "How many Inhabited Houses are there in your Parish, Township or Place; by how many Families are they occupied; and how many Houses therein are Uninhabited?" This question was enlarged in 1811 with an additional enquiry asking "How many Houses are building and therefore not yet Inhabited?" These questions also appeared on the censuses of 1821 and 1831. But thereafter enumerators were required to make a return of the houses (a) inhabited, (b) uninhabited and (c) in the course of being erected. The 1831 Census omitted the last category.

Before the 1851 Census, the definition of a "house" was up to the enumerator's interpretation. However, for the 1851 Census, it was specifically defined as the entire space inside the external and party walls of a building. This definition was used for all subsequent censuses in England and Wales until 1911. Despite sticking with the definition for the 1861 and 1871 censuses, it became a separate issue and cause for consternation in Scotland. For the 1881 Census and every census up to 1931 in Scotland, it was decided that:

> In all statements based on the Scottish Census Enumeration of 4th April, 1881, we are now instructed to regard as a Separate House (1) every dwelling with a distinct outside entrance from a street, court, lane, road, etc., or (2) with a door opening directly into a common stair; but any such dwelling, if sub-divided and occupied by different families, is reckoned as only a single house.

For the 1921 and 1931 censuses of England and Wales, the term used was "structurally separate dwelling". This was defined in the Housing Report published after the 1931 Census as "Generally any room or suite of rooms intended or used for habitation having separate access to the street or to a common landing or staircase to which visitors have access. Thus a private house which has not been structurally divided is one structurally separate dwelling whether it houses a single family or a number of families. Similarly, each flat in a block of flats is a structurally separate dwelling. Where a private house or any other set of premises originally constructed for the use of a single family has been structurally sub-divided into maisonettes or portions each with its own front door opening on to a common landing or staircase, then each such portion is regarded as a structurally separate dwelling."

In Scotland, between the 1861 and 1931 censuses, it was a requirement to report the number of houses with at least one window or more. In 1891 and 1901 in England and Wales the number of rooms of a household occupying less than five rooms were to be returned; this was expanded to all households from 1911 to 1931.

Even registrars struggled with the room question. On 30 December 1890, the registrar for the sub-district of Ambleside wrote to the Registrar General's office: "Sir, I do not feel quite clear on the following points – In taking the number of rooms in a house should cellar, scullery, pantry or small attic be included?"

To which the RG's secretary responded with, "Only those rooms which are actually used for living or sleeping purposes should be counted as rooms occupied."[199] Just a few days later, another letter landed on the secretary's desk. This time Mr W. Arnott the registrar for Woodbridge requested clarification to which the Secretary replied, "That with reference to Clause 5 of the Census Act, which does not define what constitutes a room, no room should be counted as an occupied room, unless it is distinctly used for living or sleeping purposes and that therefore washhouses, sculleries and cellars should not be so counted, unless they are used as either sitting or sleeping rooms."[200]

Following this confusion, instructions were provided to householders and enumerators for the 1911 Census to "count the kitchen as a room, but do not count the scullery, landing, lobby, closet, bathroom, nor warehouse, office, shop." For the 1921 and 1931 censuses, the authorities handed the responsibility for obtaining particulars of the number of rooms to the enumerator.

Together with the perplexity of room definitions, some enumerators and registrars were a little baffled by the meaning of "uninhabited" when asked to note such dwellings on the schedules and elsewhere. Due to the lack of guidelines specifying what constituted a house in 1841, it could have been presumed that offices, shops, and warehouses etc., fell into this category and therefore were "uninhabited" as opposed to dwellings vacant for periods of time. Even as late as the 1890s, registrars were still querying whether offices with caretakers should be included as "uninhabited" and were told not to include them simply because the question was about spare housing capacity and as such, this type of inclusion would not reflect the true figures. In response to any query received regarding the term uninhabited, the Registrar General's secretary usually wrote "that all houses in which no person slept on the Census Night should be returned as 'uninhabited' although the Houses may be furnished & the residents only temporary absent." The problem with recording temporary absence was that these dwellings were not available to the housing market and therefore skewed any meaningful data from a question designed to measure spare capacity. As a consequence, the census authorities were determined to address these queries in 1901 by making a distinction between uninhabited houses occupied for business or other purposes and those not occupied for any purpose. Despite this attempt at clarification, enumerators appear to have been permanently baffled by the task.

Back in 1841, when they completed their enumeration books, enumerators would write in the "Place" column the names of houses, streets, and places, but rarely the house number, if it existed. The second column containing the heading "Houses" was divided into two further columns, the first of which was labelled "uninhabited or building" and the second "inhabited". For each inhabited house, the enumerator placed a number "1" next to the name of the householder in the "inhabited" column. For each uninhabited house or one being built, the enumerator was asked to indicate by writing "1 U" or "1 B" respectively in the first column. He also marked the end of a house with double oblique strokes (//) after the name of last person in the house on the dividing line between the "Houses" and "Names" column. A single oblique stroke (/) was placed to indicate where a family ended when a dwelling was shared between multiple families.

For the 1851 Census, enumerators were asked to draw a line across the page from left to right as far as the fifth column under the last name in each house. Where there were multiple occupiers in the same house he was asked to draw a similar line under the last name of the family of each occupier, but starting the line a little on the left-hand side of the third column. In his study of households in Yorkshire, Peter Tillott discovered enumerators did not always follow the instructions exactly, some left a space when they had to draw a line, others only began to write in a new household when approaching the foot of the page and they had sufficient lines on that page to complete it. Lines were sometimes ruled or drawn freehand and drawn beyond the fifth column, or even across the page. Occasionally, a "ruled in error" would appear if the enumerator had drawn a line under a new head instead of under the last person of the previous household.[201] Higgs also noted similar errors and discovered long lines and double strokes occasionally omitted at the bottom of pages; he also found errors in the "Houses" column where the number "1" should have been inserted in the "inhabited" column, but was erroneously excluded.

To indicate uninhabited or buildings under construction, the enumerator wrote in the address column, in the row under the last name of the last inhabited house, "one house uninhabited", or "two houses building", etc., and then he would draw a line under this in a similar manner for inhabited houses.

For the 1861 Census, the 1841 "Houses" column was restored and an inhabited house was marked by the enumerator with a number "1" in the first column next to the name of the first person in the house. For each uninhabited house or one being built, the enumerator was asked to indicate by writing "1 U" or "1 B" respectively in the second "Houses" column. The double oblique strokes returned for the 1861 Census and were inserted after the name of the last person in the house on the dividing line between the "Houses" and "Names" column. Where there was more than one occupier in the house, a single stroke was required to distinguish each family in a dwelling shared between multiple families. This system continued for the censuses of 1871, 1881, 1891, albeit with the double oblique strokes drawn in the opposite direction (\\).

> As one who had charge of the census papers in one district, I unhesitatingly state that, as far as the number of "monoglot" Welsh people is concerned, the returns are utterly worthless.
>
> *Evening Express*, 27 August 1894.[202]

It was a last-minute decision to add a question enquiring about Gaelic speaking individuals to the 1881 Census in Scotland. Pressure was brought to bear in Parliament and the disinclined census commissioners for Scotland, who had expressed opposition to expanding the census schedule, had to concede to a language enquiry. Such was the lateness of the enquiry, the question was added vertically along the crease on the reverse of the schedule with the explanation “This line was inserted in red ink after the schedule had been printed.” In the “Where Born” column of the schedule, householders were required to write the word GAELIC opposite the name of each person who spoke Gaelic habitually.

No sooner had news of the Gaelic question become known then the detractors started with their criticisms. “The Gaelic census”, one wrote, “like everything else wrung from ‘my lords,’ is given with a grudge, and given in such a manner as to render it worse than useless.” They argued further that instead of it being a correct census of all those who were able to speak Gaelic, it didn’t account for those who spoke it daily but were unable to do so within their families due to various circumstances. This included the thousands of Highlanders living in Glasgow who weren’t in the habit of speaking Gaelic at home, as well as young adults living in lodgings without a family to speak it with.[203]

Following the census, it was reported that some enumerators had been over-zealous when dealing with the answers to the language question and others were charged with plain interference. Hugh M. Matheson, a law clerk, living in a lodging house with fellow lodger James Simpson, both native of Sutherland, were called upon by the enumerator on the Monday of the 1881 Census. They had completed their schedule and returned themselves as Gaelic speaking. A little later, their landlady approached Hugh and informed him the enumerator asked her whether she’d heard Hugh and James conversing in Gaelic often or at any time, to which she responded negatively. Upon receiving the answer, the enumerator crossed out Gaelic from Hugh’s schedule.[204] The report of this event caused a minor uproar in the newspapers and naturally many believed such interference by the enumerators was widespread after having heard numerous complaints. As a consequence, a few individuals sought clarification on the matter. On 3 May, the Lord Advocate was asked in the House of Commons, whether he would allow the returns to be amended in all cases where it was clear enumerators acted in contravention to the instructions they were given. The Lord Advocate, in response, said the instructions given to the enumerators were they should include only those actually speaking the Gaelic language.[205]

To add to the confusion, a letter had appeared in the newspapers on 2 April 1881 from George Seton, secretary to the Registrar General for Scotland, who was responding to a query from the registrar for Fort Augustus dated 18 March 1881. The registrar asked “Are the enumerators, when taking the census, to include among the Gaelic population those who can,

Above: Local Enumerators for Bexhill. *Bexhill-on-Sea Observer*, 1 April 1911. (Content provided by THE BRITISH LIBRARY BOARD. ALL RIGHTS RESERVED. With thanks to The British Newspaper Archive)

Below: Paterfamilias filling up the census return. *Illustrated Times*, 13 April 1861. (Author's personal collection)

Left: An enumerator visits… *Illustrated Times*, 13 April 1861. (Author's personal collection)

Below: Being taught their duties: enumerators listening to a lecture. *Illustrated London News*, 15 April 1911. (Author's personal collection)

Above: The census enumerator in a Grays Inn tenement. *Illustrated Times*, 13 April 1861. (Author's personal collection)

Right: Advertisement. *Illustrated London News*, 15 April 1911. (Author's personal collection)

Left: George Graham. *Illustrated Times*, 13 April 1861. (Author's personal collection)

Below: Registrar General's room at Somerset House. *Illustrated Times*, 13 April 1861. (Author's personal collection)

Above left: Census Office, Craig's Court. *Illustrated Times*, 16 April 1861. (Author's personal collection)

Above right: Indexing department of the Census Office. *Illustrated Times*, 16 April 1861. (Author's personal collection)

Teaching children to fill up the census papers. *Illustrated London News*, 15 April 1911. (Author's personal collection)

Left: Taken for the tax collector. *Illustrated London News*, 11 April 1891. (Author's personal collection)

Below: The enumerator endures some chaff. *Illustrated London News*, 11 April 1891. (Author's personal collection)

Above left: Counting the census papers. *Black & White*, 25 May 1901. (Author's personal collection)

Above right: What's this? *Illustrated London News*, 11 April 1891. (Author's personal collection)

Right: The lady of uncertain age. *Illustrated London News*, 11 April 1891. (Author's personal collection)

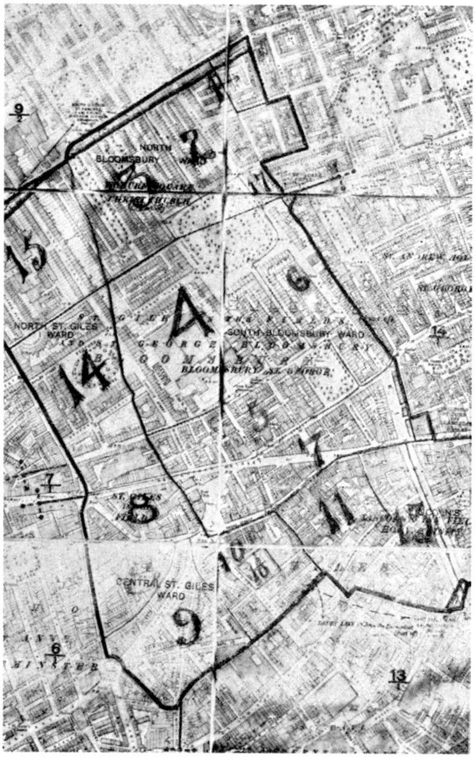

A map divided into enumeration districts. *Illustrated London News*, 15 April 1911. (Author's personal collection)

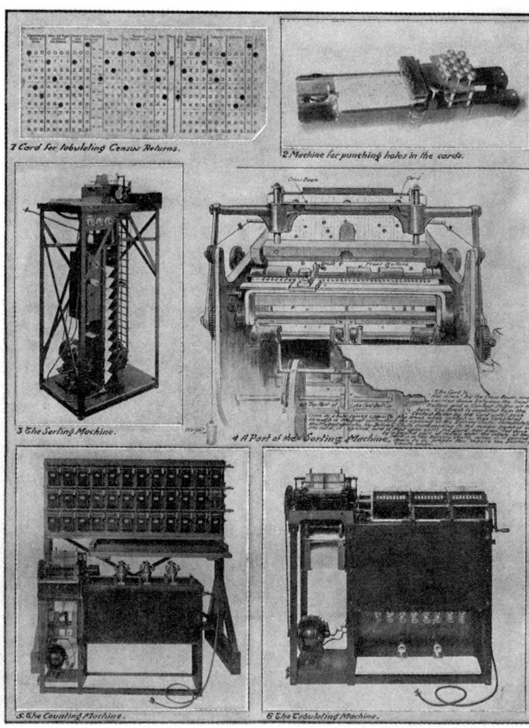

Electric census clerks. *Illustrated London News*, 15 April 1911. (Author's personal collection)

Above: The lady who sent her schedule in a sealed envelope. *Illustrated London News*, 11 April 1891. (Author's personal collection)

Below: The census in the West End. *The Graphic*, 13 April 1901. (Author's personal collection)

Above left: The man who refuses to fill up the schedule. *Illustrated London News*, 11 April 1891. (Author's personal collection)

Above right: The man who lights his pipe with the schedule. *Illustrated London News*, 11 April 1891. (Author's personal collection)

St Marylebone Workhouse. *Illustrated London News*, 1867. (Courtesy of Picryl)

Above left: Alessandro I Gonzaga (1797–1869). (Public domain)

Above right: Carte-de-Visite of Boston Corbett, 1865. (Courtesy of Picryl)

Regent's Park skating catastrophe. *Illustrated Sporting and Theatrical News*, 26 Jan 1867. (Public domain. The British Newspaper Archive)

Above: Isola Pescatori. Home of the Zanetti family. 1890s. (Courtesy of Picryl)

Below left: Middle of Market Street, Ralston, c.1822. The Zanetti family traded from the large building in the centre of the drawing. From Old Manchester by James Croston. (Courtesy of Hathitrust)

Below right: Frances Zanetti, *Reynolds Newspaper*, 15 March 1908. Content provided by THE BRITISH LIBRARY BOARD. ALL RIGHTS RESERVED. With thanks to The British Newspaper Archive.

Above: Workhouse inmates being prepared for census day. *Illustrated London News*, 15 April 1911. (Author's personal collection)

Right: The numbering of the sick. *Illustrated London News*, 15 April 1911. (Author's personal collection)

Above: The enumerator taking the census in St. James's Park. *Illustrated Times*, 13 April 1861. (Author's personal collection)

Below: At a lodging house. *Illustrated London News*, 11 April 1891. (Author's personal collection)

Above: Taking the census on the Regent's Canal. *Illustrated Times*, 20 April 1861. (Author's personal collection)

Below: An enumerator in a gypsy encampment. *The Graphic*, 13 April 1901. (Author's personal collection)

Above: Taking the census in the dark arches of the Adelphi. *Illustrated Times*, 13 April 1861. (Author's personal collection)

Left: The grave of George Edward Douglas and his wife Ann. East Finchley Cemetery. D10 55. (By the author)

and who actually do occasionally, though certainly not habitually, speak Gaelic fluently?" In reply Seton wrote, "I am directed to inform you that the Registrar-General thinks the expression in question may properly be held to apply to all persons who are so familiar with Gaelic as to be able to converse fluently in that language."[206] This should have been the end of the matter, but the messaging, no doubt due to the lateness of adding the query to the schedule, was not clear to some persons nor did the message actually get through to some quarters.

The population was also confused as to whether they should indicate if they spoke Gaelic due to the wording of the question. In some areas, a few individuals cited under-reporting of Gaelic speakers with commentators suggesting this was down to a combination of misunderstanding the question and a sense of shame in admitting use of the language to the enumerator. It was not always the case and there was at least one instance where the entire schedule was completed in Gaelic.[207]

Member of Parliament Charles Fraser-Mackintosh sought answers from local registrars based on his suspicions of misinterpretation and under-reporting. He asked that an enumeration be made of persons omitted from the census in view of the confusion surrounding the word "habitually". Based on the returns he received, Fraser-Mackintosh believed the Gaelic census population was incorrect and that the total number omitted was about 5,000. Other authorities believed the figure was actually higher.[208]

The 1891 Census included Gaelic in column 10 of the schedule requesting that the householder write "Gaelic opposite the name of each person who speaks Gaelic only, and 'G and E' opposite the name of each Person who speaks both Gaelic and English." The result was an increase in speakers, though this was mainly due to the under-representation seen a decade earlier. In 1901 and in subsequent censuses thereafter only those of three years of age and upwards were enumerated.

The Census Office commissioned the printing of Welsh language schedules for use in Wales from 1841 onward. The enumeration books and the questions asked remained the same as those used in England until 1891. In that year, a new question was added specifically for Wales and Monmouthshire asking about the language spoken – this consequently led to an update of the English and Welsh household schedules used in Wales. On the schedule, occupiers were instructed to indicate if they spoke only English, only Welsh, or both languages by writing the corresponding term in the column. A separate enumeration book, in English, for Wales and

Monmouthshire was printed which contained this extra column. In 1901, the same arrangements were made, however, children under 3 years old were not included in the language data collection.

The census authorities began organising the printing of the Welsh language schedules in early 1891. On 21 January, they contacted J. Morris Jones of Llanfair, Anglesey and asked how long it would take him to deliver the Welsh translation of the household schedule. After the schedule was made public, the *Evening Express* commented that Jones did a decent job, writing, "the translator has wisely used English words, such as engine-driver, draper's assistant, grocer, staymaker, &c., instead of ransacking his brains for Welsh equivalents."[209] The translation was arguably the only thing that went well for the census authorities in terms of the language question in 1891, and they found themselves in a similar situation to their Scottish counterparts with accusations and counter-accusations of incompetence, meddling, and "cooked" returns.

Instructions were sent out to registrars in the January asking them to appoint Welsh speaking enumerators in areas where Welsh was widely spoken, with the Registrar General emphasising they should be "preferred" above English monoglot enumerators.[210] This appears to have been something of a task for registrars who already encountered difficulties finding enumerators fitting the usual requirements of the job. It was reported in the sparsely populated Welsh hills, where there were 186 Welsh speaking homes and only 6 English speaking ones, an English monoglot enumerator was appointed to the task. Unsurprisingly, it was believed he had great difficulty understanding the Welsh vernacular.[211]

In addition to nominating Welsh speaking enumerators, registrars were assigned the task of calculating the number of Welsh language schedules required for their area. In Merthyr Tydfil registrars asked for 15,000 English schedules and 2,500 Welsh schedules, but due to a misunderstanding at the Census Office only received 13,500. A quick wire to the Census Office requesting a full complement quickly remedied the situation.[212] But elsewhere there were similar problems: there were not enough Welsh schedules sent to Welsh speaking areas. There was even a case of English schedules intended for use in England, therefore without the language column, sent to Welsh registration districts. Enumerators were requested to carefully examine their schedules in case the twelfth column was missing and to immediately communicate with their registrar if they found any deficiencies.[213] In Hawarden, a number of local residents complained to their MP Samuel Smith about receiving English schedules without the language column. This inspired *The Wrexham Advertiser* to spend a whole day making enquiries with local residents "and in no instances had the schedule containing the Welsh column been distributed, except that the enumerators in some instances had Welsh schedules for the use of those who knew no English." The newspaper pursued the beleaguered Registrar Hugh Roberts for an explanation. Roberts elucidated that as Hawarden was a sub-district of the Chester Union, he did not think about schedules with the language column. He saw a mention of the Welsh census, but wasn't "much interested" and when he received the schedules from Chester, he had no idea there were two forms of English schedules printed.[214]

On 10 April 1891, *The Herald* newspaper reported the Census Office hadn't received any complaints regarding a shortfall of household schedules; in instances where English forms were supplied bearing no language column, it was possible the packers may have mistakenly included bundles of the said form in the parcel sent to the registrar. The paper then went on to explain the Registrar General had only received information concerning two cases in which a mistake was made.[215]

A few days later the Registrar General's secretary responded to a number of allegations put to the office from MP Sir Hussey Vivian. The MP received a complaint that a few houses in a district in Neath were omitted completely by the enumerators and the residents were unable to find suitable schedules. The secretary informed Vivian the allegations were unfounded and explained all the enumerators had enough schedules in the Welsh language for occupiers who couldn't understand English; that they were also able to supply schedules in the Welsh language to all who wanted them, and neither the registrar nor his enumerators received any complaint made to them on the subject.[216]

Another area of contention was the actual content of the language column. One registrar, who was rather late in asking the question on 14 April 1891, queried with the Census Office whether individuals who spoke both Welsh and English could return themselves as Welsh only. The answer from the Registrar General was no.[217] It was clear enumerators stuck to this instruction too, for in the House of Commons, MP David Lloyd George asked whether there had been any complaints regarding the alleged tampering by the enumerator at Machynlleth, Montgomeryshire, who changed the words from "Welsh only" to "both". It wasn't tampering, the enumerator was just doing his job.

Elsewhere, the *Wrexham and Denbighshire Advertiser* reported: "Whether to put English and Welsh spoken, or Welsh only, on the census papers seemed to be a grave question with the men, and what age seemed of vital importance to the women. One gentleman whose family of seven could speak English fluently, put Welsh, only to give 'that Raikes a snub'."[218]

Due to pressures from organisations like the Welsh Language Society, which urged householders to fill out the entire schedule in Welsh, even if it was provided in English, and to request Welsh forms even if they understood English, the exercise became politicised.[219] There was no better endorsement according to the *Evening Express*, than the Archdruid of Abergele who put down his infant son of 2 years old as a "Welsh" speaker.

Despite accusations enumerators were tampering with the language column, it seems many understood their tasks and performed them very well. They were required to translate the Welsh schedules into English and if they made changes to the form, they could only do so in front of the householder. It seems there was just one incident of an enumerator refusing to translate his schedules as reported by the registrar of Criccieth on 15 April 1891. The registrar was instructed by the Registrar General's office to find someone else to provide the translations and refuse the original enumerator his pay.

The Registrar General was quick to defend the distribution of the schedules and his enumerators in a letter dated 24 April 1891:

> Sir, – have the honour to acknowledge the receipt of your letter of the 21st inst., with enclosure, which has had my attention. I have addressed circulars to all my registration officers in Wales, and I find that it is not true that the supply of census forms printed in Welsh was quite inadequate to the requirements of the Welsh-speaking population.
>
> Every specific case of complaint under this head brought under my notice has been investigated, and I have found that many were groundless. In all places where it has been proved that, owing to the altogether unprecedented demand for Welsh schedules, the supply fell short, efforts have been made, and, so far as I know successfully, to rectify any omission or error. I think it quite possible that some enumerators, finding that persons habitually transacting their business in English applied for schedules in the Welsh language, or filled up their

> schedules incorrectly – by stating that they spoke Welsh only, may have pointed to the penalty incurred for making false statements; but it is impossible to inquire into the truth of this assertion without full particulars which would enable me to identify the enumerators; and, in fact, nothing more is charged against the enumerators than that they did their duty...
>
> I am quite satisfied that an honest attempt has been made by the registration officers to obtain for the first time an accurate return of the Welsh-speaking community, and from inquiries I have made I am strongly of opinion that if any error has been made it will turn out to be that, worked upon by proclamations, sermons, and newspaper articles, a great many people have returned themselves as speaking only Welsh who had no right to do so. – I have the honour to be, sir, your obedient servant, (Signed) Brydges P. Henniker.[220]

In 1894, an enumerator who acted during the census wrote he encountered families where English was almost exclusively used, but who returned themselves as "monoglot" Welsh. And in one instance a "monoglot" Englishman wanting to return himself and his family as Welsh in deference to someone he admired.[221]

All the above raises doubts regarding the results of the Welsh language census. And there was a similar unequivocal opinion expressed regarding the inaccuracies in the General Report of 1891. Higgs attempts to explain the results by pointing out some people believed that if they primarily spoke Welsh and only occasionally or poorly spoke English, they were justified in reporting themselves as Welsh-speaking only. He also indicates that rather than the influence of Welsh nationalism, it's more likely that householders were confused by what was required from them.[222] The truth of the matter is probably somewhere in between.

For the 1901 Census, individuals aged 3 years or above were required to make a statement in the language column and it was believed this led to more successful results compared to the 1891 Census. However, the 1911 Census, where the tables were compiled directly from entries on the schedules, revealed some doubtful data; many schedules only contained information for the head of the household. It was considered that if this happened during the 1901 Census, the enumerators may have assumed the language spoken by the head of the household applied to all members listed on the schedule, and such defects may have been concealed during the copying process.

During the 1921 Census, the same information regarding language was requested on the schedules. However, the Order of Council for the 1931 Census, made no mention of those who only spoke English. As a result, the survey focused solely on whether the individual could only speak Welsh or if they were able to communicate in both Welsh and English. This deliberate omission was made because the "English only" category was originally included in previous censuses to ensure all questions were comprehensive and every person provided an answer.

Chapter Nine

A Life Beyond the Census: George Edward Douglas

On our own particular genealogical journey we see fragments of a life and are sometimes guilty of defining a person by the fragments we see. With our own ancestors, we seek to familiarise ourselves with how they engaged with their environment socially, economically and culturally, but unless our ancestors were enumerators, we may forget that they too had an existence outside the census. It takes a moment to recognise that beyond those few weeks once a decade, a life was lived, marriages were made, children were born, accolades were won and loved ones were mourned. Moreover, these individuals commuted to their usual job, had professional successes and disappointments; were enraged by their grievances with the tax man and government; visited the theatre, played sport, and skated on winter lakes.

For officiating officers such as George Edward Douglas, master of the St. Marylebone Workhouse, from 1862 right through to his retirement in the 1890s, the census was a natural extension of his occupational role. Within that professional remit he engaged on a daily basis with individuals and families in the similar way a parochial or urban enumerator would have done in his or her brief time enumerating citizens and visitors. Douglas was also dedicated to service and radical change, and by being such a focal point in one corner of the metropolis, he invited calls for his organisational skills and knowledge when the community needed him. Such calls were often in tragic circumstances, but not always: in 1891 Douglas helped unravel the mystery surrounding the origins of a vulnerable young woman, which subsequently led to a reunion between her and her family.

By exploring Douglas' eventful life and in the next chapter that of Frances Zanetti, the enumerator is no longer a grey individual, hidden behind handwriting and our tunnelled focus on ancestors, he or she exists beyond the census in sharpened view.

Douglas was born in Ireland about 1832. His father died before his fifteenth birthday leaving him, as the eldest son, more or less the main family bread winner for his Scottish mother Ann and siblings William, Ellen and Edward. The family moved to England and when he was in his late twenties Douglas made the journey south from the Manchester suburb of Hulme and settled in London. There he applied for a position at the St. Marylebone Workhouse. The workhouse minute books record his appointment at the meeting of 29 March 1859: "That George Edward Douglas be employed as Clerk in the Master's Office on probation for three months at a Salary of £40 per annum with rations, lodging and washing in the workhouse."[223]

George remained in that position for a year until he eyed the vacancy for the more lucrative position of storekeeper. He had competition from thirty-eight fellow candidates. These were eventually whittled down to twenty-seven after a round of interviews in front of the Board of Guardians. After making the shortlist of two, George was appointed storekeeper by a majority vote on 21 December 1860, aged 28.[224]

The 1861 Census enumerates George in St. George Hanover Square where he was recorded as storekeeper at the workhouse and, curiously, landlord of the Southcott family who were sharing his residence in North Row. Later that year, he married Ann Elizabeth Eaton at Holy Trinity Church, St. Marylebone. For the next thirty years she would be his wife, confidante, friend, colleague and mother of his children.

On 17 October 1862, Charles Cooper, master of the Marylebone Workhouse, sent his letter of resignation to the Board citing an opportunity to take charge of the Birmingham Workhouse as his reason. The Marylebone Board moved swiftly to advertise the opportunity and received fifteen applications including one from Mr and Mrs Wakelin and one from George and Ann. At the meeting of 14 November 1862, George and Ann were resoundingly voted master and matron of the workhouse by twenty votes to four. Knowing the Board would be in dire need of a new storekeeper, duty conscious Douglas put himself forward to undertake both jobs until a new storekeeper was appointed.

His wife Ann was four months pregnant with their second child May Eaton Douglas when late in the afternoon on a rainy 7 June 1863, a distressed woman and her three children took shelter under a gateway on the south side of Oxford Street close to Bond Street. A man stopped and asked her if she needed assistance. She explained her husband had abandoned her, leaving her and her children without support in a strange city. He advised her to apply for admission at the workhouse in St. Marylebone and promised to join her within thirty minutes.

At 4.30 pm, he found her standing in the rain after being turned away. He knocked on the door, demanding to know why a desperate woman and her children were being refused. Douglas, standing nearby, explained the Board of Guardians had resolved to close the casual ward, so no casual applicants would be admitted. Unimpressed, the man declared, "I am a member of the House of Commons", and questioned whether the Board even had the authority to pass such a resolution. When Douglas admitted he did not know, the man replied, "In my belief, they have no such legal power, so you must admit these parties."

Douglas, irritated by the man's tone, warned him to leave immediately, accusing him of causing a disturbance during visiting hours. The man, undeterred, waved his green silk umbrella at Douglas and insulted him as insolent, threatening to report him. Fearing violence, Douglas called his porter, Edward, and asked him to escort the gentleman from the premises. After three requests to leave, the man finally departed. According to his account, he took the woman and her children to a milk-shop for refreshments and, after only about five minutes, returned to the workhouse. There, he knocked and kicked the door and was eventually granted admission after he produced his calling card identifying him as Lord Raynham.

Once inside, the Lord sarcastically addressed Douglas, "Oh, you can be civil now. Rank makes a difference." Writing a few days later, Douglas set down his official version of what happened:

> I heard the Gentleman, who was kicking at the gate, call loudly to be let in. I opened the wicket, and told him I could not admit him. He said, I am Viscount Raynham. I answered, how was I to know that? his [*sic*] conduct had been so unlike that of a Gentleman, that he must produce his card before I would admit him. He then gave me his card, and on being admitted, I said, My Lord, your conduct has been so exceedingly ungentlemanly, and you have behaved yourself in such an insolent manner to me that you cannot be surprized at the

reception you have met with. His Lordship, (who is not a ratepayer of this Parish), then demanded to see the order by which Casual wards were closed. I told him it would be found in the Minutes of the Board. He demanded to see the Minutes. I told him they were in the department of the Secretary, who did not attend on Sunday. He then observed, you can be civil now, rank makes a difference; make no apology – to which I replied, your Lordship does not deserve any apology. I think one is due to me; he then left, saying, that we should hear more of this.

Lord Raynham was so much excited, that he did not give me an opportunity of informing him that this Parish, with many others in the Metropolis, were, through the prevalence of Small-Pox in the workhouse, unable to receive casual poor. And that I always relieved, either with Money, or in kind, Women with Children who applied after 7 o'clock, P.M. I have this Week relieved two families, who stated that they were refused admission at the Paddington and Mount Street Workhouses, for the reason above stated.[225]

Geo Ed Douglas, Master

Throughout the 1860s, the workhouse struggled with overcrowding due to increasing poverty and smallpox in London. The problem had grown to such an extent Douglas reported to the Board of Guardians casual admissions had to sleep in the corridors.

Lord Raynham filed his complaint, leading to an inquiry by Poor Law inspector Mr Cane at the workhouse. Douglas faced both the investigation and negative press. A key part of his testimony, omitted from his official version, was neither he nor the porter saw the alleged woman and children near the workhouse, a claim supported by a pauper. Lord Raynham dismissed this as lies, despite inconsistencies in his own account, such as denying kicking the door and forgetting he had an umbrella. It might have been the case those connected with the workhouse closed ranks to protect Douglas and the porter. Certainly all the guardians and the workhouse chaplain swore they never encountered anything other than civility and kindness from Douglas,[226] but perhaps they were protecting their own.

A few weeks later, the Poor Law board submitted their decision to Lord Raynham, saying in light of contradictory evidence and the lack of testimony by the woman, they could not uphold the complaint. Effectively, they circled the waggons around Douglas and Edward in respect of Raynham's accusation of rudeness stating:

> With regard to the alleged insolence of the master and porter, the statement of yourself on the one hand, and that of the officers on the other, are so conflicting that the board are unable to say that the charge had been satisfactorily established; but after the testimony borne by the guardians and the chaplain to the general good conduct and civil demeanour of the master, the board are led to believe that any discourtesy or rudeness, of which he might have been guilty, may not unreasonably be attributed to the somewhat abrupt and unexpected manner in which he was interrogated by your lordship (who was entirely unknown to him at the time), as to his duties, and the regulations of the guardians.[227]

Even if the guardians did close ranks to a degree, their response shows what a deeply valued individual Douglas was and given his behaviour throughout the many public incidents in his life, it is unlikely Douglas would have turned the woman away. On each occasion he revealed himself to be a humane and tactful individual. Further, his regard and empathy for his workhouse charges meant that with the help of the Marylebone Guardians he transformed institutional life. No small feat when dealing with London's largest workhouse.

A Lacabane! Penh! I laugh at him! I am a Gonzague, I say!

It is something of a myth that workhouses only dealt with the very poorest individuals in society. There were many reasons individuals of all ranks may have walked or were guided through the main gate.

On a September morning in 1865, an impoverished princess was admitted to the workhouse in a distressed and agitated state of mind. Of English ancestry, Maria Eliza Gonzaga was the daughter of Colonel Coke of the Indian Army and of "modest fortune". In 1833 she married John Escudero or De Escudery at the St James's Roman Catholic chapel in Spanish Place, Marylebone, then after his death,[228] Alexander de Gonzaga-Mantua (Alessandro Gonzaga, Prince of Castiglione) in 1841.

Alexander's travails regarding his inheritance were well documented in the press. A biography written by "an old diplomatist" seemingly with a view to engender sympathy for Alexander's plight described his loss of status: from heir to the lands of a dukedom to the victim of despoilers.

Born in Dresden in 1797 to Giuseppe Luigi Gonzaga and the Princess Esterhazy, he entered military life at the age of 13 after leaving college in Krakow. His biography reveals him to have been a soldier of extraordinary ability. Recruited into the 9th Vistula Infantry Regiment by Marshal Ney, he became a non-commissioned officer on 1 May 1812. Later that year, he received the Military Cross of Poland following the Battle of Mozhaysk. In 1813, for his bravery at the Battle of Leipzig, Prince Poniatowsky awarded him the Golden Cross for Military Valour. His notable actions continued during the Dantzig and Bautzen campaigns, all while he was just 14. Although he received many honours for his achievements, his greatest wish was to be recognised and admired by Emperor Bonaparte. This wish was fulfilled after the Battle of Craonne. In March 1814, Napoleon's forces confronted the combined Russian and Prussian army. Stationed near Berry-au-Bac, young Alexander spotted two Russian officers near the French defensive lines and suspected they were spies. He charged at the two riders and as soon as the boy was within range, he fired the first shot, causing one of the officers to leap from his saddle. Clenching the horse's bridle with his teeth, Alexander wielded a sabre in one hand and a pistol in the other, and rushed at the remaining officer. Gonzaga was about to fire, but then recognised the officer as none other than the Russian General Prince Gagarin. After seizing the horse's bridle, he disarmed the general and took him prisoner.

According to Alexander's biographers Napoleon asked to speak to him after such exploits. "Your valour deserves a reward", said the emperor, "and I leave you free to choose between the rank of captain and that of officer of the Legion of Honor."

With a large dose of hubris the lad accepted the Legion of Honour claiming he would eventually be made captain anyway. That promotion didn't come until 1824 following his service for the Grand Duke Constantine in the Caucasus. The 25-year-old must have thought life was treating him well until he returned to Warsaw and killed a colonel in a duel resulting in him having to flee to Berlin.

Four years later he was still performing feats of derring-do. Three months into the Siege of Braila during the Russo-Turkish War of 1828–1829,

Gonzaga, who was now a colonel, led a handful of soldiers through fog on a mission. His brilliant strategy led to the storming of Braila and its eventual fall.

Following the death of his brother in 1828, he sought to establish his rightful inheritance, but discovered his dominions had passed into the hands of the Empress Maria Theresa in 1748. For years he continued to petition and seek assistance from diplomats and the royal houses of Europe, though to no avail. It seemed the Austrian government was determined to stop him ascertaining how his lands fell into the hands of the Austrian royal house.[229]

Unperturbed, he continued as a professional soldier fighting in the Polish insurrection, in Lithuania, where he and his men swept like a "thunderbolt" into a wing of the Russian deployment, while the men were sleeping. After years of dispatching Russian enemies to untimely ends, he signed up for service in Spain in 1837 and was almost immediately involved in rescuing four women from sexual assault by fellow soldiers. He served in Spain from 1837–1839 (though he may have served again later). This is one of the few documented facts about him – his name appears in a soldier's list in the *Archivo General Militar De Segovia* where he is shown as a Carlista.[230]

After having achieved so much in his professional life despite the Austrian state trying to poison him at every opportunity (according to him), he arrived in London and married Maria Eliza. It is very unlikely his bride was aware of the claims against him until it all came to a nasty climax.

For years, he tried to secure his inheritance rights and eventually contacted the editor of the *Annuaire de la Pairie et de la Noblesse de France, des Maisons Souveraines de l'Europe et de la Diplomatie* in Paris. Unfortunately, his attempt to legitimise his claim didn't go as planned. The editor, André Borel d'Hauterive, was a formidable genealogist and researcher who graduated as an archivist-palaeographer in 1837. He examined Alexander's case and not only found a reason to reject the claim, but he also investigated Alexander's visit to the Bibliothèque Royale de Paris, revealing Alexander was involved in fraudulent shenanigans.

Borel d'Hauterive questioned Alexander regarding his claim of being a descendant of Filippo Luigi Gonzaga, pointing out it was a well-documented fact that the heir died at the age of 8 in 1748. Alexander responded by saying he could prove his lineage courtesy of the esteemed Italian genealogist Count Litta. But, if the young Filippo Luigi didn't die as Alexander suggested, Borel d'Hauterive asked, why has his descendants been silent about their rightful inheritance for a hundred years? Why did

Napoleon's soldier of fortune Alexander de Gonzaga appear in Stuttgart in 1836 under another name, that of "Graf Myrzinowski" and make a claim then?[231] Why not earlier? When asked to produce the evidence regarding his rightful status, Alexander made a peremptory objection, saying Austria, having seized all the family papers, made it impossible to justify his filiation.

At this stage, Borel d'Hauterive thought it wise to refer to Count Litta's esteemed work, *Famiglie celebri di Italia (Gonzaga di Mantova)*, housed in the Bibliothèque Royale de Paris. It verified Filippo Luigi Gonzaga's death at a young age – *morì tenera età*. So, when Alexander appeared again with a genealogical table (tavola 17) from the same book, which extended the lineage of the Castiglione branch up to himself, Borel d'Hauterive was quite shocked. However, he quickly noticed an inconsistency: there were two tables labelled tavola 17, with no indication one was an addition or supplement, suggesting one of them was apocryphal and interpolated. In Borel d'Hauterive's account he noted, this "remark cut short the discussion, and M. de Gonzague withdrew." After Alexander's departure, a library employee responsible for bookbinding informed Borel d'Hauterive that when the book was returned by a reader, he found a second tavola 17. Unsure which one was authentic, he sent both to be bound. A detailed inspection revealed differences in paper and printing between the tavola 17 cited by Alexander and the other pages in the book.

The copy currently in the Bibliothèque Nationale de France, successor to the Bibliothèque Royale de Paris shows no second table. This was either removed or the book is a different copy. There was only one individual who would benefit from inserting a fake table into Count Litta's book and that was Alexander. According to one source, Alexander filed a lawsuit against Borel d'Hauterive or the publishers of the *Annuaire de la Pairie et de la Noblesse de France, des Maisons Souveraines de l'Europe et de la Diplomatie*.

It was not before too long the so-called Prince Alexander de Gonzaga was exposed as a fraud to the Parisian public. He was arrested in Paris on 23 July 1852 on the triple charge of swindling, an unauthorised stay in France, and illegally wearing the Legion of Honour. The latter charge was immediately withdrawn upon evidence of his nomination of the Legion of Honour by Emperor Napoleon I. Records from the Légion d'honneur archives indicate that a Jean Murzynouski, who attained the rank of captain in the 1st Regiment de la Vistule, was awarded Chevalier by decree on 22 March 1812. However, there is no mention of a Gonzaga.[232]

As for the other two charges, he endured a stay in Mazas prison while the authorities conducted a twelve-month investigation. Reporting on his trial, the *Globe* described him as having a military appearance, his buttonhole ornamented with various coloured ribbons and sporting a large moustache. His defence was that in his capacity of chief and hereditary grand master of various Chivalric Orders he distributed more than 500 crosses in different countries paying the expenses for all of them, save 5 or 6. The president of the tribunal of correctional police disagreed, saying Alexander was not authorised to award orders because it couldn't be proved he was heir to the dukedom of Mantua and therefore his actions were fraudulent.

The tribunal consulted genealogist Professor M. Lacabane from the Ecole des Chartes, who was unable to verify Alexander's genealogy. He pointed out Alexander's identity documents were either forged or his claim of being born in Dresden and baptised in the church of Wolla was illogical, as there was no record in Dresden and no church by that name in Wolla. Alexander responded with "A Lacabane! Penh! I laugh at him! I am a Gonzague, I say!"

The court received a declaration from Polish priest Stankeviez, who initially claimed to recognise Alexander as Murzynowski from Poland. However, when called to testify, he retracted his statement. Other Polish witnesses attested the man on trial was not the soldier Andre Murzynowski, noting that the real Murzynowski was a prominent soldier residing elsewhere.

When questioned about his identity, Alexander asserted, "I am still the Prince de Gonzague, still the Count de Murzynowski. The latter name is not one of my birth, but that of an estate in Poland." He reiterated his documents had been seized by the Austrian government.

The Tribunal's President accused him of being a man named Yorbeck, who was educated at a Jesuit college and later served a Murzynowski. To this, the defendant responded he had always been Gonzague Murzynowski. Although, he did admit he was expelled from the army in Spain due to "incapacity and cowardice", and also confessed to marrying the daughter of King Ferdinand of Spain's secretary, which led him to adopt the title Prince Gonzague.

The Tribunal sentenced him to three years imprisonment and a fine of 3,000fr[233] for illegally issuing decorations and for remaining in France after he had been asked to leave. He appealed the sentence at the Court of Paris and demanded through his advocate Monsieur Avond to know the grounds for the accusations. The Court rejected his demands and refused an adjournment to sift through the case, subsequently increasing his fine to 5,000fr and his imprisonment to five years. Alexander claimed he was originally denied a defence. Despite lodging a supplementary brief in the Court of Cessation which illustrated the violations of law committed by the Court of Paris, his plea went unheard.

After such a long stay in Mazas, his health was waning. He petitioned Emperor Napoleon III who ordered his immediate release and his expenses paid. He finally received his freedom on 1 January 1854 at 7 am. From there he turned his back on France and headed to England.[234] He was no doubt a fraud, even though he maintained his right to be identified as Prince Gonzaga up until thc 1860s. Nevertheless, while he may have illegally created orders and dished out honours, he decided to confer on the ladies of the Order of the Starry Cross, established in 1668 by Empress Eleonora Gonzaga-Nevers, a unification with the Order of the Redeemer, renaming them the "Order of the Ladies of Mary Elisa" after his wife.

On Sunday, 24 September 1865, Maria Eliza was in her home at 20 Edward Street, Portman Square and had reached such a stage of agitation, her doctor was summoned. With no place to take her because of the sabbath he brought her to the St. Marylebone Workhouse. Due to her aggressive and uncontrollable state, it was decided by the medical officer in agreement with George Edward Douglas, to place her in a private room. For the duration of her stay, she was superintended by a paid nurse which was a crucial detail when controversy struck a month or so later. The patient was removed to Hanwell on 29 September where she was assessed by Dr John Randell. His notes describe her as a 62-year-old married Roman Catholic who had been ill for ten days, showing no signs of epilepsy and or any suicidal tendencies. However, she was violent, restless and excitable: "She has constant and vague hallucinations about events and persons. Her delusions are so varied that it is impossible to select any. She is spiteful and dangerous to others."

By 6 October he was reporting she was still restless and excitable and had become very feeble; on the 10th he wrote in his case notes she had died from exhaustion as a result of the acute mania she had suffered for three weeks.[235] Alexander was noted as her next of kin.

It was not until mid-November 1865 that Douglas was confronted with scurrilous claims in the *Pall Mall Gazette* concerning the late Princess, stating she died in the workhouse and whilst there she was robbed of her valuable jewellery by some of the pauper nurses. Douglas promptly wrote to the paper with a correction, describing Maria Eliza's private accommodation and treatment by paid staff at the workhouse before she was removed to Hanwell. He then went on to say it was regretful her relatives should be pained by the publicity revealing her admission to the workhouse. Then further stating, that after her death at the asylum, it was discovered the rosary beads she possessed while in the workhouse, were missing.

After Maria Eliza's sad and troubled death, Alexander de Gonzaga was still defending his inheritance, claiming his honour had been "wantonly assailed" in a letter to the editor of the *Morning Post* in December 1866.[236] He never gave up, but with his reputation tarnished throughout Europe, Alexander had no place to go and died in Norwood on 7 July 1869.

For Douglas, the never-ending admissions and discharges to and from the workhouse rarely abated; just as he was seeing off one extraordinary case, another appeared. A month after overseeing Princess Maria Eliza de Gonzaga's care, Douglas admitted another patient to the workhouse who was gravely ill and mentally delirious. He had received the key to the patient's small residence at the top of a house on Chapel Street from the landlady and entered the lodgings with assistant overseer, Mr Tubbs. To their astonishment the patient, Bartholomew Corbett, had amassed a collection of books, papers, and stuffed birds from his taxidermy work spanning many years. Each item was meticulously stacked and labelled. In one part of the room, Bartholomew had constructed an "avenue" made of the stuffed birds, measuring about 3 feet high and 2 feet wide. This avenue led to a recess not much larger than the inside of a large travelling bag and it was believed Bartholomew had slept there for many years.[237]

The 84-year-old had gradually withdrawn from all social interaction. Despite offers of help and kindness, he never accepted the assistance of his landlady Mrs Allen during his seven-year residence. That October she noticed he hadn't emerged from his room for several days and decided to call the police. An officer came swiftly with two constables but was unable to open the door due to Corbett's papers and books blocking the entry. The three men forced the door open and were confronted with a mess from floor to ceiling which they navigated by crawling on all fours until they reached Corbett.[238] The man was so dreadfully ill from erysipelas they did not think he would survive many more hours.

Among his numerous letters was a note indicating he had joined the renowned American ornithologists Alexander Wilson and John James Audubon on their expeditions through the forests and prairies of the distant west to study America's native birds. These journeys must have occurred before Wilson's death in 1813. Then in 1840, Corbett sailed for New York on the ship Zenobia with his children John, Thomas, and Emma Corbett.[239] Ten years later he was listed in Doggett's directory of New York as a naturalist. He must have returned prior to 1861 when he was recorded on the 1861 Census as one of the poor brothers of Charterhouse.[240]

At Marylebone infirmary the staff managed to prolong Bartholomew's life and he remained in the workhouse until his death at 3 pm on 19 February 1866. While staying there, he kept his room at 41 Chapel Street, paying the weekly rent of 2s. 6d. until 16 December 1865. From that date his rent went unpaid until his death. Miss Lowe from 31 Chapel Street helped cover some of this debt, along with the costs of his upkeep while he was in the workhouse, but the remaining debt would not be paid until his son Sergeant Corbett of the United States cavalry arrived to administer his father's affairs.[241] The previous August, Sergeant Thomas Corbett was discharged from the army and upon returning to civilian life, headed home to Boston where he resumed working as a hatter. He focused on silk hat finishing, using mercury-based compounds to stiffen fur and remove it from hides. Utilising heat and liquids, hatters molded the felt around silk hats while simultaneously inhaling the mercury-laden mist. The inhalation and the ingesting of residue left on fingers led to slurred speech, irritability and unsteadiness, with advanced poisoning resulting in paranoia; hence the phrase "mad as a hatter."

Throughout his life Thomas "Boston" Corbett displayed signs of instability and when combined with religious fervour and the grief of losing his wife, it brought about devastating consequences. On 16 July 1858 he castrated himself. Surviving this, he joined the army in 1861 but was then court-martialled for his disruptive behaviour and constant proselytising. Remarkably he was allowed to re-enlist and he joined the 16th Cavalry in 1863.

A few months prior to his father's illness, Thomas who by this time had changed his name to Boston, was sent with his regiment to track down the man who shot President Abraham Lincoln: John Wilkes Booth. On 26 April 1865, Corbett and his fellow soldiers tracked Booth and one of his accomplices to a tobacco barn in Virginia belonging to Richard Garrett. The accomplice surrendered, but despite an attempt to flush Booth out with fire he remained resolute. With the barn burning, the assassin inside put his rifle down and picked up a small table to try and suppress the flames. A shot rung out and Booth fell forward. He did not die instantly but lingered two hours before he breathed his last breath.[242]

Corbett admitted firing the shot after God had told him to do so. For years following the incident, there were doubts about Corbett's claim he had sent Booth to his maker; there were contradictions in the accounts of eyewitnesses at the scene and Corbett himself said he acted in self-defence despite others seeing Booth setting down his rifle. Irrespective of what actually happened, Corbett lived out the rest of his life as the man who avenged the assassination of a president. When he could no longer work due to his increasingly erratic behaviour, he took to the lecture circuit and recounted the time he shot John Wilkes Booth.

It is unlikely he returned to England following his father's death. In the spring of 1866, Douglas received a letter from a Barton Corbett son of Bartholomew authorising Miss Lowe to sell the property of his father. With the proceeds from the sale, she was to reimburse the workhouse for the fees incurred while nursing and maintaining Bartholomew.[243] It is possible Douglas read the name on the letter incorrectly and it was actually from Lincoln's avenger Boston Corbett. The fate of Thomas "Boston" Corbett has not been properly established. There was no further correspondence between him and Douglas and it is thought he died in a fire in 1894.

While the Corbett saga came to an end for the workhouse authorities in 1866, the following year they found themselves at the centre of a major catastrophe.

On New Year's Day 1867, a north wind sprang up across London after the capital enjoyed a mild end to 1866. The arctic squall brought ten inches of snow on Wednesday, 2 January and the temperature on the Thames gradually fell from 41 degrees Fahrenheit to 31 degrees at night. It was estimated 455 people lost their lives directly or indirectly (from succumbing to bronchitis or other afflictions) during the cold period.[244] Further lives were lost in one tragic incident on Tuesday, 15 January 1867.

On that day, emboldened by the frost of the night before, ice skaters and sledgers set out for the lake in Regent's Park. They continued to arrive in great numbers throughout the day with as many as 500[245] skaters dancing across the frozen water. Little did they notice the fissures beginning to appear upon the icy surface, brought about by the great mass of bodies. When the merriment reached its peak, an eruption, or an explosion according to some witnesses, caught their attention. What they heard was the sound of an acre of ice splitting and the water swallowing 200 people.[246]

Earlier that afternoon, George Edward Douglas and his wife Ann Elizabeth crossed the Marylebone Road from their residence at the Marylebone Workhouse and were taking an afternoon stroll when they saw the commotion. The vision horrified them: heads appearing above the water, trying to grab the broken slippery ice only to be submerged again; men and women floundering while holding terrified children; individuals jumping from the ice to the shore and by doing so toppling others into the freezing water – such was the trauma of the scene that numerous observers testified they would never forget it as long as they lived.

While many were stunned and unable to move from the shock, a number of individuals jumped into the water, including icemen and park keepers, and began to pull the unfortunate ones to the banks of the lake. Ropes and grappling hooks were utilised, but some of the ropes were rotten and fell apart when force was applied to them. In the end the sheer strength of the rescuers managed to pull the soaked men, women, and children out of the icy water. Douglas immediately sent for the police, some brandy, and blankets, while his wife Ann quickly returned to the workhouse and began to make arrangements to receive the injured at the infirmary. Ann's organisation meant surgeons were on hand as soon as the first fifteen victims arrived in cabs. It was soon discovered not all of the persons were alive and those who had survived were delirious. One man of twenty-five died later that day.[247]

In the park, the Royal Humane Society set about the dreadful task of recovering the bodies. By the end of the day they had delivered seven corpses to the Marylebone Workhouse mortuary for identification. Hearing the news, a crowd of some 2,000 gathered at the workhouse gates to pass by the dead, many anxious for missing family or friends. Some would find their loved ones laid out on mattresses, one father telling Mr Douglas, "Oh, he can't be dead; he only left me two hours ago, strong and cheerful."

As daylight faded, the Royal Humane Society ceased their onerous task. Duties at the workhouse, however, continued without abeyance: fourteen victims were now in the care of Drs Randall and Fuller. Douglas, as the senior officer, was preparing for a visit from Dr Hardwicke, the deputy coroner, and Police Inspector Burrows, who were there to take descriptions of the deceased.

On the Wednesday morning, relatives of the missing continued to appear at the workhouse. Douglas had the duty of informing them all of the bodies had been identified, though he allowed parents to enter the mortuary to allay fears their child was one of the dead. In addition to the stream of anxious parents, there were also the grieving families pleading Douglas for release of the bodies. He could not of course legally comply, instead he appealed to the coroner, Dr Lankester to hold an inquest as promptly as it could be arranged. Indeed, the first inquest regarding the circumstances surrounding the deaths of thirty-three individuals took place in the boardroom of the Marylebone Workhouse at 5 pm that day.[248] Curious inmates, the general public, and relatives of the dead were all in attendance, however the inquest was adjourned until further searches of the lake had been undertaken.

Douglas quickly assumed a new position as treasurer, managing the charitable funds allocated to compensate the men responsible for retrieving bodies from the lake. A number of unemployed men were recruited at 2s. per day to smash through the ice and further the effort to locate the missing. Most of these labourers had been deprived of work in traditional industries due to the harsh winter and required employment to feed their families.[249]

On the Saturday following the disaster, some 40 men were employed just to clear the ice. This was increased to 207 in addition to dredgemen. Clearing the ice meant divers could descend into the freezing waters, working in thirty-minute shifts, however it was hard going and thick black mud obscured their view.[250] They also contended with effluvia from the sewer.

After some unpopular demands to drain the lake, a decision was made on 26 January 1867 to terminate the recovery mission. This appears to have been a temporary measure despite Douglas' view the recovery had been successful and there were no further bodies to be found. This assumption was based on the testimony from witnesses and on the experience of a man named Poole, the self-proclaimed "Champion Skater of America" who was an expert on the behaviour of ice in various environments. Despite their opinions, the authorities continued dredging until the beginning of February, one week after the inquest found a verdict of accidental death for the forty individuals who had lost their lives in the accident. It appears no further bodies were discovered after this date.

Douglas' services and actions in the midst of tragedy did not go unrecognised. The workhouse guardians awarded an additional £50 per annum to the joint salaries of Mr and Mrs Douglas. Further, at a small ceremony held in the boardroom of the Marylebone Workhouse, in front of local dignitaries, Douglas received a purse containing £120 and a testimonial on vellum.[251] No doubt a public acknowledgement of his and his wife's quick-thinking, kindness, and hard work during a lamentable catastrophe.

Douglas' extraordinary encounters with individuals from various social backgrounds and unique predicaments exemplifies the working life of the parish official, but he was also a man with a family and a life beyond his role of Master. Likewise, every enumerator who stepped across the thresholds of rural cottages or tenements in the city courtyards to gather and complete schedules, came home to their families, ate their dinners, and played with their children by the fire.

Chapter Ten

A Life Beyond the Census: Frances Zanetti

Lying just off the shore from Stresa on the western side of Lake Maggiore are the Borromean Islands. Tourists, artists, and writers have visited this area for centuries, mostly drawn to the palaces and cultivated gardens of Isola Bella and Isola Madre, two centrepieces set against a backdrop of blue hills.

The architects of the grand palazzos and contrived vistas of the two islands were the Florentine Borromeo family, who in a frenzy of building activity, changed Bella and Madre into their own exotic garden paradises. Among the long boulevards laid out by the family it is still possible to hear the call of parrots or watch the spectacle of parading peacocks.

In contrast to Bella and Madre, the third island, Isola Pescatori, has retained its rock stairs and fisherman's cottages. On the lane lining the shore, hotels, eclectic restaurants and cafes serve the wandering tourists who have navigated the tight winding alleyways leading from the centre of the village. Tucked away on the southern tip of the island is the Chiesa di San Vittore. In the small graveyard behind the church stands two mausoleums one of which belongs to the Zanetti family, one of the oldest and most influential families on the island. Francesco Zanetti, a doctor of some renown was born there on 29 May 1729 and Vittore Zanetti, who was either a son or relative of the doctor, was born on 4 May 1770.[252]

At some point in the late eighteenth century, Vittore and his relative Vincent left the island and headed west eventually settling in the north of England. They went into partnership with fellow picture dealer John Fiorino and operated as Vittore, Zanetti and Company, serving Manchester's new brand of wealthy merchants born out of the flourish of the industrial revolution.[253] In 1801, the partnership was dissolved and Vittore expanded his business, typically providing prints and decorative arts in the form of chimney glasses, chandeliers, bronzes, mosaics and china as well as optical equipment and musical instruments. Vittore also founded an exhibition space and annually invited patrons to view the works of the old masters. His focus on art and opulence led one employee to exclaim "There is not any other shop in Manchester that comprises such a variety of articles of taste."[254]

Zanetti needed a practised eye and a flair for spotting craftsmanship in order to assess the quality of materials and finish of the objects he supplied. How he came by these skills is anyone's guess, but they were forwarded to both his son Joseph and apprentice Thomas Agnew. Joseph's birth must have swiftly followed Vittore's marriage to Elizabeth Frith of Great Budworth on 5 July 1800. He would later join his father's flourishing business in 1817, experiencing the high of expansion and a partnership with the 24-year-old Thomas Agnew, and the low of dealing with the Blackfriars Commissioners and eventually, bankruptcy.

In the October of 1823, Zanetti and Agnew were issued with a notice by the commissioners to prepare for removal from their premises at the Repository of Arts in Market Street, Manchester. The notice followed an Act of Parliament which gave the commissioners far-reaching powers for street and sanitation improvements in Manchester and Salford including lighting and widening streets and thoroughfares.

While the improvements may have been welcomed by the general public, it proved devastating for many businesses in Market Street. Vittore had refitted the shop seven years earlier, making improvements to the picture gallery and workshops.[255] Thomas Hopkins, an employee with vast experience of working with businesses all over the north-west remarked he had never been "in any shop as good as Messrs. Zanetti and Agnew's..., both the gilding shop and the show shop."

After having invested so much money and effort in the refurbishment, the order to move came as a blow. While they had identified a new premises in Exchange Street, it was far from adequate: the ceilings were high and had to be lowered, it was actually far too commodious for their purpose measuring 55 square yards in comparison to the 38 yards at Market Street. With a staff of fourteen including six gilders, five apprentices, two joiners, front of house staff Thomas Agnew, Joseph Zanetti and John Grundy, there was no concern about the workshop or showroom space, but rather the quality of the environment.

Joseph had raised the issue of potential damage to items hung high to cover the capacious walls, while the gilders were having serious reservations about the effects of sunlight on their work. As Thomas Hopkins commented,

> In consequence of the sun there will be a very considerable loss, and they will not be able to do their work well. It is almost impossible to gild above a certain temperature. I feel it very difficult to estimate the loss, but I conceive that in time, gold, &c, it will be very moderately reckoned at one fourth of the labour of five men and five apprentices in the hot season, say £31. 15s.

The commissioners argued Exchange Street was more fitting for their carriage-owning clientele and that the firm would also benefit from the footfall of the casual customer – a demographic Agnew and Zanetti had demonstrated returned the most income.[256] There was no doubt that the commissioners were intent on having their way; they agreed to pay the firm damages of £1,210 when the enquiry was settled in 1825, this being somewhat short of the £2,307 requested by the firm to cover the cost of removal.

The following year Vittore dissolved his partnership with Thomas Agnew, handing over his interest in the firm Zanetti and Agnew to his son Joseph.[257] Thomas was now the senior partner. Vittore headed back to Lake Maggiore and retired to his home on the Isola Pescatori. After his death on 13 November 1856, his legacy ensured the islanders had access to doctors and medicine; it also ensured the continuing education of poor girls by founding a school on the island. The school is now an office for civil marriages.[258]

A decade after Vittore passed his interest in the Repository of Arts to Joseph, a notice appeared in *The London Gazette* informing the public that the partnership between Thomas Agnew and Joseph Zanetti was dissolved. Thomas would run the business alone absorbing all of its debts.[259] He would go on to greater things, establishing a gallery and art dealership in Old Bond Street, London and becoming one of the foremost dealers of the nineteenth century.

Joseph, on the other hand, declared bankruptcy in February 1837, one month after announcing the dissolved partnership.[260] Later that year, following a move to King Street, Manchester and by order of his assigns, Joseph was forced to auction off a major portion of his stock including paintings by Rubens, Teniers, Van Dyck, Guercino, and Sir Joshua Reynolds. He was able to resume trading as a carver, gilder, and dealer from his temporary premises in King Street after the auction.

The 1841 Census records him and his family including wife Ann, whom he had married in 1829, and children Joseph, Sarah, and Edward at Garden Lane, Manchester. If the bankruptcy had not been traumatic enough for the family, what happened next was devastating. On a Friday morning in late January 1843, Patrick Brady, who was hired to work as an excavator on a new lodge for Blair's bleach works in Mill Hill, Little Bolton, ventured to the brook beyond the works. While there he noticed a black object in the water. Moving closer towards it he realised it was a man's body. Calling for assistance from two fellow employees, they lifted the body from the brook onto the grass and found some change and a pocketbook on the body. The gilt lettering on the pocketbook left no doubt as to the identity of the victim, it was Joseph Zanetti.

The day before, Joseph had set out for Garstang and asked a boy to accompany him on his journey presumably with some form of work in mind for the lad. Instead of paying the boy a shilling, he mistakenly gave him a sovereign. By the time he arrived at the railway station to return home, it was too late to retrieve his money from the boy and he was left stranded. He walked to see his acquaintance John Walmsley of the Commercial Inn in Great Bolton who supplied him with ale, whisky, a sandwich, and a cigar. John gave him 5s. for his onward journey and Joseph left about 3.45 pm only to return 20 minutes later, possibly to kill time before the 6 pm train. He drank more whisky and played billiards with Robert West who was an old friend; Robert thought Joseph was out of sorts and seemed bewildered. He did not ascribe this to the alcohol intake, but something else. As far as Walmsley was concerned Joseph was no different from normal and he saw him off about 5.40 pm never to see him again.

For days following the discovery of the body, there had been gossip about town that Joseph had been murdered. There was a wound on the back of his head, and his body appeared to have been dragged to the water. Perhaps the greatest mystery of all was how his handkerchief had ended up under a stone. During the inquest at the Crown Inn in Folds, Little Bolton, the murder theory was first challenged by surgeon Joseph Denham. He testified that the bloody head injury was merely coagulated blood from a cheek wound and that Joseph was alive when he fell into the water, not dragged there. Police Sergeant Thomas Beech further suggested that Joseph likely tripped in the dim light and accidentally knocked the stone onto the handkerchief. Eventually the jury returned an open verdict of "found drowned" permitting further enquiry if necessary.[261]

The tragedy for Ann and the family was the loss of Joseph at the age of 43; he had also left them with the additional worry of dying intestate. After administering his estate, Ann continued the business in her name, advertising "her very superior assortment of chimney and toilet glasses, hall tables, bagatelle tables" in the *Manchester Courier and Lancashire General Advertiser* in March 1843. In the years following, her eldest son Joseph entered into the trade and eventually became a carver and gilder. But at some point a decision was made about the business and Ann put up for sale her entire stock on 23 and 24 December 1851.[262]

In July 1862 Joseph's son and namesake married Teresa Jane Hughes in Mortlake, Surrey. The ceremony was celebrated by his cousin the Rev. Vincent Zanetti who spent part of the next decade dealing with the spiritual needs of Fenian convicts imprisoned in north London. After leaving behind the former textile centres in King Street and St. Ann's Square, Joseph junior and Teresa headed to Cheetham where they set up home with Teresa's father. Following the births of two children, both baptised at St. Chad Roman Catholic church, Teresa gave birth to daughter Frances on 6 July 1866.

The church of St. Chad would be at the centre of the Zanetti family spiritual life for years to come. Thanks to the zeal of the Very Rev. Canon Sheehan, the church was augmented with large two-light windows during a period of renovation. At a time when Manchester's "gloom reigned supreme", Sheehan's flock now enjoyed the spectacle of coloured light from the newly installed stained glass. Sheehan also commissioned the reredos to be gilded, and three new panels painted by Charles Goldie depicting the Sacred Heart, the Blessed Virgin, and the Blessed Margaret Mary. A new tabernacle in gilt bronze with enamel and precious stones was ordered from eminent metal worker M. Chetier of Paris. All the work combined affected a striking change to the interior of the church.[263]

While the silhouette of St. Chad dominated the summit of Cheetham Hill, it stood among a cluster of Catholic buildings which included a Presbytery, a convent, and a number of schools; they, like many of the

Catholic structures scattered around the city, were reminders of the fight for Manchester's Catholic soul.

In early nineteenth-century England and Wales, the Church of England dominated education seeing itself as the protector of the nation's Christian faith, believing education was the church's duty rather than that of the state. It viewed challenges from figures like Quaker Joseph Lancaster – who, in 1810, founded the Royal Lancasterian Institution for the Education of the Poor of Every Religious Persuasion – and from Manchester's Dissenters, who promoted education to make labourers more efficient in an industrial setting, as threats to its authority. For many Dissenters, universal education was a means to create wealth among the already prosperous. The 1833 Factory Act marked an early victory for education reform by mandating two hours of schooling six days a week for factory children under 13, with further acts in the 1840s extending part-time education to mill children as young as 8.[264]

While Dissenters' schools received state grants, Catholic schools were excluded from parliamentary funding. Despite the Catholic Emancipation Act of 1829, few Catholics had the influence to drive social change, prompting the Catholic Church to establish the Catholic Poor School Committee. Amid a surge of Irish arrivals due to the potato famine, secretary Scott Nasmyth Stokes appealed to the Committee of Council on Education for help in addressing the severe educational needs. Although parliamentary grants were finally offered, a lack of teachers persisted until orders such as the Sisters of the Cross and Passion and the Sisters of Notre Dame intervened. In 1849, Elizabeth Prout's order, the Sisters of the Cross and Passion, took up residence at St. Chad's School in Stocks Street, Manchester, using a modest grant to procure books and maps for the new school.[265]

In 1852 the clergy of St. Chad invited the Sisters of Notre Dame to open a day "middle school" in a renovated coach-house at Cheetham Hill. Such was the reputation of the order founded by Marie Rose Julie Billiart and Françoise Blin de Bourdon in 1804, they held a prominent position among religious communities' teachers. The sisters first arrived in England from their mother house in Namur, Belgium in 1845, setting up in Penryn before transferring to Clapham in 1848. By 1895, they had opened foundations across the country from Manchester to Glasgow.[266] They appealed to many Catholic parents because despite being English, the schools were French in character and offered the prestige of the French convent school. They provided broad educational opportunities which went beyond the usual curriculum of reading, writing, and domestic duties for girls.

Writing in 1908, George Alston described a typical convent school education to include:

> English in all its branches, French, Latin, mathematics, science, drawing, needlework, class-singing, and drilling, while such subjects as music, singing, dancing, Greek, German, Italian, elocution, shorthand, book-keeping, dressmaking, cooking, etc., are generally taught as optional extras. Pupils are entered for the Oxford and Cambridge Local Examinations, the Higher Locals, the Higher and Lower Certificates of the Oxford and Cambridge Joint Examination Board, the Matriculation Examinations of the London and Liverpool Universities.[267]

It was into this environment that Frances Zanetti's parents Joseph and Teresa enrolled her and her older sister Annie. At St Chad's Sisters of Notre Dame High School, Frances would receive one of the best educations in Manchester equipping her for future roles in local government and also preparing her for a life as a devout Catholic.[268] In later years she was engaged in the proceedings of the Catholic Truth Society and appointed chairman of the Catholic Women's League. It wouldn't be a stretch of the imagination to say her faith must have influenced her commitment to improving the lives of the poor children of Manchester.

In 1881, Frances took the Lancashire and Cheshire Unions Institute exam in French while at the Manchester Mechanic's Institute.[269] Despite a thirst for education and self-improvement, her early years were not entirely devoid of fun and tied to further education. She developed a love for lawn tennis and while not as devoted to amateur dramatics as her sister, presumably because it interfered with her role in local government, she appeared in a number of theatre productions between 1882 and 1901.

At the age of 25 she was working as a school daily governess. Mildred M. Cullen suggests school governesses hadn't sat government teacher training certificate examinations,[270] but sought school positions such as those advertised in the *Manchester Courier and Lancashire General Advertiser*:

> DAILY GOVERNESS requires Situation in school or family, in or about Manchester; English, French, mathematics, drawing, theory, and drill; testimonials if required. – Address G 33, at the printers.[271]

Following the implementation of the Infant Life Protection Act in 1897, Frances Zanetti was appointed Inspector of Child Protection for the Manchester and Prestwich Union. This new role, initiated by local authorities and mainly undertaken by women was designed to protect children from what were the perceived cruelties of baby farming.

Negative attitudes towards single mothers and illegitimate children had prevailed for centuries. It was believed children conceived in sin would inherit the moral indiscretion of their parents and pass on their lack of rectitude to legitimate children. Up until 1834, Poor Law assisted single mothers and gave responsibility to the putative father, but many believed Poor Law as it stood encouraged licentious behaviour due to the availability of parish relief. The change in the law in 1834 immediately absolved the father of any responsibility and placed the burden solely on the mother up until the child was 16.[272]

Mothers were humiliated and were socially and economically sanctioned in an effort to restore female morality. Nineteenth-century authors and artists fetishised the fallen woman, presenting ideals of womanhood and advocating the respectability of marriage. While many unwed mothers tried to find work to support their child and regain their moral identities, they had few options. Factory and domestic employment meant they were unable to conceal their condition and avoid the scrutiny of their employers. Working after the birth of their child was also impossible because of the lack of childcare facilities.

Social reform to protect the lives of innocent children was rejected due to the fear of state intervention violating the Victorian ideal of the family. As a consequence, many unwed mothers had little choice but to turn to several equally unpalatable solutions. If she were to choose a foundling hospital or a workhouse she would be questioned about her situation and perhaps forced to relive any trauma associated with the pregnancy. She could seek an abortion and risk death or commit infanticide and risk the courts. Alternatively, she could scour the newspaper advertisements to locate a couple willing to foster her child until she got back on her feet. These substitute parenting services permitted many young women to manage the stigma associated with unwanted pregnancy and allowed them to work towards restoring their respectability. They gave mothers the liberation to seek employment as an interim measure and unburden the stresses brought about by the pregnancy. They also created a way to "dispose" of a child legitimately and without criminality. Mothers could pay foster parents to look after their nurse child by the week with the view it would not be a permanent arrangement.

Extreme abuse within the baby farming industry meant it quickly became an emotive umbrella term used not only for the malpractice and systematic murder of children, but also for the respectable services of fostering and adoption. The focus on the killing of children provided a generalisation that all baby farming services were identical when they were not.

Women associated with providing services were characterised and labelled as monstrous entities:

> BABY-FARMING, the opprobrium of Britain, the darkest stain upon our religious character as a nation, continues to flourish. Babies in dozens are sent literally as lambs to the slaughter. The slaughterers are vile old harridans, in whom every spark of womanhood has long been extinguished; wretches ... hateful and devilish Canidias, who watch the last agonising convulsions which end the little life with the same coolness as they would watch the struggles of a drowning fly, and who rejoice when all is over that they are now ready for another piece of murder. This frightful race of witches and hags must be exterminated.
>
> *Islington Gazette*, 15 July 1870[273]

Despite its reputation, adverts continued to be placed in newspapers and desperate women continued to respond to them. At face value the advertisements appeared respectable and all offered a similar service. Rarely were references asked for or personal information exchanged. When the transaction was complete some mothers knew they would never see their child again. Those who wanted a clandestine disposal may have later claimed they had been hoodwinked by the lies of the disreputable baby farmer. For others it would have been seen as an innocent adoption process.[274] Deviant baby farmers would solicit for infants under two months knowing the frailty of their life. For the period in which they "cared" for the infant they would extract money from the mother while simultaneously starving and dosing the child with laudanum or other poisons. The bodies were then wrapped in old newspapers, dumped on waste ground or thrown in the Thames. When appalling murders such as those perpetrated by Charlotte Winsor in 1865 and Margaret Waters in the late 1860s became headlines, reform finally arrived in the shape of the Infant Life Protection Act 1872. It was no longer possible for a baby farmer to care for more than two children from one family longer than twenty-four hours unless their house was registered. The Act failed because it did not include a plan for the registration and inspection of the baby farmer's home.

The 1896 case of Amelia Dyer brought the shortcomings of the 1872 legislation into sharp focus. Suffering from severe mental health problems, Dyer was apprehended when caught in the act of disposing of baby corpses in the Thames. The general public and campaigners for further child protection were horrified and the government had no recourse, but to produce a bill for the Infant Life Protection Act 1897. The new bill brought amendments to the previous act by changing the maximum age of children covered by its remit from 12 months to 5 years. Not only did the carer have to be registered with the local authority, they had to allow access to the infant life protection officers, who if required, could remove any child they believed to be neglected or in danger. The 1897 Act also gave authorities the power to actively seek out baby farmers. For many like Frances Zanetti, it would soon become clear the Act had its flaws particularly in view of those paying £20 or more to adopt a child, who did not fall within its remit. In his article "More Ignorant and Stupid than Wilfully Cruel", Daniel Grey suggests this aligned with the widespread belief that child abuse and neglect were mainly perpetrated by working-class parents.

Frances hadn't been in her role long when she appeared in court to testify at an adoption trial. During an inspection on 28 October 1898 at the home of Mrs Hamman in Rusholme, she discovered a 9-month-old child who had been adopted for the sum of £10. Mrs Hamman's failure to register the transaction under Section 5 of the Infant Life Protection Act had led to the court appearance. According to Frances the child was healthy and treated well and the court adjourned for twelve weeks to monitor the child's situation.[275]

The following year she was involved in a more serious case in Moss Side which warranted a hearing before the Chorlton Guardians. The family in question were caring for three nurse children all aged under 5 when they received an infant aged 5 weeks. A midwife delivered the baby to the family admitting it was very sick and would not last another week. The child died the following day, but the coroner was not notified and the funeral took place before any action was taken. The woman caring for the children pleaded ignorance of the provisions of the Infant Life Protection

Act. The Guardians dismissed her claim as absurd – after all she had been a registered carer for some time. With this in mind, they pressed for a prosecution.[276]

Two months later, Frances delivered her annual report to the Joint Committee of the Chorlton and Prestwich Unions. During the previous twelve months she had made upwards of 1,300 home visits. From those visits, seven new cases arose from failure to comply with the Act; another 87 cases were those of children received for hire or reward who did not fall within the provisions of the act simply because they were taken as single children. This was a loop-hole the authorities desired to see amended at the earliest opportunity.

At the Chorlton Board of Guardians meeting on Friday, 19 January 1900, Dr Rhodes, a board member emphasised the value of Frances' work. She had prevented many cases from becoming abject and where possible children received the correct care due to them. In recognition of her services the Board reappointed Frances in the role of inspector without objection.[277]

In the autumn of 1900, the Registrar General Reginald MacLeod sent out communications to the Registrars and Superintendent Registrars of England and Wales about the forthcoming census. Notices were soon placed in the newspapers informing the public the census was almost upon them, and the recruitment of enumerators would soon commence. Frances' local newspaper the *Manchester Courier and Lancashire General Advertiser* announced, "it is held that women are eligible to serve as enumerators, and their employment may be freely resorted to when the local conditions are suitable." This was the second time women were formally hired as enumerators, although it took a while for the public to fully accept the idea women could be hired.

As Frances saw it, being an enumerator afforded her the rare opportunity of observing the conditions of children nursed away from home. She would also be able to check on any suspected baby-farming activities while on duty for the census. On this basis she submitted an application to become an enumerator. For the application she was required to supply her full name, postal address, age last birthday, occupation and whether she was well acquainted with the district. At the time, she was resident in Bignor Street, Cheetham, roughly a forty-minute walk from her selected district, enumeration district two in the Manchester sub-district of Ancoats. District two was one of the poorest quarters of Ancoats, dotted with lodging houses and the red brick galleried tenements of the labouring class. It was also the home to many Italian migrants who were attracted to this area of Manchester. Frances' selection for Ancoats was probably due to her roots and her ability to speak a little Italian. The psychology of familiarity was an important tool for the enumerator; a householder was more likely to be compliant if they felt safe with the visitor or so it was thought.

Like all enumerators, she received instructions in advance of the census. She familiarised herself with the schedule and the boundaries of her district and armed herself with a stylograph or a fountain pen and some blotting paper. She was allowed to deliver the schedules from Monday, 25 March and had up to Saturday, 30 March to make sure the job was completed. For thoroughness Frances made two visits to the district in case she missed people on her first round. She soon discovered it took significant time explaining to the householders the nature of the schedules, how to complete them and the penalties for non-compliance – all this had to be achieved while simultaneously completing her memorandum book. The Italian community told Frances of their fears regarding the census. Were the forms a prelude to their repatriation? Would there be injunctions against their large families crammed into two rooms? Or was the form a summons for their failure to whitewash their walls? All these concerns were familiar to enumerators up and down the country and had to be allayed by a simple explanation about why the census was needed.[278]

On the morning of 1 April 1901, it was raining heavily. Frances returned to her district during the downpour and began the task of collecting the schedules. Immediately she discovered only one in twenty were correct. Failure to include the correct number of rooms or county of birth were common errors, but there were also a few blank papers. Thankfully she carried spare blank schedules with her and was able to rewrite the erroneous forms assisted by the householder. An enthusiastic lady offered all the details of her children only to later inform Frances they were in the army or married and living elsewhere. At which point the schedule was disposed of and Frances started again. There was a great deal of confusion surrounding occupations. Cap makers had to be clarified by industry. Were they cloth cap makers or paper cap makers? Also, the pedlars and hawkers, of which there were many in Ancoats, when confronted with a question regarding the nature of their goods, answered with anything they could sell.

As the day progressed, the job became more onerous. Tiredness set in for many enumerators, though probably not as much for the tennis mad Frances. On her round individuals were still in bed or had gone to bed, shouting out to her when disturbed, "Call again!" Another woman answered the door bleary eyed and shoved her rent book into Frances' hands believing her to be the rent collector. In another house she was invited in to take shelter from the rain. Inside a woman apologised for the state of her schedule explaining it was completed by her youngster, adding "My old man's no writer. He's under the Eye Institution." To which Frances replied with a twinkle in her eye, "He's got a load on his shoulders then", but her attempt at a joke clearly fell flat and the woman rattled on about her husband's heavy burden and her lack of literacy.

The inability to write was a common excuse. "There were no School Boards in our time" or similar words were often uttered among the poorer classes. One man gave himself two wives and when this was pointed out to his real wife she replied he was "no scholar, which to her explained everything." Despite the frustrations involving literacy or inaccuracy, it was not the most frustrating task of all. When confronted with a lodging house in the neighbourhood of Jersey Street or Henry Street, it was the laissez-faire attitude of the lodging housekeeper that tested her patience. After receiving instructions during the delivery of the schedules he ignored them because he did not want to press the guests for information. Half an hour was wasted trying to locate individuals who had stayed the night. In the end, messengers were dispatched to find the ones already gone.

Back in the Italian neighbourhood where she quelled fears of deportation, Frances discovered a cooperative community who made an honest attempt to complete their schedules efficiently despite knowing very little English. Frances' enumeration book records a group of migrants who either arrived as a family unit or who settled and then had their children in Manchester. They worked mainly in the music, organ grinding, biscuit or ice cream trades, the latter of which was observed vigilantly by the authorities. They did not identify as British subjects, holding on tightly to their Italian citizenship, even going as far as preferring to register their children with the Italian consulate.[279]

The collection of the schedules in the Italian neighbourhood marked the finale of this stage of Frances' journey as an enumerator. She returned home to begin the mammoth task of transferring over 200 households and 1,162 individuals into her enumeration book. The documents were neatly completed with care and when she inserted words into the text she had already written, she tried to be legible. She made no comments nor did she make any marginalia. The only time she felt compelled to write something beyond her remit was when she visited the Women's Shelter at 29 Great Ancoats Street noting "These women take their share in the work of Institution [*sic*] until situations etc. can be found for them."[280]

After her census duties were concluded she returned to her quest for further amendments to the Infant Life Protection Act. She also began to write and speak publicly about broader issues surrounding childcare. Speaking at the Poor Law Guardians' Conference at Preston in 1902 she articulated the ignorance of mothers in bringing up their children. Many were unaware of basic hygiene: they were not washing their babies and were keeping them by blocked drains and ash pits or in stifling dirty kitchens. They were not feeding them a healthy diet, instead they were giving them bread, bacon, potatoes, currant buns, stewed tea and beer, in addition to condensed milk or water from filthy bottles. In order for improvements to be made and the death rate lowered, she advocated that elder girls learn hygiene and the care of infants in school.[281]

A year later she wrote a paper for the Society for the Study of Inebriety in Women entitled *Inebriety in women and its influence on child-life.* In language common for the period, she describes the poor as parasitic and uses anti-Semitic stereotypes, paradoxically calling for social reform to alleviate the stresses that encouraged intoxication. Drink, she argued was used as a remedy for overcrowding, poor sanitation, wretched working conditions and bad pay. The offspring of drunk parents became "neurotic, vicious children", affected by alcoholism and disease. Many of them, if they survived a neglected early childhood, grew up rickety and weak, further diminishing national productivity by contributing to the issues of poverty and crime. In order to alleviate the conditions leading to alcohol abuse, she suggested it would be better to build wide open park spaces with places of refreshment for "innocent entertainment"; to invest in tramways and cheaper fares to induce working people to move out of the slums and live where fresh air and cleaner surroundings may prove beneficial.

> I know, also, that a mother who loves her babe is glad of its protection.

In 1908 Frances was asked to testify before the Select Committee on Infant Life Protection. At this point in her life, she had given ten years to her role as an inspector and ever since undertaking the tenure, she had called for amendments to the 1897 Act. It was with this experience she was perhaps the most influential of the testifiers. In the first four years of her work, she told the committee, only 167 out of the 809 children she encountered came within the provisions of the 1897 Act. Many of the homes she visited had a lone foster child and although she had no authority in the circumstances, she was allowed to inspect the children with the goodwill of their carers. This led her to conclude a competent caring foster mother with nothing to hide would never object to an inspection. The committee agreed and it was suggested the Act should be extended to cover homes with a single nurse child and all foster children aged 7 years and under. The £20 lump sum limit should also be abolished. Eventually, the amendments were consolidated with the Children Bill and the result was the Children Act 1908.[282]

There were objections to the amendments from certain quarters including the Church of England Society for Waifs and Strays. In a March 1908 article for *Reynolds's Newspaper*, Frances argued that concerns about a lack of foster homes, higher prices for care, and an increase in abortion and infanticide as a result of the act were diametrically opposed to her experience. She reiterated good mothers welcomed inspection; the indifferent ones needed it.[283]

She continued in her role as Inspector for a number of years appearing at the Catholic Truth Society conference in 1908 and giving a lecture to the Blackpool Suffrage Society on the subject of child protection in 1909. In 1919 she stood as Labour candidate for the Longsight ward in the local council elections and by 1921 she was the Registrar of Births and Deaths for Rusholme.

Having spent much of her life dedicated to the welfare of children, she died in 1956 aged 90, single, and without children of her own. It can be argued given her experienced testimony before the Select Committee, that the Children Act 1908 was her child and as a result of her dedication to see it implemented, thousands of children were given lives free from neglect and cruelty.

Chapter Eleven

Institutions

> In the meanwhile, it seems that if she had come down to the earth from the moon she could not have been more hopelessly stranded.

Few travellers entering London via the Royal Albert Dock in the 1890s would have recognised the area if they had viewed it some fifty years earlier. In 1840, they would have observed the cattle grazing on the Plaistow Marshes and if they surveyed further, they may have found a residence known as the Devil's House. Apart from the house, the marshland was devoid of any activity. As such, if someone had said to the traveller "I will build a railway here", they would have thought them quite mad. Therefore, in 1847 when George P. Bidder completed his railway across the marshland, it became known as "Bidders Folly". George was unperturbed by what his detractors thought. He must have recognised the Metropolitan Building Act 1844 prohibiting toxic and harmful trades operating in the metropolis, made land outside its boundaries quite lucrative. He soon purchased the whole of the area between Bow Creek and Galleon's Reach and then sold the land for docks and factories making a very nice profit.

One of the earliest industries to arrive was Samuel Silver's waterproof clothing works which lent its name to the new settlement of Silvertown. Later, both Henry Tate and Abram Lyle would set-up their own separate sugar refining operations in Silvertown and on the Plaistow Marshes, before merging in the 1920s. The new industries and the building of the Royal Victoria and Albert Docks attracted migrants from all over the world. These migrant men and women who disembarked their ships and stood on the dockside with but a few coins in their pockets may have had plans for the next stage of their journey. Some took the train to Fenchurch Street, while others joined established family members in the new communities of Hallsville, Canning Town, and Silvertown.

In the March of 1891, a young woman arrived at the docks carrying some Russian and German money with the objective to seek out her family in Silvertown. Unfortunately, she had lost the address and was unable to ask for directions due to having no knowledge of English. When all of her attempts to communicate failed, she was eventually rescued from her situation by representatives of the Travellers' Aid Society.

The Society was founded in 1885 and afforded the opportunity for women travelling alone to be met by a safe and friendly face when they reached their destination. Agents from the Society would arrange to meet the traveller at a railway station or port; they would check the suitability of any employment the woman was offered and find her decent lodgings. If the woman made no prior arrangements before travelling, placards were displayed at transport hubs informing her not to trust unauthorised persons who might lead her astray. It was in these situations the Society also relied on the goodwill and cooperation of porters and dock officials to notify them of any stranded young women, particularly ones who couldn't speak or read English.

Once the Society made contact with the young traveller, it did not take them long to find her a situation in Marylebone – presumably domestic service within a household. However, this did not go well due to her ignorance of all languages. Not knowing what could be done for the young woman, she was soon dispatched to St. Marylebone Workhouse.

George Edward Douglas was now in his twilight years in charge of the workhouse, having entered into his twenty-ninth year as master the previous November. He was now tasked with providing for the young woman and establishing who she was and where she intended to settle. The task was not his alone, he was ably assisted by barrister Sydney Holland, later Viscount Knutsford, who sat on the Board of Guardians and made it his own quest to establish the identity of the young woman. On 31 March 1891, he visited the workhouse and trying a little French and German he endeavoured to communicate with her. When this failed, he tried Italian, Swedish, Servian (Serbian), Russian, some Romany, Polish, and Yiddish, all to no avail. He then started to establish names for various parts of the body and objects, and by using phonetic spellings, he wrote them down: a hand was ranke, eyes was arkese, an ear was ancise, and money was penegri. After having compiled a list he then sent out letters to the national press asking for their assistance stating "unless, when discovered, someone will help her to return, she will have to stay in the workhouse for the rest of her life. I am bound to say she seems happy and contented and disposes with ease the rations of two ordinary paupers. When will England do as other nations do, and stop this cruel importation of foreign paupers?"[284]

Holland was no doubt echoing the thoughts of many when he voiced his concerns regarding "pauper aliens". There had been a swell of anti-immigrant feeling growing since the Jewish migration from eastern Europe with activists such as William Wilkins blaming Jews for stealing jobs and increasing rents by living in cramped spaces. Wilkins was so incensed by the situation he joined thc Association for Preventing the Immigration of Destitute Aliens founded by Arnold White in 1891. While their campaign for anti-alien legislation claimed to have the support of forty-three trade unions including the powerful Dockers' Union, public opinion overall was unmoved.[285]

Newspapers such as *The Sportsman* joined in the anti-immigrant chorus when it came to the St. Marylebone traveller. Jumping on the huge interest in the young woman's story, the newspaper repeated sentiments expressed elsewhere with its repulsion for her "outlandish yibberish" and the bewildering attraction of London to migrants, before asking why does she choose to live here rather than in the land of her own people?[286]

The fear of losing out to migrants in terms of housing and employment led many to support their arguments for anti-immigrant legislation with unsupported assertions. Claims that pauper aliens were frequent users of the workhouse and were strains on the rate payers were swiftly dealt with by the 1891 Census report published in 1893. In the East End of London, it said, where there should be an excess of pauper aliens more than in any other city in the kingdom, there were 36,871 European foreigners. Of these 36,871 migrants, "only 105, or 2.85 [per] 1,000, were inmates of the workhouses, while, out of the other 6,68,243 inhabitants [of London], 950, or 13.5 per 1,000, were pauper inmates."[287] Therefore foreign migrants dependant on workhouse relief made up a small percentage of the pauper population. Of the 105 inmates, 51 were Germans, 16 were French, 14 were Russians or Poles, and five were Swiss – the remainder from other countries contributing no more than four to the total population.

In terms of the total population in workhouses, the report shows there were 182,713 inmates in England and Wales. The male inmate population exceeded females in almost every county except for Rutland where numbers were equal and in Cornwall where women outnumbered men. Conversely, in Scotland[288] and Ireland female inmates marginally exceeded males in all asylums, poorhouses and workhouses.[289] One of the reasons cited for the excess of men in workhouses in England and Wales was they were more prone to serious illness than women and as a rule their occupations required extra physical labour. This meant any incapacitation would prevent them from earning. While this reason made sense in explaining excess among the over 35s, it did not explain why boys under 15 were shown in such high numbers. According to the report the excess of boys could be ascribed to the availability of charitable schools and institutions favouring girls. In addition, the practice in some Poor Law Unions of allowing widows applying for relief to remain out of the workhouse with some of their children, while sending their boys who were more expensive to clothe and feed into the institution, may have been a contributing factor.[290] Inmate figures for other census years for Britain and Ireland can be consulted on the HistPop website.

Among those included in the 1891 Census workhouse returns was the enigmatic young woman in the St. Marylebone Workhouse. Within hours of Sydney Holland's plea for help in the national press, he was inundated with offers and enquiries from the general public. In one newspaper, a journalist wrote that Holland's phonetic word list provided all the clues needed for "our travelled Newcastle polyglots." Based on the contents of the list they suggested she was either Lithuanian or a Laplander (and not Welsh as someone suggested!), particularly as she possessed some Russian and German money. It did seem strange, they continued, that in a city the size of London, not a soul could understand a word she said. If she had fallen to the "earth from the moon she could not have been more hopelessly stranded."[291]

On 3 April 1891, Polish author and journalist Edmond Naganowski visited the workhouse and sat down to speak to the young woman. This gentle, well-mannered girl, explained to him her name was Anna Bordanaitys and she was 20 years old. Her father, who was a soldier in the Russian Army, had disappeared many years ago leaving behind her mother and herself in the village of Borodynka in the region of Suvalki (Suwalki, Ostpreußen). Like most of the inhabitants of that district, she spoke only Lettish, a mix of the ancient, and almost extinct Lithuanian and Finnish languages. The family suffered persecution for being members of the branch of the

Roman Catholic Church known as the United Greek Church. Religious intolerance divided the community and many were forced to convert and some transported to the Tzar's furtherest dominions. A relative managed to escape to England some three or four years earlier and so to avoid further persecution, it was agreed between mother and daughter they should travel separately to elude the authorities. With that in mind Anna journeyed first to Koenigsberg and then to Hamburg where she boarded a ship to London.[292]

Both Sydney Holland and George Edward Douglas were determined to reunite Anna with her relative despite the difficulties due to her losing his address. In the meantime Douglas found her another job with a lady who spoke the same tongue.

On 10 April 1891, the newspapers reported Anna was included on the census despite having left the workhouse on Sunday morning to join the brother she was seeking. He was found in Silvertown working in a sugar factory. As Anna left the workhouse, she fell to her knees, kissing the hem of Douglas' coat in gratitude for his help.

Anna's inclusion in the workhouse enumeration book despite having left early on the Sunday provides a small clue about census taking in some of the larger institutions. While it is apparent there was no widespread rubric to follow, there is also little evidence regarding the method used to record institutions with inmates of 100, 200, 500, or 1,000 individuals and even less knowledge about how it was achieved prior to 1841.

From 1801 to 1831, the overseers of each parish or "other substantial householders" in England and Wales and local schoolmasters in Scotland were asked to record the number of families and the men and women in their parishes together with information about economic activity. During this period, there was no separate provision for answering questions about inmates in institutions in England, Wales, and Scotland until 1841 and in Ireland until 1821. As Higgs has suggested, due to Rickman's lack of clarity surrounding the recording of prisons, workhouses, hospitals, and schools etc., each institution may have been treated as a "family".[293] In the preliminary observations of the 1821 Census enumeration abstract, the difficulty of defining inmates was discussed by Rickman:

> What is to be deemed a distinct Family? One single person inhabiting a house cannot but be returned as a Family, although the word Family usually denotes more persons than one. But there is difficulty regarding Inmates, who in the various

> degrees of connection arising in domestic arrangements, may be deemed of the same family, or a distinct family.[294]

Plans for the 1841 Census in Britain, the Isle of Man and the Channel Islands included procedures for identifying institutions in advance of the census date. Superintendent registrars, sheriffs, provosts and lieutenant governors were requested to draw up a list of all charitable and public institutions (every gaol, prison, penitentiary, house of correction, hulk or prison ship, workhouse, poorhouse, almshouse, hospital, infirmary, asylum, madhouse, public school, endowed school, college, barrack, and other public or charitable institutions) in their district and to include the total number of inmates for each institution.

From this list, institutions which did not fit the definitions were expunged and included in the normal returns. The idea was to reduce the number of institutions requiring separate enumeration books sent directly to them by the census authorities. Those in receipt of the institutional books were chief officers or masters who were then expected to complete the returns for their individual institutions. Despite the initial preparation, some institutions which were considered too small for the separate books received them while some large institutions were included with the normal households.

For the 1851 Census, institutions with inmates of 200 or more received Enumeration Books for Public Institutions (EBPIs) and were placed in their own enumeration districts. Each book was marked on the outside with letters denoting the kind of institution it was for: "W" for workhouse, "P" for prison, "L. A.", for lunatic asylum and "B" for barracks.[295]

To avoid confusion, registrars were requested to make sure their house-to-house enumerators were aware of all the institutions in their district. It was vital the smaller ones, with inmates below 200, were not overlooked and to facilitate their inclusion, enumerators were supplied with the special schedules printed in red.

This same system continued until 1881 in England, Wales, the Isle of Man and the Channel Islands, but with changes to the special schedule which was printed in black for 135 persons.

For the 1861 Census in Scotland it was the general rule public institutions with inmates exceeding 50 persons were treated as separate enumeration districts. Institutions whose inmates did not amount to 50 persons were treated as ordinary houses and were noted on special schedules printed in red by the enumerator on his route. This changed for the 1871 Census and the number of inmates in residence to qualify for a EBPI was increased to 135. We learn from the 1871 Census report for Scotland the EBPIs were furnished with fetching pink covers and the special schedules continued to be printed in red.[296]

The 1901 Census brought England, Wales, the Crown dependencies and Scotland into accord: institutions with inmates numbering 100 or more would receive the EBPIs and other institutions would still receive the special schedules.

Despite changes to the system following the decision to abolish enumeration books for the 1911 Census in England and Wales, what remained was the requirement for registrars to include institutions on the last pages of their plan of division and for them to then supply the officers or head of the establishment with an enumeration book now entitled "Enumeration Book for a Public Institution or Large Establishment." Registrars could recommend the heads of other large establishments with over 100 inmates e.g. hotels, a business house, college or school to be appointed the enumerator. In the case of registered lodging houses they could recommend the appointment of the keeper or deputy as the enumerator in their plan of division. As with the previous censuses, the special institution schedules in red were still issued, but in two sizes one for 40 names and another for 100 names.

Institutional enumeration books can be viewed on a number of websites, but coverage is not always complete in terms of preliminary matter. *The Genealogist* has digitised title pages and prelim material such as summary tables, enumerator's instructions and declarations as well as the schedules for the 1841–1911 censuses. A survey of the EBPIs for England, Wales, the Channel Islands and the Isle of Man reveals there were several sizes produced for each census.

The institutional books utilised for the 1911 Census in Scotland, were different from what was used in England and Wales and were aligned with the Scottish householder enumeration books. The book for Kirkland Asylum, Bothwell consists of 10 pages with 35 lines for inmates on each page. It has 3 pages of preliminary matter with the geographic data and the title *Enumeration Book for the undermentioned institution or establishment* on page i.

For the 1921 Census, there were changes in regards to the schedules issued to the Chief Resident Officer of institutions. HistPop has schedules from the National Archives (Kew) class RG 27/9 for England and Wales which indicate the following forms were used:

I schedule for institutions for 40 names.
II schedule for institutions for 70 names.
III schedule for institutions for 195 names.
P schedule for prisons for 40 names.
PP schedule for prisons for 70 names.
PPP schedule for prisons for 345 names.
NM schedule for all Armed Forces for 95 officers and other ranks, and 45 persons other than officers and ranks.
NM schedule for all Armed Forces (large).

Separate schedules were issued in Welsh (size CC for 25 names) and in English for Welsh households (size WW and WWW for 25 and 70 names respectively); for the Channel Islands (size AA for 25 names) and for the Isle of Man (size MM for 40 names). These schedules were for large private households, lodging houses, boarding houses, hotels, clubs, and institutions.

The schedules issued for the 1931 Census did not differ greatly from the 1921 Census, though some sizes diverged in terms of spaces for names. In Scotland, enumerators were supplied with the Large Schedule A for families and establishments exceeding 10 persons, but not greater than 30 persons and Schedule B for institutions and large establishments for 50 names and 110 names respectively.

Structure of the Enumeration Books for Public Institutions

As with the household enumeration books, the EBPIs from 1841–1901 for England, Wales, Scotland, Channel Islands and the Isle of Man (and the standalone books in 1911) do not differ greatly in terms of structure or indeed content. The preliminary pages include the name of the institution and its geographic data including address where applicable; the authority under which the census was taken (e.g. The Act for taking the Census...) along with directions for filling up the book; an example of how to fill up the book, tables with the number of males and females per page, and the number of officers, staff, their families, servants and visitors; then the declarations signed by the enumerator, registrar, and superintendent registrar. The 1841 Census did not follow this format entirely and the summary tables and the declarations were included after the institutional return.

With the exception of the 1851 and 1911 Census (which had 20 and 30 lines respectively), each book had 25 lines in which the master or chief officer could enter the names of the inmates, patients, and soldiers etc. The first page of the book recorded the officers their families and staff at the institution. There was often a gap between the end of the staff enumeration and the beginning of the inmates' enumeration, but this was not consistently adhered to and was only directly instructed once for the 1851 Census.

Some large institutions such as the St. Marylebone Workhouse often needed more than one enumeration book to record the large number of inmates within their walls. Notes for "Book 2" and "Book 3" can be found typically on the summary tables page and indicate more than one book was used.

The column structure also largely remained the same as the household returns with some minor differences: there was no column for either a schedule number or an address. Instead, line numbers were added, and the address was incorporated into the geographic data on page i of the preliminary pages. The column headings were adapted from 1851 onward to the various types of institutional return as it evolved from census to census. The initial wording in column one referring to the "Master" and "Head of Institution" became "Chief Resident Officer" by 1901 and changed again by the 1911 Census. The directions for the 1861 Census provided enumerators with the choice of either entering the name and surname of the inmates or their initials. Even though the instruction hadn't been included in the previous enumeration books, enumerators of some asylums and prisons used this method for the 1841 and 1851 censuses.

There was clearly some flexibility when it came to providing initials as shown in the case of Sarah Bradbury who was the proprietress of Earl's Courthouse, Old Brompton. Sarah provided an asylum for rich women suffering from mental health issues and had flatly refused to complete the 1841 Census return saying she acted from motives of delicacy. When she appeared before Kensington Magistrates, she informed the court she preferred to pay the fine rather than distress the friends of the inmates. Prior to her appearance in court the local registrar tried for several weeks to encourage Sarah to complete the schedule, but she ignored him. It was at this juncture the authorities sent a letter informing her the initials of the inmates would suffice. All to no avail, Sarah would not complete the return. Eventually she was fined the full penalty of £5 plus costs and informed the court her friends approved of her determination.[297]

In 1921 there were at least ten asylums enumerating inmates either by initial only or by last name then first name initial. They were: Bicton

Heath, Chester, Lancaster, Hampshire with 1,400 inmates, Mickleover, North Riding, Nottingham with 900 inmates, Rubery Hill with 450 inmates, Sedgefield with 1,284 inmates, and West Riding with 2,250 inmates. The number of inmates for each asylum was estimated by the registrar and included in the plans of division and unless stated may have included staff and officers. The latter were more or less fully enumerated in each institution, though there were exceptions: Sedgefield did not provide full names for its domestic staff. In addition to the lack of full names in the asylums, the places of birth for the vast majority of inmates was given as "not known" or left blank.

For the home barrack returns introduced for the 1911 Census the heading given to column one was "Name in full", but there was also a main heading placed across the page indicating it was a return for officers, soldiers, and the "rank and file". On page 11, after the nominal pages for the officers and soldiers was another page formatted for enumerating the wives, children, servants and the staff such as canteen managers, store men, and housekeepers etc.

An additional table was added to the preliminary pages for the 1911 Census. Similar to the household returns in which householders were instructed to indicate the number of rooms in the dwelling, enumerators were asked to indicate the number and type of rooms in use in the institution or barracks. For barracks this included staff quarters, married quarters and barrack rooms and in other institutions fever wards, the doctor's house, and steward's house. These summary tables can be quite insightful for the researcher. For instance, Stepney Union Workhouse had 787 persons enumerated in total. In the main body of the workhouse there were 489 inmates in 81 rooms and in the sick wards 170 inmates in 32 rooms.

Remuneration

For his time and perhaps for the time spent by his staff on census duties, George Edward Douglas received a fixed fee of 10s. 6d. for each of the three censuses he supervised, but only if he gave a satisfactory performance of all census duties. In addition to the fixed fee he received 2s. 6d. for every 100 inmates enumerated above the initial 300 with proportional parts of 100 being paid at the same rate. In order to receive remuneration, masters and chief resident officers were required to complete a claim form signed by the registrar for the district and by the superintendant registrar before it was sent to the Census Office. Douglas would have anticipated receiving his pay before the end of May 1891 for the 1,500 or so individuals including inmates, officers, and their families who were returned for the 1891 Census.

Though the fixed fee had been a steady 10s. 6d. since 1871 and prior to that 10s., by the 1911 Census it was reduced to 7s. 6d. in England and Wales. In 1921 ex-gratia payments of 10s. for the first 100 persons and then a further 10s. for every 100 persons thereafter was paid to hotels, lodging houses, and institutions not administered by a local authority (RG 27/9). The ex-gratia payments were made to the enumerators of Scottish institutions in 1931 under the same proviso they were not in charge of local authority establishments. For the 1911 Census, Scotland still paid 10s. 6d. (plus the additional fee above the initial 300) in contrast to their counterparts in other areas of Britain and the dependencies.

> You go to some of our old people and shout down their ears, "Where were you born?" he observed, and they say, "I'm pretty well, thank you." *Coventry Telegraph*, 2 April, 1901.

The local and national press revelled in stories about taking the census in workhouses and asylums and in enumerator's accounts about the itinerant poor. Their fascination with the pauper population seemed to satisfy a readership who enjoyed the irreverence of the inmates and their retorts to authority figures, and who wanted to laugh at the comedic depictions of individuals in circumstances so far removed from their own lives. In 1901, the *Sheffield Independent* more or less made this admission by remarking "There was nothing at all out of the way in the lists; the inmates took the matter stolidly, and it would not have been possible to raise a laugh in any single instance." One can sense the writer's disappointment that individuals were sensible and gave no droll responses worthy of reporting.

Elsewhere journalists fared much better. One writing about the Rugby Workhouse in the local advertiser was able to report to his readers one individual who was asked if he was married, replied "No, I'm lucky." While a female in the same institution admitted she had been married three times and disclosed that each of her husbands remarked upon the beauty of her eyes, saying "they would fetch a duck off the water."[298] In 1911 the *Yorkshire Evening Press* reported on the honest admission of a man who told the enumerator he was a "drunkard up to date." Meanwhile in Brighton, it was reported that at the workhouse "there were several queer entries – or there would have been if they had all been allowed to go down." An individual described himself as the "Queen's jester", and when told this wasn't a valid occupation, he insisted on tragedian. While there are no entries in the returns for tragedian, there are a few for other professions within the theatrical sphere, so perhaps he was recorded as one of those. A casual inmate said he was "a knocker and minder" and when asked to elucidate said, "I knocks at doors and minds the policeman" – in other words, he lived by begging. A woman said she was single before adding in resolute handwriting, "Not my fault" and another woman, after describing herself as single, added "Thank goodness!"[299] This suggests the inmates were asked to write down their particulars before the official came around to complete the return.

In many institutions, the inmates were primed in advance of the census date and were encouraged to think about their answers. For the 1911 Census, the master of Leigh Workhouse, Mr France started "in good time and by means of a preliminary discourse with the inmates" informed them they would be asked certain questions hoping to jog their memories as to where they were born, their age, and occupation.[300] In both Sculcoates and Chesterfield workhouses, rough copies or drafts were made first before entering the final details onto the special schedule or into the enumeration book. Transferring details from the rough copy onto the schedule took Mr Rylatt of the Sculcoates Workhouse most of the night of 2 April.

A decade earlier, William James Hill of the Guildford Union Workhouse gathered all the particulars regarding staff and inmates the week before the 1901 Census. This only made it necessary for him to *strike from his list* those who had either left or died before Sunday night.[301] This striking out was not on a rough copy, but on the actual enumeration book. Evidence for this method of enumeration can be found in the returns where three names are crossed out on page 3 and one on page 9 (RG 13/605 F. 64–67). Hill may have been pleased with himself for using this method, but whoever wrote out the return made the mistake of entering all the last names first followed by first name and as a consequence a note was added to the declaration page.

When entering surnames some enumerators grouped individuals together by initial letter of surname; others entered the institution's residents in no apparent alphabetical order but by type of inmate starting with resident paupers, followed by the sick, then the casuals. They may have based their drafts on the quarterly roll of inmates kept by the workhouse. At Firvale Workhouse, the roll and other records were used to check the answers given by inmates. If necessary, relieving officers would also verify the information supplied by individuals. However, problems arose with the very sick who were unable to supply information or with orphans and young children who had no older relatives in the house. At Guildford Union Workhouse it was discovered that few of these children "knew where they first saw the light, and it was only by a knowledge of the parishes from which they came when they entered the house and the fact that they had a settlement, that the enumerator was able to arrive at the probable place of birth."

It is of no surprise given the amount of checking some workhouses undertook that they started the task a week prior to the census. Then, when it came to the census day itself, they began their final verification early on the Sunday. At St. Giles's Workhouse it was reported that having taken all the necessary particulars earlier in the week, the sole remaining task was to check the names on the lists. With the inmates retiring at 8 pm, the only requirement was a tour of the wards to find out who was present and after midnight their names were then written on the return.[302] Evenings were considered the ideal time for making the official return because in theory everyone would be in the institution. However, the system elsewhere wasn't always as efficient as it was at St. Giles. At Firvale Workhouse on the night of 31 March 1901 three individuals escaped enumeration when they failed to observe the rules of the institution and stay within the grounds.

Even though some residents like the Firvale Three didn't always cooperate with the staff, most inmates did with good humour. At Ecclesall Workhouse, sixteen fleeting casual paupers who sought respite for the night, were entered onto the returns late on Sunday. The particulars they gave were surprisingly full and detailed and without any nonsense regarding occupation or birthplace. In fact the list was a model of neat completeness.[303]

Keeping tabs on those who entered the casual wards could be difficult for the officials and the superintendent in charge of the ward at St. Giles's Workhouse kept a rough list open throughout Sunday evening. Late into the night he had already listed thirty-three individuals. Elsewhere, the task was left until the following day. The master of Epsom Workhouse paraded the inmates at 6.30 am on Monday morning and each one was questioned individually.

In hospitals and asylums across Britain the procedures and hurdles were very similar to those demonstrated in the workhouse. In the days leading up to the census, patients and staff were prepared for its arrival by engaging in chat and small talk until the final taking of particulars. When the census day arrived, the system pursued was almost the same in every hospital according to the *Todmorden Advertiser and Hebden Bridge Newsletter* in 1891. A separate schedule was supplied to each ward, which was filled up by the sister. At Guy's Hospital, Southwark the sisters were busiest during the earlier part of the evening and when necessary, had to alter their returns before they were finally handed to the enumerator if there was a death or new arrival. The patients' names, approximate ages, and occupations, were already entered in both the general books of the hospital when they came in, as well as in the smaller records kept by the sisters. This facilitated entering the details of those who were unconscious or so incapacitated they couldn't provide their own particulars, though in some circumstances relatives had to be contacted for information. The official enumerator, Dr John Charles Steele, then toured the wards and stopped here and there with gentle questions regarding the patients' answers.

At the general hospital Tonbridge Wells the census was taken on the Monday morning by the matron who went from bed to bed collecting details from the patients. Likewise, at Surrey County Hospital a special return was used by the matron for the female patients and for the males enumerated by other medical staff.

The quote at the beginning of the chapter from Thomas Martin, the master of the Coventry Workhouse, regarding his old deaf residents is no doubt true and is illustrative of the type of hurdles some institutional enumerators faced. It also highlights the fascination with the elderly and how age was portrayed in the newspapers. Centenarians and near centenarians were regularly reported whenever the workhouse was mentioned. In 1891 the *Newcastle Daily Chronicle* told its readers that Polly Thompson of the Camberwell Workhouse was 104 years of age. Indeed, a Mary Thompson aged 104 can be found on the returns (RG12/472 F.124. p.5). The paper goes on to say that in the "same institution several of the inmates were stated to be 99, 98, 97, and 95 years of age."

Prisons, barracks, and asylums rarely received attention in the newspapers when it came to the census, presumably because they did not generate as much interest, but in 1901 the Birmingham City Asylum received a mention in the *Birmingham Mail*. This was due to an inmate called "old Maria" who was not even included on the census because she had recently died, but the newspaper thought her worthy of recognition. Maria was 90 years of age and was resident in the asylum since it had opened in 1850, having been the first patient to enter through its doors.

In some of the institutions, there was a degree of scepticism about many of the stated ages. At St. Marylebone Workhouse it was reported in 1891 that "there are no reputed centenarians here, but great caution had to [be] exercised in accepting the greatly-advanced years claimed by some of the old folks."[304] This quote sounds like it's from Douglas. At St. Giles's Workhouse, the assistant master responsible for enumerating the inmates told the *Westminster Gazette* there had been no difficulty with women lowering their ages (as seen elsewhere), in fact "it is all the other way. People who enter the workhouse as a rule are more often inclined to overstate their age than otherwise."[305]

Another subject of fascination for the newspaper readership was the former occupations of the inmates. For the 1841 Census enumerators were instructed that after having recorded the details of the master or chief resident officer, their families, and staff, they didn't have to record the occupations of inmates unless they were in hospital. Patient's professions were to be recorded and prefixed with the letter "P". The example page in the 1841 Census institution books indicated how this should be achieved.

In 1851, the instructions were changed and the enumerator was asked to state the ordinary occupation of the inmate before admission in all workhouses, asylums, and hospitals etc. By 1891 if an inmate followed more than one occupation each one had to be recorded in order of their importance or by which the living was mainly earned, but in practice it was not always that simple. At Leigh Workhouse in 1911, the male inmates had worked in such a variety of occupations it was difficult to determine which occupation they strictly belonged to. A decade earlier the officials at Winson Green Gaol were confronted with a different problem when trying to ascertain the trades of the prisoners. Some must have prevaricated about their jobs while others blatantly admitted they had no calling beyond thieving. Meanwhile at Guy's Hospital in 1891 the men were averse to defining themselves as costermongers and requested to be recorded as "fish merchants" or "vegetable dealers".

While practically every trade under the sun was represented in the institutions, it was the most curious that attracted the newspaper editors. In the *Portsmouth Evening News*, it was reported that in the local workhouse there was one John Williams, a Black British subject, born in Barbados, who was an elephant tamer. In keeping with census confidentiality, the newspapers changed the first name of their subject from Robert to John and 61-year-old Robert Williams, the elephant tamer can be located by searching the 1901 Census of Portsmouth Workhouse (RG 13/991 F.32. p.11). Elsewhere in the institution there were governesses, and hospital nurses, and (among several well educated women) a girl who was reputed to be the daughter of a titled lady.[306] For many observers, like our old friend from the *Sheffield Independent* who reported on the lack of humour on show at the workhouse, those who fell on hard times were something of a mystery or to be regarded with scepticism:

> Were the inmates of the Firvale Workhouse isolated from the rest of their kind it is absolutely certain, supposing the information on the census papers to be correct, that they could supply themselves with home manufactured goods of every possible description. One wonders how it is that they come to be in such circumstances, for in no single instance does a full-grown and able-bodied male inmate tacitly confess that he has no craft at all and never had one.[307]

Irrespective of how they came to be in the institution, it was noted by many there was some difficulty in ascertaining where the inmates came *from*. At Chesterfield, Hull, Guildford, and Leigh Workhouses it was a common problem, for some of the elderly had hazy notions of their age, and where they were born. At Guy's Hospital, there were some 500 patients, including many young children, and *one fourth* of them were unable to tell where they were born.

For George Edward Douglas, who made use of the quarterly roll to facilitate the census taking and who encouraged garrulous reminiscing among the inmates at St. Marylebone, places of birth were still a problem. Even though he was knowledgeable and very literate, he still "puzzled over the rural names, pronounced according to local fashions, which have been given to him, generally without the faintest idea of spelling."

Like many other chief resident officers, he was the ultimate administrator of the census in his own institution, but it is clear other staff played their roles. There are at least two separate sets of handwriting in the EBPIs and neither belonged to Douglas. His handwriting only appears on the summary tables and in a number of comments such as writing a child was an orphan or deserted by its mother. It is not surprising in a union as large as St. Marylebone's, which had a master's clerk, a senior clerk, five assistant clerks, and six relieving officers, the work would be spread among the staff. Other institutions were no different.

At Chesterfield Workhouse the information collected in draft form was entered on the schedule under the supervision of the master. At Firvale, the census was taken by the assistant master and staff at the workhouse and was supervised by the stand-in master.

When the "Lithuanian girl", Anna Bordanaitys, left the workhouse on the morning of Sunday, 5 April 1891, her name was still included in the enumeration book. She appears on page 34 and was one of the last inmates out of the 850 or so to be entered into Book One. After completing Book One they still had Book Two with 673 individuals to record, presuming they worked in that order (the books may have been numbered after completion). This suggests the workhouse staff began their efforts early, perhaps one or two days beforehand and hadn't bothered to delete Anna's name when she left.

The institution enumerators were given a few days after the census to make sure everything was in order. In theory any outstanding details about individuals were entered into the enumeration books during this time. If necessary, staff and officers ventured out into the community to call on the family of the institution's residents or to check other records concerning an inmate. In 1891 Douglas and his team were required to make sure the EBPIs were returned to the district registrar by Monday, 13 April. After the census business was finalised institution staff could refocus on their usual duties. For Douglas it was the continuation of over thirty years of work to establish St. Marylebone Workhouse as an exemplar in the humane and intelligent treatment of the poor. To outsiders it became an object-lesson in the Poor Law system, where inmates made their own clothing, made furniture, carried out repairs, bound the books and magazines in the library, and cut and sold firewood for a profit; where the children could indulge in a "palace of toys" for the three weeks they were in the workhouse before being sent off to school and where the elderly inmates were not exposed to the cruel task of oakum picking: a form of hard labour Douglas hated. Instead, the older inmates were given gentle occupations, a bed of their own and a wash kit. If there were couples, they had their own room with a large bed and night-dresses in embroidered red cases. Each room had two armchairs, a chest of drawers, a washstand, and a fireplace with a mantel and ornaments.[308]

When George and Ann Douglas retired in 1894 due to his ill health, they left behind a legacy of kindness and compassion at the workhouse. They were also the oldest master and matron in London, having held their position for over thirty years. Two years after their retirement, Ann died, leaving George to live out his final years in Brondesbury. He died in 1900, following a battle with cancer, and was buried by her side in Marylebone Cemetery.

Just over a decade later the 1911 Census would ask individuals a question about their nationality if they were born in another country. In an institution in Hull, an old inmate requested that, even though he was English, he did not want to be recorded as English. "I have renounced England", he said, "and I now want to be Austrian!" His request was denied.[309] For those who were actually born on foreign land, like the Lithuanian girl, and who chose to come to Britain to settle and work, they would present further challenges for the enumerators.

Chapter Twelve

Movers and Evaders

In 1881, a man sat in a damp and draughty courtyard just off Petticoat Lane, while a jovial woman perched at the bottom of some stairs relayed his questions to her parents in the tenement up above. It was fortuitous, or perhaps the exact reason he was chosen to enumerate the little pockets of European diaspora found along the lane, the man spoke several languages. For in these courts set back from the main thoroughfare were little congregations of Irish, Dutch, Germans, Poles, and Jews, each with their own challenges and difficulties for the enumerator. Like so many of his colleagues navigating the clusters of foreign-born souls, he soon discovered most of the schedules handed to him were blank and he would be looked upon with honest eyes devoid of any comprehension of the process. Thankfully the joyous woman sitting on the steps assisted him with her good grasp of English, shouting, "How old be you, father!" to the elderly gentleman up near the roof. All was going well until the question regarding whether there were any idiots or lunatics in the household sent her into hysterical laughter.[310]

It was of course difficult enough for registrars to find enumerators who fitted the required characteristics let alone ones who were polyglots. For the 1911 Census, registrars were instructed that it was desirable, if possible, to select enumerators with a knowledge of Yiddish. Not only did the enumerator have to hear and distinguish names such as Dabbelovitski and Simanovitch, but they would also receive local street directions from newly arrived migrants who were only conversant in their own tongue. Then, when he finally arrived at his first street, consisting of some eighty houses or so, the enumerator would spend the next four hours in this one street collecting his papers, most of which he had to fill in for the householder. If the enumerator didn't understand a name and asked for it to be spelt, he was met with a limited knowledge of English orthography and a mispronunciation of English letters. One Polish tailor lodging with a Russian family in Leeds could barely muster enough English to make a guess at his own surname.

In some instances it was evident the person could write English well enough, but were disinclined to put pen to paper for fear of some legal consequences; others from nations where conscription was familiar believed they were signing a document of the same kind. Further, there were those suspicious and anxious of being deported leading them to reluctantly give up any information.[311]

Many of their fears were allayed by local rabbis or clergy who held meetings at synagogues and churches in London and Leeds to explain the purpose of the census. Emissaries of the chief rabbi toured east London with the enumerator or ahead of his visit, armed with schedules, ready to complete them for the householder who was unable to write in English. Not that they did so without complaint, "It's worth a guinea an hour!" exclaimed one emissary who was accompanying the enumerator. On his round every room was teeming with migrants, all of whom trooped out into the passages curious to see what was going on. Many had made gallant attempts to fill in the schedule often in "Polish-Hebrew" or "Hebraic-German", and in such a topsy-turvy fashion, amending it was hopeless. Another schedule had to be substituted and held up against the passage wall, while the enumerator put the questions to the interpreter against the din of children playing, and carts rumbling along the stony street. They all laughed and found common ground, bandying jokes until finally an answer was given which was interpreted by the enumerator.[312]

In 1911, large crowds of men, women, and children thronged the east London synagogues and other local institutions in a joint arrangement organised by the census authorities and the Jewish Board of Deputies. There, persons with no grasp of the local language received assistance with their forms from synagogue officials or received advice about completing the schedules.[313] Full example schedules in Yiddish and German were produced for the 1911 Census together with a circular in Yiddish stating where it was possible to obtain assistance in filling up the schedule. For the censuses of 1891 and 1901 brief example household schedules were produced in Yiddish and German for the Jewish population of east London to use as a guide for filling in the normal English household schedule.[314] Where there was no assistance, the next generation stepped in. These were the English-speaking children who were born in various countries while their parents travelled across Europe or in various counties until their parents settled. In one corner of a Polish community, a girl of about ten positioned herself in every room in the house and played the part of interpreter.[315]

A good few of the settlers called themselves British subjects, were proud of it, and would write this on the schedule even if they were not naturalised. But in their homes and community they still held onto their distinct cultures and habits. Along the roads and thoroughfares enumerators were met by black bread filling bakers' windows and little wine shops replete with bottles of Kosher wine and Pommeranz liquor; women absorbed by their house cleaning duties in preparation for Passover which fell during the 1901 Census, or, those working at machines in their rooms whether it be slipper makers, ice cream makers, or countless tailors.[316] There were lodging houses run by "Pashas" and their young apprentices engaged as pedlars or hawkers who canvassed the whole community with their silk wares. There were some opium dens, but these were never described as such on the census schedules.[317] Down the exotic streets of areas such as Pennyfield in Limehouse lived men and women from almost every country on earth. The Chinese seafarers of Limehouse were observed paying homage at mysterious shrines or to the guinea pigs, pigs, and rats kept as religious symbols. While there were some difficulties with the clan names, many of the Chinese men in this area had European English-speaking wives to fill in the schedules. These women had quite a good time according to one newspaper: the Chinese husband takes care of all the household chores efficiently. He cleans floors, chairs, windows, does the dishes, and so on.[318] These were not the only insights the enumerators garnered during their travels around their respective districts, there were snippets of extra information that didn't make the enumeration books. For instance there was a preponderance of affectionate names such as "Solly", "Jakey", "Abey", and "Ikey", and some enumerators soon realised their districts were inhabited by migrants all from the same place. The Irish, who were more or less recorded as being from Ireland on the vast majority of the censuses often specified to the enumerators exactly where they were from. The enumerator for a Whitechapel enumeration district in 1901 discovered his community were mostly from Belfast; in an area of Bolton they were from Dublin, while in a part of Leeds in 1881 an enumerator found the labourers, flax mill hands, and rag sorters were almost exclusively from County Mayo.[319]

Aside from the language and comprehension difficulties, the suspicion and the anxiety, all of which subsided as the nineteenth century progressed, enumerators found their migrant communities affable and willing to help. From the Italians in Dundee to the Polish Jews in Whitechapel, everyone who could assist and make the enumerator's job easier, did what they could do. Of course, there was the odd funny story too:

> "At one house," says an enumerator, "a German lady answered the door, and informed me that she did not speak English. I asked her if there was anybody in the house who spoke English, and she replied, 'Yes, I will send dem.' Another German woman then appeared, and in answer to my question as to how many families there were in the house, promptly replied, "Eighteen shillings."[320]

> "Aye, its all along o' the drink", said one of the deputies... "plenty of men with good trades in their fingers need not have been here but for that." – Lodging House Keeper

On arrival in Britain these migrant families often found refuge in licensed lodging houses or in the house of an occupier with rooms for rent. For enumerators, the initial instructions of how to deal with lodgers who took rooms with families were somewhat ambiguous. Schedules were to be "left at every house in his district for the occupier and where a floor or room is let separately, a separate paper for each occupier of every such floor or room." These instructions from the 1841 Census do not provide any assistance with regards to what to do with those who sub-let from the occupier.

For the 1851 Census the instructions were rewritten and the enumerator was instructed to leave a separate schedule with each occupier. The "occupier" was defined as either the "resident owner or any person who pays rent whether (as a tenant) for the whole of a house or (as a lodger) for any distinct floor or apartment." This was repeated for the 1861 Census, but with additional clarification distinguishing families with servants and visitors, families with servants and boarders at the same table, and sole lodgers or two or more lodgers boarding together.

The 1861 Census instructions were used again in 1871 and 1881, but in Scotland another sentence was appended to the one concerning lodgers, adding "but not occupying the same apartment as the family with whom they lodge." Also in 1871 a distinct reference to licensed lodging houses was inserted: "Visitors staying in hotels or inns are to be included in the schedule to be filled up by the proprietor or manager; and persons in licensed lodging houses are to be returned in the same manner."

In 1891 the enumerator was instructed that a household schedule should be left with "the occupier of a tenement living alone, or for two or more lodgers living together in one tenement." As Edward Higgs points out, the examples given to the enumerator were confusing in light of these instructions. On the one hand the lodger who was in a separate household in 1881 but was still a "lodger" in relationship to the household head was now "head" in his own right.

Clarification was finally achieved for the 1901 Census when enumerators were instructed to leave a household schedule "for a lodger (with or without family) separately occupying a room or rooms, and not boarding with any family in the house." In 1911 this was rephrased and expanded to "every separate Lodger occupying a room or rooms in a house and not boarding with any family in the house. When two or more lodgers share a room or rooms they must be treated for Census purposes as a family."

In many cities there were districts awash with lodging houses. In Glasgow there were men's homes, women's homes, and lodging houses full to capacity when the proprietors took up their pen and ink bottles ready to take the census. Hydepark Street Home had 350 inmates as did North Woodside Model Lodging House; McAlpine Street Working Men's Private House had 336 lodgers and in the Female House in Carrick Street there were 88; Portugal Street Model Lodging House had 345 lodgers, while the Model Lodging House for Females in East Russell Street had 127 women sleeping overnight. While no doubt referencing some of the cheaper houses, the *Glasgow Herald* warned that many of the returns from the lodging houses were erroneous. Some through stupidity, some through design, with many keepers understating the number of lodgers under their roof for fear of the law and any fines coming their way.[321]

It was often stated that those who kept a lodger or two at home were reticent to reveal to the enumerator that they had a lodger when he or she delivered the schedules. Subsequently, they discovered they may face a fine for concealment and so when the enumerator came to collect the schedule, they were more forthcoming with the information. Then there was a mad rush to gather the required details from the lodger (if he or she was still there) and add it to one of the spare schedules the enumerator carried in their bag. There may have been many reasons for lodger denial: overcrowding and illegal subletting made individuals nervous, but confidentiality may have been a factor. One woman who first denied she had a lodger ran after the enumerator and explained her denial, informing him she thought he was a detective. Elsewhere it was reported that many householders had described their lodgers as visitors – perhaps for the same reasons as above.[322]

It was not unknown for enumerators to receive verbal abuse when enquiring about lodgers. In Manchester in 1891 an enumerator enquired of a lady if she had any lodgers to which she replied, with considerable wrath, "No, never had, and don't want any."[323] Such sentiments were repeated elsewhere.

Like Glasgow, Edinburgh had a number of lodging houses of varying quality. At the cheaper end, there were some filled with 100 persons, three to a room and two persons to a bed. Ventilation was poor and the odour was likened to rivalling the sewers. In one particular house the task of taking the details of each lodger extended well into the night due to half the inhabitants having gone to bed. A good many were not happy to be disturbed by a knock on the door. Those who were still up, gathered together around old stoves in rooms strewn with sawdust upon the floor, found the whole process amusing, particularly when asked about age, employment, and marriage. Unmarried women were found to be reluctant to reveal their age in front of male lodgers.

According to one newspaper, the proprietress of a boarding house in London devised an original plan for recording the ages of her guests in confidence. She coated the edges of the schedule with gum, and after each boarder entered their details, they moistened the gum, and gently folded the paper so their particulars were completely hidden from view. After all the boarders were entered onto the schedule, the document was placed in an envelope and sealed. When the enumerator called to collect the schedule, he or she had to cut the edges with a pair of scissors before they could see the written contents![324]

It was not just the ladies who were touchy about their ages. In one establishment, where a privacy screen was erected in the drawing-room, the resident ladies completed their census duty without much protest. The men on the other hand were prone to levity, to evasion, to giving ridiculous answers, and some even objected to being disturbed during a game of bridge. While it tried the patience of the proprietress, after some cajoling and some entreating, she managed to get the process complete, though not before commenting, "Oh, these men... they are much more touchy about their ages than the women are."

In Sheffield in 1911, the manager of a lodging house in one district engaged an assistant to take the particulars of the 300 or so men who made up his "little family" when they paid their 4d. for the privilege of a bed. The manager then transferred the details to the schedule. He found that determining their ages was the most difficult task because many only had a vague idea of their birth year (or so they said) and made their best guess. Some were also rather hazy about where they were born. In contrast, they were eager to have their correct names stated. "Not one in twenty using the lodging-house gives his right name", said the manager, "and the world does not know that half of them are alive. But as soon as they knew that I was taking the census, they would say, 'Come here, I'll give thee my right name. It may be wanted if I get t'owd age pension.'" The manager found men who had assumed a common alias like Brown would then submit a fancy surname. Yet he was quick to say few, if any, of his residents had fallen from the high ranks, many were hawkers, navvies, cutlers, butchers, shoeblacks, and bottle-sorters. Just a handful were former bankers or veterinary surgeons. Quite a considerable number of them were farm labourers who were too old for regular employment, and who made a living following thrashing machines from one farm to another within a radius of 5 or 6 miles of Sheffield. In the summer they were employed in hay-making. It was said that many of these men were not the type to get married and entries in the "married or single" column consisted almost entirely of a continuous line of "singles". They spent their time roaming up and down the country remaining single all their lives, though some of them had escaped relationships and wore the mask of single status.[325]

> Doubtless amongst the outcast population a considerable portion have brought the misery upon themselves by idleness, dishonesty, and intemperance.
>
> *Illustrated Times*, 13 April 1861

For those not lucky enough to have a bed for the night, who roamed the streets with nowhere else to go, the early census returns made no special effort to record them. For the 1841 Census, the enumerators were instructed to state in their summary tables the number of persons sleeping in barns, sheds, tents or in the open air, or anyone not in a dwelling house. No particulars were taken. For those travelling overnight, enquiries were made with railway, canal, and coaching companies to get an idea of the numbers on the move. The system remained the same for the 1851 Census, however those who were travelling would have their details taken where they stopped, or at their hotel or residence the next morning. This also applied to night workers. The Census Office continued to use this method for recording travellers for the rest of the century. For the 1861 Census, those sleeping rough were fully enumerated and their particulars were given in the CEBs under the heading "List of Persons not in houses"; in 1871 individuals were entered where they were found in the roads, fields, and outhouses where they slept.

In 1891, the Census Office called for assistance from local police forces to help with policing "low neighbourhoods" when the enumerator was at large and to also assist with returning the number of "houseless persons sleeping in the open air." This request was repeated in 1901 where specifically they were asked to record on a schedule the sex, age, and where the person was found sleeping on 1 April 1901. This information was then given to the enumerator when he or she called at the police station.

In 1910, after considering the difficulties of enumerating the homeless, the Census Office asked the then Home Secretary, Winston Churchill for police assistance during the forthcoming census. It was agreed the police would only record those persons sleeping in barns, sheds, kilns, under railway arches and in the open; any individual or family sleeping in vans or tents etc. would be returned by the regular enumerator. For this duty, the police were issued with special instructions and the Police Return of Homeless Persons schedules based on the normal household schedule used in 1911, but with adaptations. The same requests for police assistance were made in 1921 and 1931.

In some quarters the police assistance in 1901 was considered something of a failure, with news of their arrival clearing the streets of Westminster faster than a blizzard. The homeless were not in their usual spots such as Piccadilly and the embankment at Lambeth. Despite an organised police presence very few homeless were actually recorded by the end of the night. Those further north thought they had found the answer or one possible explanation at least. It was stated the empty streets were due to the weekend influx of individuals entering the casual wards of the workhouse. A vagrant would enter the casual ward on Saturday, have a rest on Sunday, and only do a few hours' work on the Monday morning. If he or she entered on any other day they would be compelled to do two days' work.[326]

For many, the Vagrancy Act would have been sufficient cause for them to find a hideaway in some secret nook for the night. Some of these recesses were unknown to the police and the homeless could confidently avoid the census, but others, where the daily congregations of the homeless met, were familiar to the authorities. In 1911, a miserable crowd of men gathered in search of warmth found around the coke ovens in Attercliffe Road, Sheffield. In the small hours of the morning their rest was disturbed by the sound of a policeman's voice as the officers formed a ring around the ovens. Some of the homeless managed to slip away unnoticed, but the rest, a hundred or so sullen men were marshalled, handcuffed, and led to the police station. Here they reluctantly gave up information about themselves or professed they didn't know their age before spending the night in the cells. A few days later they appeared in front of the magistrate to answer a charge of sleeping out. They were used to it. The raids came frequently and many of them had notched up a number of previous convictions for the same charge, but where could they go?[327] The Salvation Army and Mission Halls offered some respite in the form of soup and shelter, but not everyone was so lucky to find a place.

Fifty years earlier, in the London rookeries those found wandering the street were sometimes the sick who were unable to pay for lodgings after their discharge from hospital, the orphan who had no guardian or the ill-treated child turned out by a parent. Some of the children gathered together by the vegetable markets, looking for food scraps, while others took possession of ruined or deserted buildings. The census authorities knew they were lucky to capture such unfortunates on the census. In general the system worked well and few slipped through the net even if they were living in places that didn't officially exist.

> ...the train passes the station of Batty Green – or Batty Wife Green, a village created by the railway operations, for before the advent of the navvy there was nothing but purple billowy moorland for many mile and no sign of habitation to be seen.
> *Carlisle Express and Examiner*, 6 May 1876.

In 1891, quarryman and lodging housekeeper William Goddard was enumerated with his "spouse" Eleanor at their home in Stoney Middleton. Aside from their 6-year-old son, there were twelve lodgers clearly providing an income for William and Eleanor. However, due to the nefarious types of individuals who frequented the lodging house, being a lodging housekeeper wasn't a safe occupation. In 1887, Eleanor discovered this to her cost when she was stabbed in the arm by one of the drunk lodgers who also attempted to stab her in the head. Thankfully she survived this encounter.

In 1881, William Goddard's life had been very different. He was enumerated as single and was himself a lodger working as an iron miner in Ulverston. On the face of it, the census entry for William seems straightforward enough, though as ever with a census snapshot, there was more to William's life than on display. Miles away in Hardingstone, Northamptonshire was his estranged wife Dora and her new man Joseph. William and Dora must have parted ways sometime after 1871 because on that census, they were located far from where they were born at a place called "Jericho" at Ingleton Falls. William was working as a miner on the railways and was surrounded by railway labourers who had migrated to the very same spot from across Britain, Ireland, and the furthest reaches of the empire. For such hazardous work, the men might have anticipated earning between 3s. and 6s. per day.

This body of workers had assembled for the construction of the Settle and Carlisle Railway. Their numbers inflated the population returns of many local townships from Crosby Garret where out of 580 inhabitants, 364 were railway workers, to Ingleton which saw an increase of 1,247 souls from the 1861 to the 1871 Census. The construction of the railway was divided into four separate contracts or sections of the track, the first of which was 17¼ miles in length starting from Settle. The engineers were undaunted by the challenge of cutting through the peaks and dales of the Pennine chain and paid a high wage to find men and families willing to spend the winter on the bleak, remote, and often treeless moorland, where peaty bogs could swallow a horse up to his belly. Many of the workers, including some from foreign shores, professed they had never visited such a wild place before.

Alongside the construction, temporary settlements for the workers were expedited. At the wonderfully named Batty Wife Green, which stood beneath Great Whernside, 500 to 600 navvies and their families lived in scattered wooden huts covered in black felt. Nearby, wooden services were built in the form of a mission-house, schools, library, post office, hospital, a hotel, and a good few pubs. Pedlars and purveyors of provisions sold their goods and produce, while temporary tram lines were laid to carry goods, railway materials, and people across the muddy valleys and peaks. Despite these attempts to provide everything the residents might need, Batty Wife Green was not a safe place. During the course of construction there were a number of murders and crimes including a fatal dispute between English and Irish navvies. The inhabitants also had to cope with a smallpox outbreak and a number of accidents. Not far from Batty Wife Green were other wonderfully named temporary settlements: Sebastopol, Jerusalem, Inkerman, Salt Lake, Belgravia, Winterscales, Oxgang Huts, and many many others including William and Dora Goddard's own settlement at Jericho near the Blea Moor sidings.

On Monday, 3 April 1871, the temperature dropped with the advent of low pressure. The wind changed direction from a westerly to a north-easterly bringing with it plenty of cloud and rain and some sleet on the coasts. Up on Blea Moor where it was devoid of cover, the wind must have been a challenge for the enumerator as were any conditions under foot. If Thomas Taylor was from Ingleton, getting to Blea Moor was a trek even by cart or trap. If he had travelled in the evening to catch the men finishing their work, he may have benefited from about two hours of light in which to collect and check the schedules before the dark made conditions worse. With the elements bearing down on him, Thomas traipsed from hut to hut. He noted there were 560 individuals "temporarily present" in his district out of 688. He visited a number of local farming families scattered across the Ingleton Falls township before encountering his first railway family at Blea Moor Huts. The head of the household was John Richardson, an engine driver and a native of Scotland. No exact place of birth was supplied in this instance, nor were there in many other instances in the enumeration books, only "north Wales", "south Wales", "London", "Middlesex", were given. In one instance, Taylor gives a place of birth as "Ashover, Denbyshire", which was corrected by another hand to Derbyshire; he also writes "Campden, Middlesex" instead of Camden, "Havershot" instead of Evershot, and "Boslem" for Burslem. On another occasion he writes Hammersmith as a county and records other places without adding the correct county. There were also inconsistencies when numbering the huts in Jericho and Jordan. Some were numbered, some were not. This may have been down to the inhabitants or the builders though, with many not bothering to number their accommodation. By the time Taylor arrived at writing up Sebastopol in his CEB he was flagging, entering ages in the wrong column and no doubt wishing it was all over.

At Batty Wife Hole, enumerator Thomas Moore, had 349 migrant workers out of a total number of 437. He experienced a similar wide variety of places of birth and lack of detail, supplying just counties in some instances. He seems more accurate than Taylor – though both men through their work reveal the difficulties enumerators encountered not just with overseas visitors, but with large internal migration. Local knowledge was definitely an advantage for enumerators and it's not difficult to feel some sympathy for Moore and Taylor.

I won't see him; I don't want to see him.

In Brighton, an elderly couple irritated at the appearance of the enumerator during the 1901 Census, loudly refused to cooperate. Neither of them could read or write and would not impart any information about themselves which resulted in a deadlock. The census authorities were aware the vast majority of census refusals and stalemates were either down to ignorance, not willing to admit to misunderstanding the schedule, or for fear of revealing information such as illiteracy, age, and places of birth etc. Where possible they took a softly, softly approach. In Brighton, the enumerator carefully and patiently explained to the couple why he was there and what happened to the information they gave him. The deadlock was broken and the couple complied.[328]

Sometimes, enumerators could see off a potential rebellion if they told the householder they would fill in the form on their behalf. This suggests illiteracy, in the minds of the householder, was a major factor when refusing to cooperate. If cajoling failed, the enumerator returned to their registrar to report the incident but would then be told to visit the household again, perhaps with a little advice on how to tackle the situation. This guidance might be the threat of a visit from the police in addition to a reminder of the £5 penalty for refusing to comply with the census regulations.

In the meantime, the householder has gone outside to consult with neighbours for another opinion of the nature and purpose of the census. After having understood all that and noting the neighbour's opinion whether it was an infringement of personal liberty or not, the householder was much more obliging when the enumerator called and there was no need for the cops. As the *Birmingham Mail* commented, "Very rarely indeed has it been found necessary in the past to resort to prosecution."

The threat of the fine could mollify the most stubborn of householders. In Wales in 1901, someone wrote "Mind your own business" across the schedule but soon changed their mind about the whole process when told about the penalty.[329] One man danced on the schedule, others tore theirs up, and a householder in Berkshire refused to disclose his name, age, and occupation while impertinently asking why he should have to fill up the paper and get nothing for it, while the enumerator was paid for collecting the same? All complied for fear of the £5. Sometimes though, this did not resolve the issue, and the next stage was for the registrar to make a personal call. If they still refused to complete a schedule, a decision would be made as to whether to issue proceedings against the householder.[330]

Out of all of those prosecuted, the most high-profile personality was Sir Ernest Benn publisher and president of the Society for Individual Freedom, and uncle of British politician Anthony Wedgwood Benn. Benn was fined £5 with two guineas costs after receiving two summonses. The first summons was for "being a person required by the Census Order (1950) to make a return for the purpose of the Census Act (1920) [and who] did refuse to make the said return" and the second alleged that he failed to give an enumerator such information as might reasonably be required for the purpose of his duties. He pleaded guilty to the first summons. It was explained in court he had received the schedule and was unavailable when the enumerator called on Monday, 9 April, 1951. The enumerator having discovered Benn was absent was given the blank schedule by a member of the household. On it Benn had written: "In view of the critical state of the national economy, 1 must refuse to take any part in this unnecessary waste of manpower, money, paper, and print." Ernest Benn, Oxted, 8 April, 1951.

On 12 April, the enumerator returned with a census officer to try to persuade him to change his mind, to which Benn responded, "How can I?" The court was later told Benn had been a champion of individual liberty all of his life. While he believed the census mattered in 1851, he thought it was unnecessary 100 years later due to other means of data gathering such as identity cards, and birth and death registration. Benn accepted the court's decision without argument, telling a reporter, "I was quite prepared for this. I have gone into it with my eyes wide open. For me there are two important questions – the growth of snooping into personal matters, and above all, the great question of public economy."[331]

In the spring of 1951, a letter written by Benn appeared in several regional newspapers protesting the cost and purpose of the census. He stated he would be sticking to his convictions and not complying with the Census Act. It received enough traction to prompt census officials into writing a response drawing attention to the numerous inaccuracies in the letter.[332] Still, Benn's letter may have had an impact in some quarters. Referring to a "Member of Parliament", which Benn wasn't, but could easily have been mistaken for one, refusers Violet Katherina Adams and Rowena Beverly Garwood, were both fined £2 with 18s. costs for refusing to complete a schedule. Both women stated they would have nothing to do with filling out the census schedule when the enumerator called at their home in Llanboidy. Upon seeing the enumerator from her window, Garwood came down the stairs and gave him a press cutting stating she was entirely in agreement with the article and that the census was just "nosey business". Neither of the women went to court and their case was heard without them being present.[333]

In 1841 Mr Clavering of Regent Quadrant in Piccadilly appeared before the magistrate for refusing to answer whether he had made a true return or not. Upon being told about the penalty, he strongly objected to the government for having enacted in law such a prying procedure. It was argued that given Mr Clavering's respectable circumstances he should receive the highest penalty and the magistrate agreed fining the hosier £5. Despite a third-party appearing to claim that Clavering was not in the flourishing circumstances stated and a softer fine was due, the magistrate was not inclined to alter his position.[334]

In 1901, Miss E. Kirby of Westminster refused to fill up her schedule because she did not believe in the census and further, thought it was a hoax given collection day fell on April Fool's Day (a hindrance suffered by many enumerators in 1901). After informing the enumerator of her opinion and that she was aware of the Census Act, she tore up the schedule, further stating she preferred to be summoned. Even though the prosecutor asked for a high penalty to deter others and to prevent such attitudes spreading, Miss Kirby was only fined 20s. and 44s. costs.[335]

Francis Gordon Pratt of Bayswater refused to give information about his servants or allow the enumerator access to them for the 1921 Census. He ordered the enumerator out of his house and wrote a four-page letter to the authorities, attacking the Government and declaring he had no more time to learn the details about his servants than he had to learn how to play the piano. In court, Pratt's solicitor pleaded that the defendant had acted under misapprehension to his rights under the Act and was finally willing to give the information. The court decided Pratt missed his chance and he was fined £5 with four guineas for costs.[336] Pratt wasn't the only one back-pedalling in court trying to avoid the fine by complying at the last minute. Others tried, but they were either fined the full amount or a reduced amount depending on their circumstances.

Rather than risk the fine, newspapers reported some individuals made themselves absent on the night of the census, sometimes by staying out and not being accounted for the following morning. Such tactics were used by the Suffragettes in 1911, though it was not the only one.

At the Bath branch of the Women's Social and Political Union, their president Mrs Mildred Mansel rented 12 Lansdown Crescent a few days before the census was due on 2 April 1911. Money was raised to cover the expenses of renting the house and to cover the penalty of evading the census should they need to go to court. From the outside, the residence appeared empty; the unfurnished rooms on the ground floor and basement showed no signs of occupation, while the windows on the first and second floors were shuttered. Leaving the ground floor empty was part of the ruse.

Behind those shuttered windows Mildred and her assistant Mrs Cave managed to create a congenial setting for census night. Thick tapestry curtains were hung over the shutters, carpet was laid, and a chandelier was hung from the ceiling. Over the fireplace they mounted the motto of the Women's Social and Political Union and in one corner of a room they placed a piano. In front of a speaker's table, they arrange a number of chairs for a meeting. They also acquired a few lounge chairs and some Chesterfields with cushions. All of this furniture was loaned to them. Any food they used was also donated with one lady providing cooked fowls, another lady contributing a ham, while others gave a quantity of butter and a number of eggs. In order to bring in the furniture and supplies without being noticed, Mrs Cave employed a few dedicated and sympathetic individuals to assist with the undertaking. It was agreed Mildred would act as "head of the family" when the census schedule arrived and that on the evening of the census, she would be joined by her "friends" about 9 pm. They would all drift away during the morning so that when the enumerator arrived Mildred, the only one in the house, would take the schedule from the mantelpiece and hand it to him. On it she wrote "No vote, no census" to which someone in another hand added "Cheers!"

It was asserted by an anti-suffragist speaker that no woman could stand the strain of an all-night sitting, but Mildred's ladies showed them. Such was their determination, one lady walked to Lansdown from 7 miles away just to be there, while another drove 10 miles. Many left their homes after fixing notices to their door displaying "deserted by women who want the vote." They all arrived to hear Mildred's address delivered at 9.30 pm and to listen to readings, music, and speeches. This was followed by supper at 11 pm and another about 1.30 am in the morning. As the early hours came, some ladies left, leaving by both the front and back doors. It was thought that no one began to watch the house until 8 am on Monday morning. From then until noon, policemen in shifts observed the house and signalled to another policeman if they saw anyone leave. The authorities used this tactic to watch other known suffragette houses and count the numbers coming and going. At Lansdown, the enumerator called in on Mildred at 11.30 am and when met with the "No Vote, no Census" note reminded her of the £5 penalty, leaving without argument. Mildred and Mrs Cave left shortly afterwards.

After Mildred signed the schedule, she added "with whom are a number of Suffragists who are boycotting the Census as a protest against the disenfranchisement of qualified women." The remainder of the schedule was completed by Registrar Mr Glover who stated the police best estimates for the number of women in the house was thirty-five. Mildred and her fellow suffragists considered the ruse at 12 Lansdown Crescent to have been successful despite a number of ladies on Sunday evening mistakenly ringing the bell at 12 Lansdown Place East, the residence of the archdeacon of Bath!

The census authorities accepted that suffragist action would be a problem for enumerators and the best approach was for the enumerator to read the penalty notice and walk away. These men and women were open to abuse at the best of times, and it was wise to avoid inflaming the agitators and placing the enumerator in danger. For the very few, death, suicide, injury, and assault were unexpected events that came with the job.[337]

Chapter Thirteen

Dangers, Troubles, and Death

On 5 April 1911, Registrar John H. Brentnall sent an urgent telegram addressed to the secretary at the Census Office at Millbank in which he wrote, "Marton, Enumerator lying unconscious through trap accident, can his son act?"[338] The son in question, Frank Brunton, was somewhat esteemed, according to Brentnall, given that he was an assistant overseer and a collector of income tax.

Just a couple of days earlier, Frank wrote out his schedule for himself and his family plus the four servants he employed on his farm at Marton, near Scunthorpe. At nearby Prissick House, his widowed father Robert had done the same, recording his three daughters and nine servants who undertook various duties on his farm. One of the servants was groom Thomas Collingwood, who Robert enlisted to help him collect the census papers on the Monday afternoon. The pair jumped into Robert's two-wheeled spring trap and set off touring the district. While Robert was off gathering the schedules, Thomas noticed the back-band of the trap's harness was worn at the edges. He alerted Robert, but the farmer was not too bothered saying he thought it would last the rest of the day, and so they continued on with the collection and returned home after several hours. Later that day, when the light was dying, they went out once more and got just 20 yards from the house when the back-band finally broke, alarming the horse who rushed forward and to the left with fright. Thomas was thrown from the trap and upon recovering he observed the horse gathering pace and dragging Robert who was trying to get out of the swerving vehicle. It was to no avail, Robert was propelled from the trap onto his head and fractured the base of his skull. He was carried indoors and lay unconscious for another day.[339]

Subsequent to his previous telegram, Brentnall contacted the Census Office again: "Confirming my telegram of this morning respecting the accident to Mr Robert Brunton, my Marton enumerator, whom I said was lying in an unconscious state, has, I am sorry to say died, and I have seen my Superintendent, and he says I could do no better than get his son... who is very reliable... and arrange with him to complete the census."[340]

On 10 April, Brentnall forwarded a letter to the Census Office from solicitor Albert Forbes who was engaged by Robert's dependents to seek compensation from the government. The Brunton's claim, along with those who suffered minor injuries, was forwarded by Bernard Mallet, the Registrar General, to the Lords Commissioners of His Majesty's Treasury. These were then considered using the Workmen's Compensation Act of 1906 as a guide for issuing compensation.

It was Joseph Chamberlain who said it was "most desirable in the interests of the Unionists [Conservative] party that this question [of industrial accidents] should be finally settled." After years of campaigning, though without any pressure from labour leaders interested in the welfare of workers, Chamberlain's quest for an effective compensation scheme resulted in the Workmen's Compensation Act of 1897.

Following the foundation of the Trades Union Congress in 1868, increased canvassing for adequate compensation for accidents at work eventually led to the Employers' Liability Act of 1880. The Act only went a short way in covering the needs of those unfortunate enough to meet with an accident; little more than half of the injuries were covered, offering up to three years' wages in damages only if the employer or an authorised foreman had been negligent.

Chamberlain's revisions for the Act of 1897 were put forward on the basis that compensation would be awarded irrespective of the cause of the accident, that an employee would be entitled to compensation for any accident, even if there was no negligence on the part of the employer. The 1897 Act still had its shortcomings, those who qualified were mainly engaged in industrial occupations. Therefore the subsequent Act of 1906 widened its provisions defining a "workman" as "any person who has entered into or works under a contract of service or apprenticeship with an employer, whether by way of manual labour, clerical work, or otherwise, and whether the contract is expressed or implied, is oral, or in writing." Under Section 13, the definition of "employer" included any body of persons corporate or unincorporated including the Crown, though the armed forces could not claim compensation from the latter.

A year before the 1911 Census, there were rumblings of discontent among registrars anxious they would be liable under the Workmen's Compensation Act of 1906 should an enumerator meet with an accident while on duty. On 8 March 1910, the Registrar General Bernard Mallet wrote to the Local Government Board requesting advice on the matter so he could reassure the Registrars' Association who had raised a concern. He quickly received a response from the Board explaining they didn't have authority to give advice.[341] What happened thereafter was an exchange of correspondence between the Treasury, the Registrar General's office for England and Wales, the Registrar General for Scotland, and insurance companies which didn't cease until early 1911. On 7 May 1910, Mallet sent a request to the Treasury solicitor for clarification and was told neither the registrars nor the state were liable for enumerator's injuries. Confirmation of this was also sent to the Lords Commissioners of the Treasury and to the Registrars' Association. Some were still not convinced. An official at the Treasury wrote in the departmental discussion notes, that if the enumerator was casually employed for the census on behalf of the state, it seemed to follow he was a workman. Further, he queried, doesn't that mean he had a contract with the state?[342]

By June 1910, the Lords Commissioners of the Treasury had set out their position based on the Treasury solicitor's advice and informed the Registrar General with the expectation it would be forwarded on to the registrars. It soon became apparent to the Treasury the registrars hadn't been informed. On 21 October 1910, they received a letter from the Royal Insurance Company stating the company had received enquiries from registrars as to whether they were willing to insure against liabilities and would the Treasury confirm whether registrars were liable?[343] The Treasury responded to the enquiry affirming their position and additionally declaring that should an enumerator become injured while on duty, they would be paid from public funds.[344] It is worth noting that the Registrar General was informed it wasn't desirable to publicly quote the Treasury solicitor's opinion as to whether registrars were liable. This was because the advice was "unofficial". Therefore there was some reluctance to disseminate information and as a consequence queries were still landing on the desk of the Registrar General in January 1911 from bodies such as the Office of Guardians of the Poor.

The Treasury admitted privately that in the case of Crown "business" the law had not been tested, but there was a precedent. Prior to the discussion concerning enumerators, the government had already compensated the casual labourers who were employed coaling for the Admiralty.

As far as the Treasury was concerned, it was deemed necessary to avoid future escalating costs should they offer no form of compensation to enumerators: "I think we shall either have to deal with them extra-statutorily or take some special power to compensate them if injured. (If we refuse to admit any liability we shall raise the price of their services)."[345]

In January 1911, the Treasury stated that all claims received by registrars from enumerators were to be forwarded to them.[346] Treasury officials would then administer the claims by using the Workmen's Compensation Act as a basis without admission of legal liability. If enumerators were unhappy with their settlements, they were at liberty to take legal proceedings. The compensation would be calculated upon their average weekly earnings as an enumerator plus their loss of earnings under other employers where enumerators were employed. The Lords Commissioners proposed to allow the aforementioned compensation to run from the day of the injury until after their employment as enumerators had ceased.[347]

On 12 April 1911, Mallet forwarded the claims of the Brunton family plus two other claims from injured enumerators to the Treasury. In total just seven claims were eventually sent to the Lords of the Treasury for consideration out of the 40,000 enumerators employed for the 1911 Census. One claim was rejected before it could make the list and it's also possible there were other accidents, but the enumerators concerned thought their injuries were too trifling to make a claim.

Of all the claims, the Brunton case had the greatest degree of severity; not only because the family had suffered a great tragedy, but because his three adult daughters Susan Ellen Brunton, Elizabeth Brunton, and Mabel Brunton were wholly dependent on their father for money, food, and home. Their brother Frank who took over his father's duties on that fateful day was eventually paid £2. 3s. 2d. for his time as an enumerator,[348] but the daughters were forced to wait before receiving any of their father's money plus compensation. To calculate the compensation it was necessary to know what Robert had earned during the previous three years and therefore the wait was due to the administrative cogs turning and turning very slowly indeed. The Brunton family were eventually paid the sum of £300 by the Treasury Solicitor on 25 September 1911.[349]

The majority of the other claims were either due to falls or dog bites. Enumerator Neate was on his rounds when he fell over a door-step and injured his right arm and was treated in hospital; enumerator Simons received a bite on his ankle after a dog rushed at him; enumerator Kirsop slipped on a banana skin (yes, really) and injured his head, foot, and dislocated his finger; enumerator Ridley's hand was crushed by a door slamming as he entered a house; enumerator Fenwick slipped in an uncovered gully hole and injured his right arm; enumerator Butcher was also bitten by a dog; enumerators Williams and Cook had bike accidents; finally, enumerator McMurtrie was descending the stairs at 75 Rose Street, Glasgow when he slipped, fell, and injured his arm.

Some of the claimants were still able to complete or partially complete their census duties, often with the assistance of friends or family. Despite being covered in water and mud, and having a suspected sprained wrist, Fenwick nobly trudged on and was able to finish the collection of his schedules. He returned home but was unable to do anything for two days. He then managed to write up and deliver his enumeration book by Saturday 8 April. Three days later, Fenwick visited his registrar with a medical certificate claiming he was unable to follow his usual employment as a gentleman's private secretary. On 28 April, he wrote to the registrar citing a loss in earnings of £9 plus "the damage which was done to my trousers, the surgeon and other expenses which I incurred at one sovereign."[350]

Fenwick and most of the other claims were awarded on top of their enumerators fees £1 per week backdated from 4 April in June 1911. The exceptions were Kirsop who received 12s. 5d. per week backdated from 4 April, Cooke who received 12s. for the same period, Neate who wasn't disabled by his injuries and was initially refused compensation eventually received 11s. 9d., and Williams and McMurtrie who were awaiting a decision pending a medical examination.[351]

To investigate the veracity of the claims regional Post Office medical officers were employed at a rate of 10s. each per claim. The injuries to McMurtrie and Williams were both deemed suspicious and they were asked to submit to a medical examination in June 1911. The reports that followed indicate both men had received significant damage from their accidents; Williams in particular had cuts and contusions on his face and knee, a badly sprained right arm, and had suffered the loss of two teeth. He was confined to his house for 14 days.[352] He was eventually awarded 3s. 10d. a week for the period from 4 April until 16 July.[353]

Registrar General Bernard Mallet was asked by the Treasury to fund all the compensation payments from his own department's payment codes. On 14 June 1911, he wrote to the Treasury to object to the direction, writing nothing was provided in the budget estimate to cover such claims because "he was expressly told neither the registrars nor my office would be liable in any way under the [Workmen's Compensation] Act."[354] He also pointed out he was told to just send the claims to the Treasury for them to deal with, which of course they had now contradicted. Eventually, an agreement was made between the two departments whereby the Registrar General's office would make the payments and the money was subsequently reclaimed from the Treasury.

In 1921, the same procedure for compensation was repeated for the census of that year. For the 1931 Census, any lump sum payments such as that given to the Brunton family in 1911, were treated in accordance with the passing of the Workmen's Compensation Acts of 1923 and 1925. In particular Section 25 of the 1925 Act meant that all settlements had to be registered at the local county court. This meant that if an enumerator was to pursue a claim, the Registrar General's officials were now required to complete new forms.

In light of this, one Treasury official told a counterpart at the General Register Office on 15 May 1931, "It seems therefore that we shall have now to regard the Enumerators as formally subject to the Workmen's Compensation Act."[355] However, the Lords Commissioners of His Majesty's Treasury still persisted with using the Act as a basis without the admission of legal liability. They qualified their decision by stating there were doubts whether a census enumerator was a workman within the meaning of the Act. Fast forward to 24 November 1931 and a letter from the Treasury to the Registrar General's office, which states the Lords, "in view of the W.C.A. 1925, were advised it was a matter of *doubt* that enumerators were *not* within the provisions of the Act [emphasis added]."[356]

By this date, though, the majority of the thirty or so claims received from enumerators working on the 1931 Census were reduced either by their lack of response to further enquiries about their accidents or by a dismissal of their claim. No further action was taken in a large majority of the cases. Two enumerators, Pennington and Wright received £2 and 7s. 6d. respectively for damaged clothing; Pennington's coat had become entangled in a garden gate and was torn, while Wright was attacked by a dog. In the case of J.G. Russell, the 60-year-old enumerator for Dingwall, he was awarded £5 for a bite on his left leg received by a dog belonging to the owner of Easter Blackwells farm. By far the two most time-consuming cases for the Treasury and the Registrar General's office concerned enumerators Gozney and Henry. Gozney slipped and fell down three wet steps following a downpour while delivering schedules in Worksop, and Henry fell off a bus near Denville Havant and damaged his knees, apportioning blame to the heaviness of the census materials he was carrying. Their cases were not settled until the end of 1931: Gozney received £3 in compensation and Henry was awarded £7.[357]

This gentleman has our sympathy.

Many individuals signing up to be enumerators underestimated the toll the work would take on themselves both physically and mentally. Those who were already in a fragile state of mind were vulnerable. In 1961 an ex-army sergeant major found himself wandering the streets of Aldershot for four days after disappearing from his census rounds in the Reading area. He had managed to deliver his compliment of schedules, but when it came to collecting them and helping people with the questions and answers, he said the job became too much for him. Somehow, he managed to catch a bus back from Aldershot to Reading and reported his situation to the police. The Census Office stated that in the end everything was all right, extending their sympathy to the gentleman and his plight.[358]

He appears to have survived, but others cut their lives short. Heanor tradesman George Barton managed to deliver the census papers to a portion of his enumeration district on the Wednesday prior to the 1871 Census. The following day he shot himself in his bedroom leaving behind a wife and five children. He was much lamented for his upright conduct and service to the local community. At the inquest it was decided he was suffering from temporary insanity.[359] Likewise, C.H. Tanner, who for some fifteen months prior to the 1901 Census had suffered from mental health issues and spent time in a private asylum. While he was somewhat recovered and was able to go about his usual business, including his job in Winchester and looking out for his family, he was vulnerable to a relapse. While delivering schedules on the Saturday evening before the census, he left a schedule with the engineer at a pumping station. Three-quarters of an hour later a young man found his extinct body lying in four feet of water. Not far away was his coat and overcoat carefully folded up on the riverbank, and alongside them were his hat, umbrella, and a bag containing his census book. [360]

Enumerators were of course exposed to viruses and diseases as well as abuse and assaults when entering any district. The 1871 Census coincided with the European wide smallpox epidemic which spiked in London in 1871, leading to one inner London enumerator contracting the disease.[361] That same year, in another part of London, householder William Collet was summoned to appear before magistrates for violently assaulting enumerator Nicholas Gray. Collet had refused to give his place of birth and threatened the enumerator; Gray said that as he started to walk away, Collet accused him of making faces and then struck Gray on the legs a dozen times with a cane. Collet was fined £2 for the assault.[362]

A decade later, while visiting a lodging house in Glasgow, enumerator John Murphy was verbally abused by lodger John Macdonald who told him he had "no right to take the census." Macdonald tried to prevent him from proceeding with his duties and threatened to knock him down. When the case came to court, Macdonald was fined one guinea.[363] During the 1891 Census, the enumerator for a Shoreditch district was assaulted by John Grey who was later prosecuted under sections 20 and 21 of the Census Act.[364]

In 1911, a Perth enumerator was in the process of delivering schedules and climbing a common stair in South Street when he was suddenly confronted by an individual blocking his passage upwards. The enraged man waved his arms wildly and made a rush at the enumerator threatening the life of the official. Any attempt to pacify the would-be assailant failed and so the enumerator reported the matter to his registrar. The schedules were eventually delivered to the residences in the area, but as the *Perthshire Advertiser* commented, "the incident serves to show the danger to which even such inoffensive and useful public officials as Census enumerators are exposed."[365]

In 1961 there was the extraordinary case of the enumerator who had left her car on a ramp at the side of a house in Admiralty Walk, Seasalter only to return and find the word "Trespasser" painted in creosote on the windscreen and bonnet. The perpetrator was former artist Miss Norah Coppin who appeared before St. Augustine's Magistrates on 23 April 1961 and denied maliciously committing damage to the car to the extent of £45. The census enumerator Mrs Marjorie Price had driven to Admiralty Walk at 4 pm and noted a "no parking" notice outside a house, so she parked her car on a ramp at the side of the road. After visiting some houses, she noticed the damage to her car and reported the matter to the police. The constabulary found two 5-gallon tanks of creosote and tar under a ramp near Coppin's house, one of which had been opened recently.

Coppin said she was furious when she saw the car on the ramp and wrote on the vehicle, though she didn't expect the creosote to have any permanent effect. Eventually, she admitted it was done out of revenge because she believed the car was trespassing. It made no difference to her the driver was an enumerator on government business; she said she had endured a number of annoying incidents and therefore claimed extreme provocation. The court did not look fondly on Miss Coppin taking the law into her own hands and fined her £10 and asked for 2s. 1d. in costs.[366]

Somewhere in Cheshire in 1901, a creature far from its natural habitat assaulted a female enumerator when she was passing into a garden. According to the *Cheshire Observer*, the lady heard a rustling in the trees over her head and before she could move, a monkey rapidly descended and gave her a light slap about the face. Apparently she beat him off with her census books, but he followed her for some distance as she continued down the road. Later, valiantly and unperturbed, she returned to collect the schedule with a packet of nuts in case she needed a bribe.[367]

Verbal and physical abuse was actually quite rare, but it often occurred when the enumerator was confronted by census refusals and evaders. Enumerators became acquainted with certain remarks, mainly from individuals frustrated with perceived government invasions of privacy and wasting taxpayers' money. On occasion, they would experience statements akin to that aimed at one Norwich enumerator who was told, "If the Government have any money to spend, it's a pity they don't give it to poor people instead of fellows like you."[368]

It was reported in Sheffield in 1911 that some enumerators experienced householder malice in the form of having a flat-iron thrown at them, or being threatened with a poker, or with a broom handle, or having a dog set on them.[369] Sometimes, there were no overriding political concerns or expressions of resentment regarding confidentiality behind the abuse. In Cardiff in 1891, one enumerator was cursed and verbally abused simply for disturbing a woman from her afternoon nap.[370]

... the ordinary jokers.

On 9 April 1881, a letter appeared in a provincial newspaper complaining about the incompetence and lack of diligence seen among certain enumerators. One enumerator was heard reading a census schedule out loud in a public place. Even though the schedule was a "dead 'un" – one that was improperly filled up – the action was still an infringement of the rules. The letter also complained about the number of schedules not delivered or even collected, which, as we have seen, was not necessarily the enumerator's fault. The letter ended by observing the most successful enumerators were the clergy, who with admirable public spirit volunteered to do the work in their own parishes. They were familiar faces and people responded to them better than "the ordinary jokers."[371] This of course was one opinion among many.

While there was widespread use of the clergy throughout Great Britain, in Scotland, they were given a further role in assessing the accuracy of the census information for their parish. In 1841 a "form of receipt" was signed by the clergy testifying to the accuracy of the returns. And on page ii of the 1851 Census enumeration books (CEBs) there was a space headed "Remarks of the Minister of the Parish." In many cases the space was left blank or the minister merely certified the numbers in the summary tables, but in a few instances the Minister took the opportunity to offer an opinion. This was mainly in rural areas where the space provided in the CEBs was larger due to smaller summary tables.

Not all Scottish ministers delved deeply into the adequacy of the work undertaken, some merely examined the population totals and the boundary descriptions or looked at a few pages. But others went further, William Lamb, Minister of Carmichael in Lanark, wrote of his confidence in the accuracy and constancy of the enumerator; George Gillespie, Minister of Cummertrees in Dumfries, examined the enumeration and considered it to be accurate, to which he added that "the condition and occupations of the inhabitants are also correct", and Robert Sandey, Minister of Tundergarth in Dumfries, wrote "there are a few orthographical slips in the following pages" but they didn't affect the accuracy of the enumeration. A study based on the CEBS used for the 1851 Census sample suggests there were no widespread allegations of incompetence towards the schoolmasters and their assistants acting as enumerators.[372]

It is hard to get a full picture for England and Wales, but census reports, newspapers and the 1891 census letter books housed at the National Archives at Kew also suggest incompetence was negligible. Minor errors, yes. A few in default of duties, yes, but little in the way of widespread ineptitude or criminality.

Some of the mistakes were dealt with in the chapter *One Penny Per Family*. These were largely to do with the incorrect use of abbreviations, incomplete information, and misunderstanding the instructions. There were also blunders calculating the summary tables and incorrectly apportioning detached areas of an ecclesiastical parish to another parish because it belonged to the same civil parish.[373] There were, however, more serious misdemeanours. In 1901 Joe Ely was fined £2 plus costs under the Census Act for failing to deliver schedules to eight houses in his district. This was not a simple matter of neglect, but of wilful default of duties. In 1891 in the district of St. Martin, Liverpool, enumerator John Purcell also defaulted his duties and his registrar was urged by the Registrar General's office to prosecute under section 19 of the Census Act. Purcell was charged with wilfully neglecting to visit a number of houses, for neglecting to make up the summaries, and for failing to sign the declaration. In addition to losing his enumerator's wages, which were taken into consideration by the magistrates, Purcell was fined.

While enumerators were often the victims in cases of assault, in 1931 Harry Noel Baggett, a clerk, of Senghenydd-Road, Cardiff was accused of assaulting a 78-year-old woman at her home in Love Lane. According to the complainant and her housemate, Baggett committed the offence against the senior woman and then asked an offensive question. Baggett denied all charges and explained he had great difficulty in making them hear due to their disabilities and had to read out the census questions to them. Baggett was found not guilty and discharged.[374]

During the 1971 Census, the boyfriend of an appointed enumerator undertook her work without informing senior census officials. It only came to notice when a householder asked him for identification and he was unable to produce any. The woman was removed from the official enumerator list and her boyfriend, who had originally applied for census duties, but withdrew due to studying commitments, was asked to sign the official secrecy form.[375]

That same census, an Aberdeenshire man claimed the enumerator added information to his form after he had signed it. The man asked for the form back so he could post it himself while the local census officer investigated the matter. His frustration began when he found out that the enumerator was someone he knew. This situation wasn't unique, as the hiring of local enumerators had previously caused dissatisfaction among residents due to privacy reasons.[376]

An enumerator, whose usual calling was selling life insurance, touted for business in 300 homes in Shepherds Bush in 1991 and was immediately relieved of his duties. A householder said he handed over his completed census form to the enumerator and was then asked if he would consider getting life insurance. The enumerator's employer, Guardian Royal Exchange, launched its own investigation when alerted about the indiscretion; their spokesman said the company was appalled that someone claiming to act for them should behave in this way. The census authorities told the local newspaper it was an isolated incident and they did their best to ensure they employed responsible and honest people.[377] A sentiment which generally can be said to be true across all censuses.

When it comes to mega blunders, rather than wilful misdemeanours, one has to feel for enumerator Darlington, one of the men appointed to the Upholland sub-district. In 1891, Darlington had the misfortune to lose all of his census documents, including the enumeration book, memorandum book, and schedules. On 24 April, his registrar informed the Census Office of the loss and embarked on a task sparing no effort to recover the missing material.[378] On 30 April, the Superintendent Registrar for the area was informed the schedules hadn't been recovered and the only recourse was for Darlington to enumerate his district again. New schedules, an enumeration book, and memorandum book were dispatched and Darlington completed the work for enumeration district No. 9 on 2 May 1891. All the materials were dispatched to the Census Office, only for them to immediately go missing! One can imagine what Darlington was thinking. Thankfully, on 25 May the Registrar General's secretary informed the Superintendent Registrar of Wigan the parcel had been found, writing rather diplomatically, "the delay in finding it was due to the fact that it bore... [a] label stating it contained Householders Schedules, and... was dispatched without the name of the District and Sub District being written on the label, which caused delay in finding it among the thousands of parcels of Schedules which have recently been received."[379]

> Never again will I undertake such body and soul tiring work for such miserable pay.

On 20 February 1841, a circular was addressed to about sixty Superintendent Registrars in England and Wales across various localities. They were requested to give their opinion on what would be considered a fair and adequate wage for enumerators occupied one whole day for ten to twelve hours.[380]

As a result of this survey, the Census Commissioners drew up a table of allowances and sent it to the Lords Commissioners of the Treasury for approval. The Treasury Lords enquired further and wanted to know details of how the census commissioners had arrived at this allowance; they were subsequently provided with a summary of the fifty-five answers the census commissioners had received from the superintendent registrars. This was enough for the Treasury Lords to agree to the pay scale on 11 March 1841.

The scale started at 10s. for less than 50 inhabited houses or less than 300 persons enumerated and then increased at the rate of one shilling for every ten inhabited houses visited thereafter, or for every sixty persons who were enumerated up to £1. 1s. The enumerator had the right of claiming to be paid according to the number of houses visited or of persons enumerated. In areas where there were more than 25 houses, enumerators were also entitled to an extra shilling for every mile above 5 miles traversed for ensuring he visited every house in his district. A further sum of 5s. was paid to every enumerator for the completion and delivery of the returns to his registrar.

After the census work was completed, payments to the enumerators were made from the poor rate after a certificate, signed by the registrar, was presented to the justices of the peace at the Michaelmas quarter sessions. In Scotland, the sheriff deputes or their substitutes and the provosts of the Royal burghs and other burghs in Scotland were responsible for making sure the schoolmasters and their assistants were properly remunerated. This was via payments made by the Collector of the Land Tax who was reimbursed by the Treasury.

For the 1851 Census, the delivery and collection of the schedules as well as all of their other duties were included in the enumerators table of allowances. They received a fixed sum of 18s., after that if a district contained more than 300 inhabitants. They were entitled to an additional fee of 1s. for every 60 persons above 300 and the same extra shilling, as for the 1841 Census, for every mile above 5 miles traversed when visiting every house in the enumeration district. However, the wage was subject to a deduction of 5s. if the schedules were not delivered to the registrar by 8 April.

In the weeks following the 1851 Census, there were several meetings of disgruntled enumerators unhappy with the rate of pay and the delays in receiving their payments (the enumerators of Dunbartonshire still hadn't been paid by September 1851). At one such meeting, a facetious Superintendent Registrar hoped that if he lived to see another census, he might have the opportunity of appointing his worst enemies as enumerators.[381]

The allowance determined for the 1861 Census was a fixed fee of £1. 0s. 0d. and an additional fee at the rate of 2s. for every 100 persons duly enumerated over and above the first 400 in the enumeration district. They would also receive sixpence for every mile above 5 miles necessarily traversed for delivery and another sixpence for every mile above 5 miles when collecting. However, there were still complaints mainly regarding the lateness of the payments. Enumerators were informed there would be delays due to the necessity of checking the enumeration books by registrars, but for some, the months and months of delays were inexplicable. At a meeting in Liverpool, one speaker blamed the payment delays on the "idle and drunken", a remark which was immediately repudiated; another enumerator expressed his regret at giving up the schedules before he had received his payment.[382] In Edinburgh, many enumerators sent letters to the press expressing their frustration. Most of the payment claims had been in the hands of the Lord Provost by 4 May, yet two weeks later there was still no sign of a payment, even Shetlanders had been paid before their Edinburgh brethren wrote one aggrieved man. Despite it being a pittance, they said, there was still widespread unemployment and hardship and any money was a godsend.[383]

In 1871, the fixed payment was increased to £1. 1s. 0d. and the additional fee went from 2s. to 2s. 6d., but the people of Inverness still contributed a sum to be divided among the enumerators. A letter to the *Dundee Courier* asked if the people of Dundee should do the same given "the enumerators have had such hard work and so little remuneration?"[384] Across Great Britain, enumerators gathered to hear that petitions about payments had been delivered to the Home Secretary. At a meeting in Charterhouse, London, one of them suggested they should form a deputation to wait upon the Home Secretary and inform him a fairer rate of pay would be 4½ d. per hour.[385] In Scotland, enumerators argued in a petition to the Lord Advocate that their duties were more onerous than their English counterparts having to deal with individual lodgers separately rather than relying upon the testimony of a lodging house keeper. This, they believed, deserved more pay. In May, the Home Secretary responded to the enumerators and declined to accede to the request for increased pay.

For the 1881 and 1891 censuses, the allowances remained the same. Government sources reported that for the 1881 Census enumerators received on average 34s. in total for their duties. Unfortunately, there were still payment delays. One enumerator blamed his registrar for allowing a fellow enumerator two weeks longer to copy his schedules into the enumeration book.[386]

The £1. 1s. 0d. remained the fixed fee for the 1901 and 1911 censuses, but the additional fee was increased to 3s. 6d. for every 100 persons duly enumerated over and above the first 400 in the enumerator's district. There was also an additional allowance for rural districts of large areas. In 1921 the fees were increased to £2. 4s. and 4s. for every 100 persons enumerated. Due to the delay in taking the census and to mitigate any hardship caused, enumerators received the fixed fee on the day they handed over their completed work. Ten years later payments to enumerators were actually reduced to £2 and 3s. for every 100 person enumerated after the first 100. During the 1961 Census, enumerators were receiving between £17 and £21 pounds for their entire efforts and in the last census, that taken in 2021, the rate of pay was £11.22 per hour up to £14.61, depending on location.

While some had always complained about the paltry amounts, many tried to use the system to their advantage, requesting larger urban areas thinking the wage allowance would favour them and their families. It was also the reason districts packed with lodging houses were a preference. The scale, as outlined above, indicated they would be paid a set amount for a specific number of names and a proportional sum over and above the specified amount, but the extra work involved was rarely beneficial to their purse. Some tried to capitalise or if one was being cynical, exploit the expenses system. In 1901, an enumerator wrote to the *Edinburgh Evening News* saying he quite understood the nature of the payment delays, pointing out that all of the enumerators' accounts, many of which included travelling expenses, &c., had to be checked by the Register House clerks. These poor scribes had been working till all hours, without the prospect of receiving overtime like masons or bricklayers, and that many of these accounts generally contained "imaginary mileages and over-estimated returns."[387] At the Census Office in London, officials and their registrars were certainly very suspicious about some mileage claims.

For all the complaints about pay, there were printed retorts to their gripes in the press. You knew the terms of employment when you signed up, they said, so stop moaning. To the defence of the disgruntled enumerators, many genuinely did not conceive how much work was involved and were therefore somewhat justified to feel aggrieved.

> Unfortunately the enumerators' suspicions re the average intellect (his own included) developed into a morbid certainty, and it was with a very heavy sigh of relief that he chucked the last schedule into his bag, and sent the necessary postcard to the Registrar that he had finished his collection. He went to bed and dreamed of Census forms, of noughts and crosses, of males and females, of people with occupations and people without, of persons married and persons single, of both alive and father dead. Census forms filled, the earth, air and sea, and even the bedding is made of them. No wonder he has avowed "Never no more." Let the Census of 1931 look after itself. One thing is certain, there wouldn't have been so much heard about Job if he had lived in the days of the Census and had been appointed an enumerator.[388]

So when all was said and done, would they do it again? Was it mainly only the moaners who sent their misgivings into the press rooms? There were of course a number of enumerators who came back for another census, or, who upon hearing the role bad-mouthed in a local newspaper column, came to its defence. Maybe it was an even split between the two, but there is no doubt the loudest voices belonged to the disillusioned. "It was not the wearisome tramping over mile after mile of ground that disheartened me," wrote one, "but the immense amount of clerical work which had to be done before one was entitled to the pittance granted by Government."[389] And another writing in 1901, "I visited that awful district three times, made 175 calls, noted down every shop and building, inhabited and uninhabited, building and built; then I collected the schedules, copied the detailed contents of each into the enumeration book, and for all this labour the Government generously allows me the princely sum of about £1. 17s. In conclusion let me say that never again will I be induced to become an enumerator."[390]

For all their reservations, one wonders how many shoes were bought for their children, how much coal, or how many bags of potatoes were bought with the proceeds of their duties as a government officer? And for all those who wanted to see a world separate from their own, when they looked into that sphere, and saw the hardship, or conversely the comforts of the better-off, did their experience engender any empathy, any understanding of what it was like to be these other people? Did they grow as people or were these memories they could bury?

No doubt a good proportion of them didn't look forward and see their contribution grow into a new park, a new road, more provision for social care, greater transport links, a greater understanding of our health and fertility, and a better health service. Most of the enumerators of the nations would not have considered their lasting legacy to statisticians, historians, and genealogists, but it's there, no matter how difficult it was to gather the information in the first place, no matter how many candles they burnt, they deserve our gratitude for that legacy.

Endnotes

Foreword

1. *Hampshire Telegraph.* (1891) Taking the Census. 11 April. p. 6c. www.britishnewspaperarchive.co.uk
2. *Fleetwood Chronicle.* (1901) The census. 02 April. p. 5g. www.britishnewspaperarchive.co.uk
3. *Lancashire Evening Post.* (1901) Humours of the census. 02 April. p. 4b. www.britishnewspaperarchive.co.uk
4. *Bucks Herald.* (1901) London letter. 06 April. p. 8a. www.britishnewspaperarchive.co.uk
5. *Fife Free Press, & Kirkcaldy Guardian.* (1901) The census. 20 April. p. 3d. www.britishnewspaperarchive.co.uk
6. Treasury Committee to inquire into questions connected with taking of census report. Minutes of evidence, appendices BPP 1890 LVIII. Testimony of Charles J. White. p. 82.

Chapter One – Know Thyself

7. *Glasgow Daily Herald.* (1861) Meeting of census enumerators. 01 April. p. 5b. www.britishnewspaperarchive.co.uk
8. University of Oxford. (2021) *New insights from original Domesday survey revealed.* www.ox.ac.uk
9. Britnell, Richard. (2011) *Entrepreneurs in the Middle Ages.* Woodbridge: Boydell Press.

10. Houston, R.R. (2015) 'Church briefs in England and Wales from Elizabethan times to 1828', *Huntington Library Quarterly*, vol. 78, no. 3, pp. 493–520. www.jstor.org/stable/10.1525/hlq.2015.78.3.493
11. Walter, John. (2017) *Covenanting Citizens*. Oxford: Oxford University Press.
12. Vallance, Edward. (2002) Protestation, Vow, Covenant and Engagement: swearing allegiance in the English Civil War. *Historical Research*, vol. 75(190) November.
13. *Ibid.*
14. Webb, Sidney and Webb, Beatrice Potter. (1906) *English local government: from the Revolution to the Municipal Corporations Act.* London: Longmans, Green.
15. Tate. W.E. (1946) *The parish chest*. 3rd ed. Stroud: Philimore.
16. Hearth Tax Digital. Beta version. http://gams.uni-graz.at/context:htx
17. Guðmundsson, Eiríkur G. (2015) *The 1703 Census our heritage.* National Archives of Iceland.
18. *The Gentleman's Magazine.* (1754) Abstract of the bill for taking and registering an annual account of the total number of the people, &c. in Great Britain. Vol. 23. pp. 9–14.
19. Young, Arthur. (1771) *Legislature for numbering the people. Containing Some Observations on the Population of Great Britain, and a Sketch of the Advantages that would probably accrue from an exact Knowledge of its present State.* Published in London.

Chapter Two – The Evolution of the Census

20. Dobraszczyk, Paul. (2009) 'Give in your account: Using and Abusing Victorian Census Forms', *Journal of Victorian Culture*, Vol. 14, No. 1 (2009), p. 21.
21. *Ibid.*
22. Records of the General Register Office. Census 1891: outward letters. RG 29/13 and RG 29/12. National Archives, Kew, England.
23. Woollard, Matthew. (2004-2007) *Census of Scotland, 1881.* www.histpop.org
24. Registrar General. (1920-1921) Methods of Enumeration: memoranda on de jure population; preparation of enumerators books and instructions. RG19/55. National Archives, Kew, England.

25. *Western Gazette*. (1921) The 1921 Census. 28 January. p. 10c. www.britishnewspaperarchive.co.uk
26. Batch, E. (1943) Letter to R.G.J. Farrow about cause of fire at Hayes. 10 March. RG 20/ 87. National Archives, Kew, England.

Chapter Three – Paper Mountain: Forms and More Forms

27. *East Anglian Daily Times*. (1901) The Census. 12 January. p. 5e. www.britishnewspaperarchive.co.uk
28. *Evening Express*. (1901) The Census. 1 April. p. 3e. https://newspapers.library.wales/
29. *Sheffield Independent*. (1911) Census and citizenship. 01 April. p. 4c. www.britishnewspaperarchive.co.uk
30. Census of England, Wales and Islands in the British Seas, 1881. RG 27/5. National Archives, Kew, England.
31. *Ibid.*
32. Treasury Committee to inquire into questions connected with taking of census report. Minutes of evidence, appendices BPP 1890 LVIII [C.6071] 80
33. *Ibid.* p. 81
34. *Burton Chronicle*. (1891) The forthcoming census. 19 March. p. [5]e. www.britishnewspaperarchive.co.uk
35. General Register Office. Recommendations regarding the Census: from Education Department (Board of Education 1899). 18 February 1901. Letter enclosing memorandum to Public Elementary Schools. RG 19/8. National Archives, Kew, England.
36. *Bournemouth Daily Echo*. (1901) A schoolmaster's census lesson. 2 April. p. 4e. www.britishnewspaperarchive.co.uk
37. General Register Office. Forms and instructions issued for taking the Census. March 1911. Memorandum as to instruction upon the census. RG 27/8. National Archives, Kew, England.
38. Board of Education. Teachers acting as enumerators during the 1921 census: papers. 4 April 1921. ED 24/1750. National Archives, Kew, England.
39. *The Sphere* (1921). For the family's benefit. 23 April. p. 5a&b. www.britishnewspaperarchive.co.uk

40. General Register Office. Correspondence with Members of Parliament and others: complaints regarding census questions, confidentiality, recruitment of and payment to enumerators. RG 19/124. National Archives, Kew, England.
41. General Register Office. Reports by GRO staff who were enumerators. 1961. RG 19/279. National Archives, Kew, England.
42. Treasury Committee to inquire into questions connected with taking of census report. Minutes of evidence. BPP 1890.
43. *Ibid.*
44. *Bradford Observer*. (1871). The Census. 9 February. p. 7c. www.britishnewspaperarchive.co.uk
45. *Cannock Chase Courier.* (1900) Next year's census. 15 December. p. 6e. www.britishnewspaperarchive.co.uk

Chapter Four: A Rather Poor Lot

46. *Morning Advertiser*. (1841). To the editor. 5 July p. 3e. www.britishnewspaperarchive.co.uk
47. School of Oriental and African Studies (SOAS). Davies, Charles. Letter to Charles Addis. 19 April 1881. PP MS 14/102.
48. *Monmouthshire Beacon* (1861). The forthcoming census. 9 February. p. 6f. www.britishnewspaperarchive.co.uk
49. Haddington Sheriff Court. Census Enumerators' Contracts etc. SC40/70/2. National Records of Scotland, Edinburgh.
50. This was so that their fees could be handed over to fund the regiment; an exception was made for the artisan volunteers who were allowed to deduct 10s. of the 25s. wage for their time.
51. Census Branch files. Administrative papers concerning the 1931 census. 1931. GRO6/479. National Records of Scotland, Edinburgh.
52. *Stamford Mercury* (1871) Moulton. 27 January. p. 4e. www.britishnewspaperarchive.co.uk.
53. General Register Office. Correspondence with Members of Parliament and others: complaints regarding census questions, confidentiality, recruitment of and payment to enumerators. RG 19/124. National Archives, Kew, England.
54. General Register Office. Correspondence with Members of Parliament and others: complaints regarding census questions, confidentiality, recruitment of and payment to enumerators. RG 19/125. National Archives, Kew, England.

55. General Register Office. Enumerators: local recruitment. RG 19/91. National Archives, Kew, England.
56. *Islington Gazette.* (1871) Taking the census.- Experience of a lady enumerator, and how I became one. 26 September. p. 3d&e. www.britishnewspaperarchive.co.uk
57. *Pall Mall Gazette.* (1890) The Axiom of Sex. 18 July. p. 1b&c. www.britishnewspaperarchive.co.uk
58. Treasury Committee to inquire into questions connected with taking of census report. Minutes of evidence, appendices BPP 1890 LVIII [C.6071] 80.
59. *Yorkshire Post and Leeds Intelligencer* (1890). Summary of the news. 19 July. p. 6d&e. www.britishnewspaperarchive.co.uk
60. Records of the General Register Office. Census 1891: outward letters. RG 29/9. National Archives, Kew, England.
61. General Register Office. Forms and instructions issued for taking the Census. RG 27/6. National Archives, Kew, England.
62. Treasury Committee to inquire into questions connected with taking of census report. Minutes of evidence, appendices BPP 1890 LVIII [C.6071] 80
63. *Manchester Evening News.* (1901). Taking the census of Manchester. 27 March. p. 5b. www.britishnewspaperarchive.co.uk
64. *Oxford Journal.* (1871) The census. 1 April. p. 5c. www.britishnewspaperarchive.co.uk
65. General Register Office. Unsatisfactory execution of Census duties. RG 19/121. National Archives, Kew, England.

Chapter Five – Tomorrow is "C" Day

66. *Halifax Evening Courier.* (1901) The Census. 01 April. p. 4e&f. www.britishnewspaperarchive.co.uk
67. *Halifax Evening Courier.* (1901) The Census. 01 April. p. 4e&f. www.britishnewspaperarchive.co.uk
68. *Hull Daily Mail.* (1915) An enumerator's round. 16 August. p. 4f. www.britishnewspaperarchive.co.uk
69. *Acton Gazette.* (1931) Lessons of the census. 08 May. p. 6f. www.britishnewspaperarchive.co.uk
70. Records of the General Register Office. Census 1891: outward letters. RG 29/14. National Archives, Kew, England.
71. *Manchester Evening News.* (1901) The census. 01 April. pp. 2–3. www.britishnewspaperarchive.co.uk

72. Lumas, Susan. (2002) *Making use of the census.* London: Public Record Office.
73. *Blackburn Standard.* (1891) The impending national census. 04 April. pp. 4–5. www.britishnewspaperarchive.co.uk
74. *West Surrey Times.* (1901) Taking the census. 05 April. p. 5a, b&c. www.britishnewspaperarchive.co.uk
75. *Evening Express.* (1891) Taking the census. 8 April. p. 4c&d. https://newspapers.library.wales/
76. *Kirkintilloch Herald.* (1901) The experiences of a census enumerator. 24 April. p.6a. www.britishnewspaperarchive.co.uk
77. *Manchester Times.* (1891) Taking the census in Manchester. 10 April. p. 2c. www.britishnewspaperarchive.co.uk
78. *Nelson Leader.* (1951) Census gave Matron a headache. 13 April. p. 8a&b. www.britishnewspaperarchive.co.uk
79. *Daily News.* (1921) Census mystery. 22 June. p. 5f. www.britishnewspaperarchive.co.uk
80. *West Surrey Times.* (1901) Taking the census. 05 April. p. 5ab&c. www.britishnewspaperarchive.co.uk
81. *Kent & Sussex Courier.* (1901) Curiosities of census collecting at Tunbridge Wells. 05 April. p. 10c. www.britishnewspaperarchive.co.uk
82. *Yorkshire Evening Press.* (1911) Incidents of the census. 04 April. p. 3g. www.britishnewspaperarchive.co.uk
83. *Daily News.* (1891) Taking the census. 07 April. p. 5e&f. www.britishnewspaperarchive.co.uk
84. Benwell, R.M. & G.A. (1978) The 1851 Census in the Llandyrnog sub-district. *Denbighshire Historical Society Transactions.* 27. pp. 199–202.
85. *The Burton Chronicle.* (1891) Humours of census taking. 30 April. p. 6.d. www.britishnewspaperarchive.co.uk
86. *Manchester Evening News.* (1901) The census. 01 April. pp. 2–3. www.britishnewspaperarchive.co.uk

Chapter Six – One Penny Per Family

87. *Oxford Chronicle and Reading Gazette*. (1901) The Census. 05 April. p. 6c. www.britishnewspaperarchive.co.uk
88. *Star of Gwent.* (1861) The experience of the census enumerators. 13 April. p. 5c. www.britishnewspaperarchive.co.uk

89. *Yorkshire Evening Post.* (1901) The census in Leeds. 29 March. p. 6b. www.britishnewspaperarchive.co.uk
90. *The Bath Chronicle.* (1901) The census in Bath. 04 April. p. 6d. www.britishnewspaperarchive.co.uk
91. *Munster Express.* (1871) Taking the census. 29 April. p. 7. www.irishnewsarchive.com
92. *Western Mail.* (1901) Taking the census. 02 April. p. 5e. www.britishnewspaperarchive.co.uk
93. *Cheshire Observer.* (1901) The census. 06 April. p. 8h. https://newspapers.library.wales/
94. *Dundee People's Journal.* (1891) The census. 11 April. p. 3c&d. www.britishnewspaperarchive.co.uk
95. *Renfrewshire Independent.* (1891) News notes. 17 April. p. 7a. www.britishnewspaperarchive.co.uk
96. Records of the General Register Office. Census 1891: outward letters. RG 29/12. National Archives, Kew, England.
97. *Liverpool Mercury.* (1871) The census. 04 April. p. 6c. www.britishnewspaperarchive.co.uk
98. *Morning Advertiser.* (1841) A hint to the enumerators of the late census. 05 October. p. 4b. www.britishnewspaperarchive.co.uk
99. *Western Mail.* (1891) Letters to the editor. 21 April. p. 6e. www.britishnewspaperarchive.co.uk
100. Benwell, R.M. & G.A. (1978) The 1851 Census in the Llandyrnog sub-district. *Denbighshire Historical Society Transactions.* 27. pp. 199–202.
101. *Hampshire Telegraph.* (1891) Taking the Census. 11 April. p. 6c. www.britishnewspaperarchive.co.uk
102. *Dundee People's Journal.* (1891) The census. 11 April. p. 3c&d. www.britishnewspaperarchive.co.uk
103. *Leeds Mercury.* (1881) Taking the Census. 05 April. p. 8d. www.britishnewspaperarchive.co.uk
104. *Leeds Times.* (1891) Taking the census in Leeds. 11 April. p. 5e. www.britishnewspaperarchive.co.uk
105. *Yorkshire Post and Leeds Intelligencer.* (1901) An enumerator's trials. 02 April. p. 5e. www.britishnewspaperarchive.co.uk
106. *Yorkshire Post and Leeds Intelligencer.* (1901) An enumerator's trials. 02 April. p. 5c. www.britishnewspaperarchive.co.uk
107. *Bolton Evening News.* (1901) Taking the census in Bolton. 01 April. p. 3g. www.britishnewspaperarchive.co.uk

108. *West Surrey Times.* (1901) Taking the census. 05 April. p. 5ab&c. www.britishnewspaperarchive.co.uk
109. Records of the General Register Office. Census 1891: outward letters. RG 29/9. National Archives, Kew, England.
110. *Nelson Leader.* (1951) Census gave Matron a headache. 13 April. p. 8a&b. www.britishnewspaperarchive.co.uk
111. *Sheffield Daily Telegraph.* (1911) Sheffield Census. 04 April. p. 8b. www.britishnewspaperarchive.co.uk
112. *Halifax Evening Courier.* (1911) Numbering the people. 04 April. p. 3a. www.britishnewspaperarchive.co.uk
113. *Kirkintilloch Herald.* (1901) The experiences of a census enumerator. 24 April. p. 6a. www.britishnewspaperarchive.co.uk
114. *The Bedfordshire Times and Independent.* (1921) The Census of 1921, by One Who Was In It. 01 July. p.11c. www.britishnewspaperarchive.co.uk.
115. Higgs, Edward. (2005) *Making sense of the census revisited.* London: Institute of Historical Research. pp.17–18.
116. HMSO. (1910) Census of England and Wales, 1911: instructions to the Superintendent Registrars, Registrars and enumerators relating to their duties in connection with the census. London: Darling & Son.
117. HMSO. (1911) Census of Scotland, 1911: instructions to the various local officers as to their duties in taking the census. Glasgow: James Hedderwick & Sons.
118. *Evening Despatch.* (1911) The census in Edgbaston. 05 April. p. 4e. www.britishnewspaperarchive.co.uk
119. *West Surrey Times.* (1901) Taking the census. 05 April. p. 5a, b&c. www.britishnewspaperarchive.co.uk
120. *Western Mail.* (1891) Letters to the editor. 21 April. p. 6e. www.britishnewspaperarchive.co.uk
121. *Evening Express.* (1891) Sold by the Census. 15 April. p. 2f&g. https://newspapers.library.wales/
122. Peter Smith. (2020) Victorian Preston's 'worst slum'. *Preston History.* https://prestonhistory.com/subjects/victorian-prestons-worst-slum/
123. Records of the General Register Office. Census 1891: outward letters. RG 29/12. National Archives, Kew, England.
124. *Ibid.*
125. *Ibid.*
126. *Ibid.*

Chapter Seven – Private Life of the Family

127. *South Wales Daily News.* (1891) The census. 07 April. p. 7c&d. https://newspapers.library.wales/
128. Thomson, David. (1980) Age reporting by the elderly and the nineteenth century census. *Local Population Studies.* 25. Autumn. pp. 13–25. www.localpopulationstudies.org.uk
129. Census of England and Wales, 1901. General report, with appendices BPP 1904 CVIII [Cd.2174] 51.
130. *Ibid.*
131. Census of England and Wales, 1951. General Report. 1958. London: H.M.S.O.
132. Tillott, P. M. (1972) 'Sources of inaccuracy in the 1851 and 1861 Censuses". In: E.A. Wrigley ed. *Ninteenth-century society.* Cambridge: Cambridge University Press. pp. 107–8.
133. Anderson. M. (1972) 'The study of family structure'. In: E.A. Wrigley ed. *Ninteenth-century society.* Cambridge: Cambridge University Press. p. 75.
134. Razzell. (1972) The evaluation of baptism as a form of birth registration through cross-matching census and parish register data. *Population Studies*, 26, pp. 123–7.
135. Perkyns, Audrey. (1999) Migration and mobility in six Kentish parishes, 1851-81. *Local Population Studies*, 63, pp. 30–70.
136. Thomson, *op. cit.* p. 13.
137. *Mid Sussex Times.* (1901) Taking the census. 19 March. p. 7f. www.britishnewspaperarchive.co.uk
138. Census of Scotland, 1911, Report on the twelfth decennial census of Scotland. Vol. II BPP 1913 LXXX. p. li.
139. *Burnley Express.* (1901) Census humour. 30 March. p. 6d. www.britishnewspaperarchive.co.uk
140. *Dundee People's Journal.* (1861) Facts and facetlae about the census. 20 April. p. 4d&e. www.britishnewspaperarchive.co.uk
141. *Stonehaven Journal.* (1861) More census facetiae. 02 May. p. 4c. www.britishnewspaperarchive.co.uk
142. *Rugby Advertiser.* (1901) Numbering the People. 06 April. p. 5b. www.britishnewspaperarchive.co.uk
143. *Bedfordshire Times and Independent.* (1901) Humours of the Census. 05 April. p.6e. www.britishnewspaperarchive.co.uk
144. *Western Gazette.* (1921) The 1921 census. 28 January. p. 10c. www.britishnewspaperarchive.co.uk

145. *Liverpool Evening Express.* (1911) Census day. 04 April. p. 4h. www.britishnewspaperarchive.co.uk
146. *Greenock Telegraph and Clyde Shipping Gazette.* (1861) Census curiosities. 04 May. p. 3a. www.britishnewspaperarchive.co.uk
147. *Westminster Gazette.* (1901) Census-collection day. 01 April. p. 5a. www.britishnewspaperarchive.co.uk
148. *Northampton Chronicle and Echo.* (1915) The Register. 16 August. p. 4c. www.britishnewspaperarchive.co.uk
149. *Evening Express.* (1901) Some census stories. 01 April. p. 3c. https://newspapers.library.wales/
150. *West Surrey Times.* (1901) Taking the census. 05 April. p. 5a, b&c. www.britishnewspaperarchive.co.uk
151. *Todmorden Advertiser and Hebden Bridge Newsletter.* (1891) The census. 10 April. p. 8b, c&d. www.britishnewspaperarchive.co.uk
152. *Coventry Evening Telegraph.* (1901) Taking the census in Coventry. p. 3c&d. www.britishnewspaperarchive.co.uk
153. *Maidenhead Advertiser.* (1911) Taking the census. 05 April. p. 3a. www.britishnewspaperarchive.co.uk
154. *The Western Mail.* (1871) Incidents of census-taking on the Welsh hills. 08 April. p. 2g. www.britishnewspaperarchive.co.uk
155. *Hartlepool Northern Daily Mail.* (1911) Farewell message on a census paper. 04 April. p. 3c. www.britishnewspaperarchive.co.uk
156. *Burnley Express.* (1901) Local. 10 April. p. 2e. www.britishnewspaperarchive.co.uk
157. *Jarrow Express.* (1881) The census of 1881. 25 March. p. 6f. www.britishnewspaperarchive.co.uk
158. *Brighton Gazette.* (1901) Taking the census in Brighton. 04 April. p. 5f. www.britishnewspaperarchive.co.uk
159. *Yorkshire Evening Press.* (1911) Incidents of the census. 04 April. p. 3g. www.britishnewspaperarchive.co.uk
160. *Leeds Mercury.* (1881) Taking the Census. 05 April. p. 8d. www.britishnewspaperarchive.co.uk
161. *Sheffield Daily Telegraph.* (1911) Sheffield Census. 04 April. p. 8b. www.britishnewspaperarchive.co.uk
162. *Monmouthshire Merlin.* (1851) Curiosities of the census. 18 April. p. 4a. https://newspapers.library.wales/
163. *Preston Herald.* (1871) Taking the census. 12 April. p. 2e. www.britishnewspaperarchive.co.uk

164. *Bucks Herald.* (1901) London letter. 06 April. p. 8a. www.britishnewspaperarchive.co.uk
165. Roberts, Jane. (2020) *"Alas Too Idle Yet Writing a Book" – Census Gems.* www.pasttopresentgenealogy.co.uk
166. *Bolton Chronicle.* (1851) [No title] 05 July. p. 5f. www.britishnewspaperarchive.co.uk
167. *Coventry Evening Telegraph.* (1901) Taking the census in Coventry. p. 3c&d. www.britishnewspaperarchive.co.uk
168. *Bucks Herald.* (1901) London letter. 06 April. p. 8b. www.britishnewspaperarchive.co.uk
169. Census. England. 1911. Chester. 2 April. TABBY, Peter. RG14/21856. RD 450. ED 6. SN 211. National Archives, Kew, Surrey. www.thegenealogist.co.uk
170. *Jarrow Express.* (1881) The census of 1881. 25 March. p. 6f. www.britishnewspaperarchive.co.uk
171. *Rugby Advertiser.* (1901) Numbering the people. 06 April. p. 5b. www.britishnewspaperarchive.co.uk
172. *Berkshire Chronicle.* (1901) Humours of the census. 06 April. p. 2c. www.britishnewspaperarchive.co.uk
173. Perkyns, Audrey. (1991) Birthplace accuracy in the censuses of six Kentish parishes 1851-81. *Local Population Studies.* 47. pp. 39–55.
174. *Ibid.*
175. *Ibid.*
176. *Ibid.*
177. *Ibid.*
178. *The Rhondda Leader.* (1901) Census peculiarities. 06 April. p. 6d. https://newspapers.library.wales/
179. *The Bath Chronicle.* (1901) The census in Bath. 04 April. p. 6d. www.britishnewspaperarchive.co.uk

Chapter Eight – Work, Home, and School

180. *Hampshire Telegraph.* (1891) Taking the Census. 11 April. p. 6c. www.britishnewspaperarchive.co.uk
181. Treasury Committee to inquire into questions connected with taking of census report. Minutes of evidence, appendices BPP 1890 LVIII [C.6071] 7.

182. *Dundee Courier.* (1921) Census humour in Dundee. 22 June. p. 4b. www.britishnewspaperarchive.co.uk
183. Higgs, Edward. (1982) The tabulation of occupations in the nineteenth century census with special reference to domestic servants. *Local Population Studies.* 28 (Spring), pp. 58–66. www.localpopulationstudies.org.uk
184. *Sheffield Daily Telegraph.* (1911) Sheffield Census. 04 April. p. 8b. www.britishnewspaperarchive.co.uk
185. *East London Observer.* (1881) Some Curiosities of census work. 16 April. p. 7d, e&f. www.britishnewspaperarchive.co.uk
186. *Mid-Sussex Times*. (1901) Taking the census. 19 March. p. 7f. www.britishnewspaperarchive.co.uk
187. *Manchester Evening News.* (1901) The census. 01 April. pp. 2–3. www.britishnewspaperarchive.co.uk
188. *Berkshire Chronicle.* (1901) Humours of the census. 06 April. p. 2c. www.britishnewspaperarchive.co.uk
189. *The Rhondda Leader.* (1901) Census peculiarities. 06 April. p. 6d. https://newspapers.library.wales/
190. *Bicester Herald.* (1911) Numbering the people. 07 April. p. 2f. www.britishnewspaperarchive.co.uk
191. *West Surrey Times.* (1901) Taking the census. 05 April. p. 5a, b&c. www.britishnewspaperarchive.co.uk
192. *Star of Gwent.* (1861) The experience of the census enumerators. 13 April. p. 5c. www.britishnewspaperarchive.co.uk
193. *South Wales Echo.* (1881) Taking the census. 16 April. p. 3a. www.britishnewspaperarchive.co.uk
194. *Star of Gwent.* (1861) The experience of the census enumerators. 13 April. p. 5c. www.britishnewspaperarchive.co.uk
195. Hutchins, J.B. (1867) *The Sanitary Act, 1866 (29 & 30 Vict., c. 90) and the Sewage Utilization Acts of 1865 and 1867 (28 & 29 Vict. c. 75, and 30 & 31 Vict. c. 113) : with an introduction to and summary of the Sanitary Act, together with notes and indexes to each of the Acts.* London: Knight & Co.
196. *Morning Post.* (1891) To the editor. 09 April. p. 2d. www.britishnewspaperarchive.co.uk
197. Daunton, M.J. (1991) Health and housing in Victorian London. *Medical History*, Supplement No. 11. pp. 126–144.
198. Wohl, Anthony S. (2017) *The eternal slum: housing and Social Policy in Victorian London.* Abingdon-on-Thames, Oxfordshire: Taylor & Francis.

199. Records of the General Register Office. Census 1891: outward letters. RG 29/9. National Archives, Kew, England.
200. *Ibid.*
201. Tillott, P.M. (1972) 'Sources of inaccuracy in the 1851 and 1861 censuses'. In: E. A. Wrigley ed. *Ninteenth-century society*. Cambridge: Cambridge University Press. p. 92.
202. *Evening Express*. (1894) Welsh census. 27 August. p. 1g. www.britishnewspaperarchive.co.uk
203. *North British Daily Mail.* (1881) The Gaelic Census. 26 March. p. 2e. www.britishnewspaperarchive.co.uk
204. *The Scotsman.* (1881) The Gaelic Census. 09 April. p. 6g. www.britishnewspaperarchive.co.uk
205. *Dundee Advertiser.* (1881) The Gaelic Census. 03 May. p. 6a. www.britishnewspaperarchive.co.uk
206. *Dundee People's Journal.* (1881) The Census. 02 April. p. 2a. www.britishnewspaperarchive.co.uk
207. *Inverness Courier.* (1881) The Taking of the Census Inverness. 05 April. p. 4e. www.britishnewspaperarchive.co.uk
208. Withers, Charles W.J. (2021) *Gaelic in Scotland 1698-1981: The Geographical History of a Language.* Edinburgh: John Donald.
209. *Evening Express.* (1891) Spirit of the Welsh Press. 21 April. p. 2f. https://newspapers.library.wales/
210. *Weekly Mail.* (1901) Welsh enumerators to be appointed. 12 January. p. 11g. www.britishnewspaperarchive.co.uk
211. *The Western Mail.* (1871) Incidents of census-taking on the Welsh hills. 08 April. p. 2g. www.britishnewspaperarchive.co.uk
212. *Evening Express.* (1901) Census gossip. 29 March. p. 2d. https://newspapers.library.wales/
213. *Weekly Mail.* (1891) The census of 1891. 04 April. p. 14d. https://newspapers.library.wales/
214. *The Wrexham Advertiser.* (1891) The census in Hawarden. 25 April. p. 3d. https://newspapers.library.wales/
215. *The Herald.* (1891) The census. 10 April. p. 5c. https://newspapers.library.wales/
216. Records of the General Register Office. Census 1891: outward letters. RG 29/12. National Archives, Kew, England.
217. *Ibid.*
218. *Wrexham and Denbighshire Advertiser.* (1891) Vale of Clwyd observations. 18 April. p. 6f. https://newspapers.library.wales/

219. *Evening Express.* (1891) Spirit of the Welsh Press. 21 April. p. 2f. https://newspapers.library.wales/
220. *Liverpool Mercury.* (1891) Census agitation in Wales. 06 May. p. 6g. www.britishnewspaperarchive.co.uk
221. *Evening Express.* (1894) Welsh census. 27 August. p. 1g. www.britishnewspaperarchive.co.uk
222. Higgs, Edward. (1989) *Making sense of the census: the manuscript returns for England and Wales, 1801-1901.* London: H.M.S.O.

Chapter Nine – A Life Beyond the Census: George Edward Douglas

223. Minute Books of General Meetings of the Directors and Guardians of the Poor. The London Archives (City of London Corporation). P89/MRY1/579. 12 Feb 1858-30 Dec 1859. p. 238, from the Saint Marylebone collection.
224. Minute Books of General Meetings of the Directors and Guardians of the Poor. The London Archives (City of London Corporation). P89/MRY1/580. 06 Jan 1860-20 Dec 1861. p. 190, from the Saint Marylebone collection.
225. Master's Report Book. The London Archives (City of London Corporation). P89/MRY1/684. 12 June 1863, from the Saint Marylebone collection.
226. *Lloyd's Weekly Newspaper.* (1863) Charge against workhouse officials. 28 June. p. 7c&d. www.britishnewspaperarchive.co.uk
227. *Lloyd's Weekly Newspaper.* (1863) Lord Raynham and The Master of The Marylebone Workouse. 9 August. p. 12d. www.britishnewspaperarchive.co.uk
228. He may have died in Argelly, Pau, France on 7 December 1837. *The Saint James Chronicle* (7 December 1837 p. 1c) has a death announcement for Don Juan Escudero late of Baker Street.
229. *Sun* (London). (1844) Biographical Sketch of Prince Alexander De Gonzaga. p. 12b&c. www.britishnewspaperarchive.co.uk
230. General Military Archive of Segovia. (1959-1963). *Index of personal files.* Madrid: Hidalguia. Vol. 4. p. 216. https://bibliotecavirtual.defensa.gob.es/BVMDefensa/i18n/consulta/registro.cmd?id=4816
231. Some sources indicate he first came forward in Vienna in 1831.
232. Archives Nationales. Leonore database. www.leonore.archives-nationales.culture.gouv.fr/ui/

233. *Sun* (London). (1844) Biographical Sketch of Prince Alexander De Gonzaga. p. 12b&c. www.britishnewspaperarchive.co.uk
234. *Ibid.*
235. Patients' records: female casebooks. The London Archives (City of London Corporation). H11/HLL/B/19. De Gonzaga, Eliza Maria. No. 3832. p. 331, from the Hanwell Asylum collection.
236. *Morning Post.* (1866) The Prince Gonzaga. 7 December. p. 6a&b. www.britishnewspaperarchive.co.uk
237. *North London News.* (1865) Singular discovery of the father of the man who shot Booth. 28 October. p. 3a. www.britishnewspaperarchive.co.uk
238. *Cork Examiner.* (1865) An Eccentric Character. 02 November. p. [4]b. www.britishnewspaperarchive.co.uk
239. Passenger Lists of Vessels Arriving at New York, New York, 1820-1897. Zenobia departing Liverpool for New York. CORBETT, Bartholomew. 3 October 1840. www.ancestry.co.uk
240. Census records. England. 1861. Charterhouse. 07 April. CORBETT, Bartholomew. RG9/188/ED 5. F. 29. p. 62. SN 401.
241. Poor Law Records. Minute Books of Committee of Directors and Guardians of the Poor. 7 Apr 1865-16 Mar 1866. P89/MRY1/546. pp. 329–330. The London Archives, London, England.
242. Jameson, W.C. (2013) *Beyond the grave.* Lanham: Taylor Trade Publishing.
243. Minute Books of Committee of Directors and Guardians of the Poor. The London Archives (City of London Corporation). P89/MRY1/547. 23 Mar 1866-8 Mar 1867. p. 4, from the Saint Marylebone Collection.
244. *London Daily News.* (1867) The Health of London. 16 January. p. 3d. www.britishnewspaperarchive.co.uk
245. *Norfolk News.* (1867) Fearful accident in the Regent's Park. 19 January. p. 2d. www.britishnewspaperarchive.co.uk
246. *Ibid*, p. 2e.
247. *Ibid*, p. 2e.
248. *Ibid*, p. 2e.
249. *London Evening Standard.* (1867) The Regent's Park Accident. 23 January. p. 6f. www.britishnewspaperarchive.co.uk
250. *Ibid.*
251. *Illustrated Times.* (1867) The Marylebone Workhouse. 16 March. p. 3b. www.britishnewspaperarchive.co.uk

Chapter Ten – A Life Beyond the Census: Frances Zanetti

252. Burba, Vilma. (2016) *Le quattro sorelle: Ricostruzione storica sulle origini delle Isole del Lago Maggiore.* http://appuntiretrodatati.blogspot.com/2016_04_28_archive.html
253. *London Gazette.* (1801) [Partnerships dissolved]. 21 March. No. 15347. p. 326. www.findmypast.co.uk
254. *Manchester Guardian.* (1825) Blackfriars Inn. 23 April. p. 4c. www.britishnewspaperarchive.co.uk
255. *Manchester Courier and Lancashire General Advertiser.* (1825) Improvements in Market-Street. 23 April. p. 3a&b. www.britishnewspaperarchive.co.uk
256. *Ibid.*
257. *The Manchester Courier and Lancashire General Advertiser.* (1826) Notice. 14 October. p.1e. www.britishnewspaperarchive.co.uk
258. Burba, *op. cit.*
259. *London Gazette.* (1837) [Partnerships dissolved]. 17 January. No. 19458. p. 125. www.findmypast.co.uk
260. *Manchester Courier and Lancashire General Advertiser.* (1837) Legal Notices. 25 February. p. 2e. www.britishnewspaperarchive.co.uk
261. *Manchester Courier and Lancashire General Advertiser.* (1843) Mysterious death of Mr Zanetti. 4 February. p. 2f&g. www.britishnewspaperarchive.co.uk
262. *Manchester Courier and Lancashire General Advertiser.* (1851) Sales by auction. 20 December. p.12b. www.britishnewspaperarchive.co.uk
263. *Tablet.* (1873) Salford. 19 July. p. 19a. www.britishnewspaperarchive.co.uk
264. Hamer, Domenico. (1996) A Phase for the struggle of Catholic education: Manchester and Salford in the mid-nineteenth century. *Recusant History*, 23(1), pp. 107–126.
265. *Ibid.*
266. Sisters of Notre Dame de Namur UK. *The Early Days.* www.snduk.org/the-early-days/
267. Alston, G.C. (1908). Convent Schools (Great Britain). In *The Catholic Encyclopedia*. New York: Robert Appleton Company. www.newadvent.org/cathen/04342a.htm
268. *The Tablet.* (1874) Subscriptions received. 28 February. p. 273a. www.britishnewspaperarchive.co.uk

269. *Manchester Courier and Lancashire General Advertiser.* (1881) Commercial examinations. 12 May. p. 8f. www.britishnewspaperarchive.co.uk
270. Cullen, Mildred M. (1964) *The growth of the Roman Catholic training colleges for women in England during the nineteenth and twentieth centuries*, Durham theses, Durham University. http://etheses.dur.ac.uk/9828/
271. *Manchester Courier and Lancashire General Advertiser.* (1891) Tutors, Governesses. &c. 12 May. p. 2a. www.britishnewspaperarchive.co.uk
272. Haller, Dorothy. L. (1990) Bastardy and Baby Farming in Victorian England. *The Student Historical Journal 1989-1990.* Vol. 21. Loyola University. http://people.loyno.edu/
273. *Islington Gazette*. [No title] (1871) 15 July. p. 2c. www.britishnewspaperarchive.co.uk
274. Stuart-Bennett, Joshua George. (2019) *Modernity and 'Baby-Farming': The Privatised Commerce of Motherhood and Respectability in Victorian and Edwardian London.* Unpublished PhD Thesis. University of Leicester. https://hdl.handle.net/2381/43792
275. *Manchester Courier and Lancashire General Advertiser.* (1898) Adopting a baby. 24 November. p. 7b. www.britishnewspaperarchive.co.uk
276. *Manchester Evening News.* (1899) Baby farming at Moss Side.10 November. p. 4f. www.britishnewspaperarchive.co.uk
277. *Manchester Courier and Lancashire General Advertiser.* (1900) Baby farming and child murder. 20 January. Supp. 8d. www.britishnewspaperarchive.co.uk
278. *Manchester Evening News.* (1901) The Census schedules collected to-day. 1 April. p. 2f&g. www.britishnewspaperarchive.co.uk
279. *Ibid.*
280. Census England. 1901. Ancoats. RG 13/3740. ED 2. pages 1–42.
281. *Liverpool Daily Post.* (1902) Poor Law Guardians' Conference at Preston. 29 September. p. 6d. www.britishnewspaperarchive.co.uk
282. Grey, D. (2009) 'More Ignorant and Stupid than Wilfully Cruel': Homicide Trials and 'Baby-Farming' in England and Wales in the Wake of the Children Act 1908'. *Crimes and Misdemeanours: Deviance and the Law in Historical Perspective*, 3(2), pp.60–77.
283. *Reynolds's Newspaper.* (1908) The unwanted babe. 15 March. p. 2. www.britishnewspaperarchive.co.uk

Chapter Eleven – Institutions

284. *St James's Gazette.* (1891) An Unknown tongue. 2 April. p. 11a. www.britishnewspaperarchive.co.uk
285. Winder, Robert. (2010) *Bloody foreigners.* London: Little, Brown Book Group.
286. *The Sportsman.* (1891) Notes on news. 6 April. p. 2a. www.britishnewspaperarchive.co.uk
287. Census of England and Wales. (1893) General Report. 1891. Vol. IV. pp. 66–67. London: HMSO. www.histpop.org
288. Census of Scotland, 1891, Tenth decennial census of the population of Scotland taken 5th April 1891, with report. Vol. I BPP 1892 XCIV [C.6755] xxi
289. Census of Ireland, 1891, General report with illustrative maps and diagrams, tables and appendix BPP 1892 XC [C.6780] 442
290. Census of England and Wales, 1891, Vol. IV. General report, with summary tables and appendices BPP 1893-4 CVI [C.7222] 1.
291. *Newcastle Daily Chronicle.* (1891) An unknown tongue. 3 April. p. 4c. www.britishnewspaperarchive.co.uk
292. *London Evening Standard.* (1891) Letters. 4 April. p. 2e. www.britishnewspaperarchive.co.uk
293. Higgs, Edward. *Institutions.* www.histpop.org.
294. Census of Great Britain, 1821, Abstract of the answers and returns made pursuant to an Act, passed in the first year of the reign of His Majesty King George IV, intituled, "An Act for taking an account of the population of Great Britain, and of the increase or diminution thereof". Preliminary observations. Enumeration abstract. Parish register abstract, 1821, BPP 1822 XV. (502).
295. Census of Great Britain, 1851, Population tables, I. Number of the inhabitants in 1801, 1811, 1821, 1831, 1841 and 1851. Vol. I BPP 1852-53 LXXXV (1631) xii
296. Census of Scotland, 1871, Eighth decennial census of the population of Scotland taken 3rd April 1871, with report. Vol. I. BPP 1872 LXVIII [C.592] x
297. *Dublin Evening Mail.* (1841) Kensington Police Court. 28 July. p. 3d. www.britishnewspaperarchive.co.uk
298. *Rugby Advertiser.* (1901) Numbering the People. 6 April. p. 5b. www.britishnewspaperarchive.co.uk

299. *Cornubian and Redruth Times.* (1901) Census Humour. 19 April. p.7f. www.britishnewspaperarchive.co.uk
300. *Leigh Chronicle and Weekly District Advertiser.* (1911) Notes and echoes. 7 April. p. 5b. www.britishnewspaperarchive.co.uk
301. *West Surrey Times.* (1901) Taking the census. 6 April. p. 5b. www.britishnewspaperarchive.co.uk
302. *Westminster Gazette.* (1901) Census-collection day. 1 April. p. 5a. www.britishnewspaperarchive.co.uk
303. *Sheffield Independent.* (1901) The Census in Sheffield. 2 April. p. 6f. www.britishnewspaperarchive.co.uk
304. *Todmorden Advertiser and Hebden Bridge Newsletter.* (1891) The Census. 10 April. p. 8d. www.britishnewspaperarchive.co.uk
305. *Westminster Gazette.* (1901) Census-collection day. 1 April. p. 5a. www.britishnewspaperarchive.co.uk
306. *Portsmouth Evening News.* (1901) The Census at the Workhouse. 3 April. p. 3d. www.britishnewspaperarchive.co.uk
307. *Sheffield Independent.* (1901) The Census in Sheffield. 2 April. p. 6f. www.britishnewspaperarchive.co.uk
308. *Cumberland & Westmorland Herald.* (1893) A London Workhouse. 11 March. p. 6f. www.britishnewspaperarchive.co.uk
309. *Hull Daily Mail.* (1911) Census Humour in Hull. 3 April. p. 5c. www.britishnewspaperarchive.co.uk

Chapter Twelve – Movers and Evaders

310. *South Wales Echo.* (1881) Taking the census. 16 April. p. 3a. www.britishnewspaperarchive.co.uk
311. *Manchester Evening News.* (1901) The census. 01 April. pp. 2–3. www.britishnewspaperarchive.co.uk
312. *Daily News.* (1891) Taking the census. 07 April. p. 5e&f. www.britishnewspaperarchive.co.uk
313. *Shepton Mallet Journal.* (1911) Taking the census. 07 April. p. 8c. www.britishnewspaperarchive.co.uk
314. Higgs, Edward. (1989) *Making sense of the census: the manuscript returns for England and Wales, 1801-1901.* London: H.M.S.O. 1989
315. *South Wales Echo.* (1881) Taking the census. 16 April. p. 3a. www.britishnewspaperarchive.co.uk

316. *Yorkshire Post and Leeds Intelligencer.* (1901) An enumerator's trials. 02 April. p. 5c. www.britishnewspaperarchive.co.uk
317. *Yorkshire Post and Leeds Intelligencer.* (1901) An enumerator's trials. 02 April. p. 5c. www.britishnewspaperarchive.co.uk
318. *Irish Examiner.* (1931) Census difficulties. 15 April. p. 4f. www.irishnewsarchive.com
319. *Yorkshire Post and Leeds Intelligencer.* (1881) Numbering the people. 04 April. p. 5a. www.britishnewspaperarchive.co.uk
320. *Evening Express.* (1901) Fun in the census. 06 April. p. 2g. https://newspapers.library.wales/
321. *Glasgow Herald.* (1861) Census curiosities. 03 April. p. 6a&b. www.britishnewspaperarchive.co.uk
322. *Berkshire Chronicle.* (1901) Humours of the census. 06 April. p. 2c. www.britishnewspaperarchive.co.uk
323. *Manchester Times.* (1891) Taking the census in Manchester. 10 April. p. 2c. www.britishnewspaperarchive.co.uk
324. *Coventry Evening Telegraph.* (1901) Taking the census in Coventry. 2 April. p. 3c&d. www.britishnewspaperarchive.co.uk
325. *Sheffield Daily Telegraph.* (1911) Sheffield Census. 04 April. p. 8b. www.britishnewspaperarchive.co.uk
326. *Lancashire Evening Post.* (1901) Humours of the census. 02 April. p. 4b. www.britishnewspaperarchive.co.uk
327. *Sheffield Daily Telegraph.* (1911) Sheffield Census. 04 April. p. 8b. www.britishnewspaperarchive.co.uk
328. *Brighton Gazette.* (1901) Taking the census in Brighton. 04 April. p. 5f. www.britishnewspaperarchive.co.uk
329. *Western Mail.* (1901) Taking the census. 02 April. p. 5e. www.britishnewspaperarchive.co.uk
330. *Birmingham Mail.* (1891) The census in Birmingham. 06 April. p. 3d. www.britishnewspaperarchive.co.uk
331. *Aberdeen Evening Express.* (1951) Sir Ernest Benn fined: census form not filled. 06 June. p. 8c. www.britishnewspaperarchive.co.uk
332. *Yorkshire Post and Leeds Intelligencer.* (1951) The census. 03 March. p. 2h. www.britishnewspaperarchive.co.uk
333. *Western Mail.* (1951) Two women objected to census, fined. 03 August. p. 3e. www.britishnewspaperarchive.co.uk
334. *Warwick and Warwickshire Advertiser.* (1841) 19 June. p. 1b. www.britishnewspaperarchive.co.uk

335. *Evening Express.* (1901) Maiden lady's fad. 30 April. p. 3a. https://newspapers.library.wales/
336. *Lancashire Evening Post.* (1921) A census objector. 14 July. p. 3c. www.britishnewspaperarchive.co.uk
337. *Bath Chronicle and Weekly Gazette.* (1911) Evading the census. 06 April. p. 8b&c. www.britishnewspaperarchive.co.uk

Chapter Thirteen – Dangers, Troubles, and Death

338. Treasury (Great Britain). 5 April 1911. Treasury board papers and in-letters. T 1/11327. National Archives, Kew, England.
339. *Darlington & Stockton Times, Ripon & Richmond Chronicle.* (1911) Tragic death of Mr Brunton, Marton. 8 April. p.3e. www.britishnewspaperarchive.co.uk
340. Treasury (Great Britain). 5 April 1911. Treasury board papers and in-letters. T 1/11327. National Archives, Kew, England.
341. Treasury (Great Britain). Establishment Department. Census enumerators: injury compensation. T 164/104/5. National Archives, Kew, England.
342. *Ibid.*
343. *Ibid.*
344. *Ibid.*
345. *Ibid.*
346. *Ibid.*
347. Register Office and Office of Population Censuses and Surveys, Establishment and Accounts Division: Correspondence and Papers. Census 1931: compensation for injuries. 7 June 1911. RG 20/1. National Archives, Kew, England.
348. Treasury (Great Britain). Treasury Board Papers and In-Letters. 15 May 1911. T 1/11327. National Archives, Kew, England.
349. Treasury (Great Britain). Treasury Board Papers and In-Letters. 25 September 1911. T 1/11327. National Archives, Kew, England.
350. Treasury (Great Britain). Treasury Board Papers and In-Letters. 28 April 1911. T 1/11327. National Archives, Kew, England.
351. Register Office and Office of Population Censuses and Surveys, Establishment and Accounts Division: Correspondence and Papers. Census 1931: compensation for injuries. 7 June 1911. RG 20/1. National Archives, Kew, England.

352. Treasury (Great Britain). Treasury Board Papers and In-Letters. 17 June 1911. T 1/11327. National Archives, Kew, England.
353. Treasury (Great Britain). Treasury Board Papers and In-Letters. 7 July 1911. T 1/11327. National Archives, Kew, England.
354. Treasury (Great Britain). Treasury Board Papers and In-Letters.14 June 1911. T 1/11327. National Archives, Kew, England.
355. Treasury (Great Britain). Establishment Department. Census enumerators: injury compensation. 15 May 1931. T 164/104/5. National Archives, Kew, England.
356. Register Office and Office of Population Censuses and Surveys, Establishment and Accounts Division: Correspondence and Papers. Census 1931: compensation for injuries. 24 November 1931. RG 20/1. National Archives, Kew, England.
357. Treasury (Great Britain). Establishment Department. Henry, J.A., and Gozney, V., Miss census enumerators: claim for injuries sustained in course of duties. 15 November 1931. T 164//113/29. National Archives, Kew, England.
358. *Daily Mirror.* (1961) Vanishing census man... 02 May. p. 3d&e. www.britishnewspaperarchive.co.uk
359. *Sheffield Independent.* (1871) Lamentable Suicide of a Heanor Tradesman. 08 April. p. 12b. www.britishnewspaperarchive.co.uk
360. *The Salisbury and Winchester Journal.* (1901) A census enumerator commits suicide. 06 April. p. 2d. www.britishnewspaperarchive.co.uk
361. *Clerkenwell News.* (1871) The census enumerators. 09 May. p. 4c. www.britishnewspaperarchive.co.uk
362. *Daily News (London).* (1871) Hammersmith. 27 April. p. 2g. www.britishnewspaperarchive.co.uk
363. *Edinburgh Evening News.* (1881) Assaulting a census-taker. 06 April. p. 2e. www.britishnewspaperarchive.co.uk
364. Records of the General Register Office. Census 1891: outward letters. 15 April 1891. RG 29/12. National Archives, Kew, England.
365. *Perthshire Advertiser.* (1911) Census: official threatened. 01 April. p. 5c. www.britishnewspaperarchive.co.uk
366. *Whitstable Times and Herne Bay Herald.* (1961) Artist painted woman's car… with Creosote. 27 May. p. 1a&b. www.britishnewspaperarchive.co.uk
367. *Cheshire Observer.* (1901) The census. 06 April. p. 8h. https://newspapers.library.wales/

368. *Norfolk News.* (1901) Humours of the census in Norwich. 06 April. p. 12f. www.britishnewspaperarchive.co.uk
369. *Sheffield Daily Telegraph.* (1911) Sheffield Census. 04 April. p. 8b. www.britishnewspaperarchive.co.uk
370. *The Western Mail.* (1891) Cardiff notes. 13 April. p. 5g. https://newspapers.library.wales/
371. *Croydon Chronicle and East Surrey Advertiser.* (1881) London letter. 09 April. p. 3a. www.britishnewspaperarchive.co.uk
372. Jones, Christine. (2007) 'The Fitness of the persons employed: Comments in the Scottish Census Enumerators' Books. *Local Population Studies,* 79(75). pp. 75–80. http://www.localpopulationstudies.org.uk
373. Records of the General Register Office. Census 1891: outward letters. 8 March 1892. RG 29/14. National Archives (GB), Kew, England.
374. *Western Mail.* (1931) A census man's denial. 30 July. p. 7d. www.britishnewspaperarchive.co.uk
375. *Liverpool Echo.* (1971) Census girl quizzed over boyfriend. 29 April. p. 7f. www.britishnewspaperarchive.co.uk
376. *Aberdeen Evening Express.* (1971) 'Let me check my census form.' 28 April. p. 4h. www.britishnewspaperarchive.co.uk
377. *Hammersmith & Shepherds Bush Gazette.* Census collector was a salesman. (1991) 03 May. p. 5b. www.britishnewspaperarchive.co.uk
378. Records of the General Register Office. Census 1891: outward letters. 25 April 1891. RG 29/12. National Archives (GB), Kew, England.
379. *Ibid.,* 25 May 1891.
380. General Register Office. History of the Census of 1841: the Registrar General's plan for taking the first Census by the Office with layout of forms and instructions. RG 27/1. pp. 31–32. National Archives (GB), Kew, England.
381. *Western Times.* (1851) The census. 03 May. p. 3c. www.britishnewspaperarchive.co.uk
382. *Liverpool Mercury.* (1861) Grievance of the census enumerators. 26 April. p. 8g. www.britishnewspaperarchive.co.uk
383. *The Scotsman.* (1861) The Census Enumerators. 20 May. p. 2g. www.britishnewspaperarchive.co.uk.
384. *Dundee Courier.* (1871) Letters to the editor. 15 April. p. 2d. www.britishnewspaperarchive.co.uk
385. *Clerkenwell News.* (1871) The census enumerators. 09 May. p. 4c. www.britishnewspaperarchive.co.uk

386. *Edinburgh Evening News*. (1891) Letters to the editor. 23 April. p. 2i. www.britishnewspaperarchive.co.uk
387. *Edinburgh Evening News*. (1901) Letters to the editor. 14 May. p. 6g. www.britishnewspaperarchive.co.uk
388. *The Bedfordshire Times and Independent*. (1921) The Census of 1921, by One Who Was In It. 01 July. p.11c. www.britishnewspaperarchive.co.uk.
389. *Evening Express* (1891). Taking the census. 8 April. p. 4c&d. https://newspapers.library.wales/
390. *Kirkintilloch Herald*. (1901) The experiences of a census enumerator. 24 April. p.6a. www.britishnewspaperarchive.co.uk

Index